THE FAT CHANCE COOKBOOK

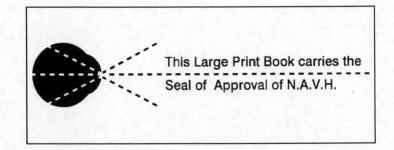

This Large Print Book carries the
Seal of Approval of N.A.V.H.

The Fat Chance Cookbook

More Than 100 Recipes Ready in Under 30 Minutes to Help You Lose the Sugar and the Weight

Robert H. Lustig, MD, MSL

with Heather Millar

Recipes by Cindy Gershen

THORNDIKE PRESS
A part of Gale, Cengage Learning

GALE
CENGAGE Learning®

Farmington Hills, Mich • San Francisco • New York • Waterville, Maine
Meriden, Conn • Mason, Ohio • Chicago

GALE
CENGAGE Learning®

Thorndike Press® Large Print Health, Home & Learning.
The text of this Large Print edition is unabridged.
Other aspects of the book may vary from the original edition.
Set in 16 pt. Plantin.

LIBRARY OF CONGRESS CATALOGING-IN-PUBLICATION DATA

Lustig, Robert H.
  The fat chance cookbook : more than 100 recipes ready in under 30 minutes to help you lose the sugar and the weight / by Robert H. Lustig, MD, MSL with Heather Millar ; recipes by Cindy Gershen. — Large print edition.
    pages cm (Thorndike press large print health, home & learning)
    Companion volume to: Fat chance. New York, New York : Hudson Street Press, [2012]
    ISBN-13: 978-1-4104-7096-6 (hardcover)
    ISBN-10: 1-4104-7096-2 (hardcover)
    1. Reducing diets—Recipes. 2. Weight loss. I. Millar, Heather, 1963– II. Gershen, Cindy. III. Lustig, Robert H. Fat chance. IV. Title.
RM222.2.L78 2014
641.5'63—dc23   2014011757

Published in 2014 by arrangement with Hudson Street Press, a member of Penguin Group (USA) LLC, a Penguin Random House Company

Printed in Mexico
1 2 3 4 5 6 7 18 17 16 15 14

Dedicated to my late father, Richard Lustig (1927–2013), who was my biggest fan. During his life, he battled all forms of adversity, and somehow beat the odds and came out on top. Every time I came up against it, I'd ask "What would Dad do?" and he always showed me the way forward. I was his biggest fan and he was my hero. I will miss him for the rest of my life.

CONTENTS

ACKNOWLEDGMENTS

This book is the culmination of the hard work of the three authors but also of the three families that support them and eat and drink with them. Robert lives and cooks with Julie, his wife of nineteen years, and their two amazing children, Miriam (fourteen) and Meredith (eight). All are on board. Julie was the brain trust behind the recent e-book *Sugar Has 56 Names: A Shopper's Guide.* Meredith wants to be a chef and has already decided she's opening an Italian restaurant when she grows up. But it will go light on the pasta and no *panna cotta.*

Cindy and her husband, Lance, a pediatrician, live in Walnut Creek, California, twenty miles east of San Francisco. Cindy and Lance have a blended family of eight children: daughters Danielle, Rose, Jennifer, and Sarah, and sons Joe, Zack, Alex, and Ben. They have nine grandchildren and three on the way. Lance helps Cindy run the family restaurant, Sunrise Bistro. Cindy loves cooking in general, but especially with her family. Her grandkids love picking tomatoes, raspberries, and strawberries in her large kitchen garden. They clamor for ricotta gnocchi and multigrain pizza (both recipes are in this book), not cookies and candy.

Heather lives just a few blocks from Rob with her husband, Pete, an editor at Bloomberg News, and her daughter Erin (twelve), who loves sugar but knows she needs to limit it. When Pete and Heather met, Pete thought two Big Macs and a shake was a good meal. Suffice to say, he's changed a lot in the last twenty-five years! Erin, like Meredith, loves to cook. Her specialties so far are whole-grain bread, salad, and spaghetti sauce.

And finally, major kudos to Cindy's "Kitchen Helpers," the people who did the heavy lifting to make this book a reality. Assistant Kristin Zellhart, fellow teachers Pam Deane and Patrick Oliver, the nutritionists who helped compile the USDA nutritional information for each dish, and all the kids in Cindy's classes — without them, this book would never have happened.

■ ■ ■ ■

1

■ ■ ■ ■

CHAPTER 1
COOK OR BE COOKED

How many times have you had, or heard, these conversations?

"I know I'm carrying extra weight, but I just can't lose it."

Or:

"I lost twenty pounds last year, but I've gained it all back and then some."

Or:

"My doctor just told me that if I don't watch my diet and start exercising, I'm on my way to developing diabetes."

This cookbook has been written to end those conversations. It will teach you to reorient your food life and your life in general. It will help you feel better, live healthier, be more productive, and — believe it or not — lose weight without dieting. You will be able to do this by taking advantage of the hormones that control energy balance and "satiety," the feeling of being full.

Drafted with my dear friend, chef Cindy Gershen, these dishes are down-to-earth, decidedly easy, and delicious. The recipes either minimize or eliminate the ingredients that do damage to our bodies and our health: fructose (the sweet molecule that makes up refined sugar); refined carbohydrates; and processed (fiberless) foods of all kinds. They emphasize ingredients that will help your body recalibrate how it uses energy and stores fat: whole grains, whole vegetables (peels and all!), fiber, omega-3 fatty acids, and high-quality protein. And here is a huge plus: most of them can be made in less than thirty minutes of active cooking time.

These recipes have not been pulled out of thin air. They are based on the science I outlined in my first book about the obesity and diabetes pandemics, *Fat Chance: Beating the Odds Against Sugar, Processed Food, Obesity, and Disease.* They have been drawn from the more than thirty years of experience that Cindy has had as a successful restaurateur and caterer in the San Francisco Bay Area, where we both live.

Why *This* Cookbook?
Frankly, you need this cookbook, no matter what your weight. It's not just because the

14

way most of us are eating today is making us fat. Even more alarming, the Industrial Global Diet is making us seriously ill. As I explain more fully in *Fat Chance,* 40 percent of normal-weight Americans suffer from the same diseases as the obese: type 2 diabetes, lipid disorders, hypertension, heart disease, cancer, and dementia. Being thin or normal weight is not a Get Out of Jail Free card.

This affects all of us, doctors included. For instance, my friend, colleague, and noted surgeon turned nutrition scientist Dr. Peter Attia discovered that he was prediabetic, even though he is young, slender, and exercises three or four hours a day. Dr. Attia recounted his personal experience with prediabetes in a TEDMED talk: http://www.ted.com/talks/peter_attia_what_if_we_re_wrong_about_diabetes.html. He lost forty pounds and reversed his prediabetes with improvements in his diet.

The bottom line is that the Industrial Global Diet is killing people while bankrupting the American medical enterprise. If we do nothing in America, Medicare will be broke by 2026 due to the enormous burden of such chronic metabolic diseases as diabetes. And America exports its diet around the world to the detriment of both developed, and developing, countries. It has to stop. But it won't stop until you make it stop.

Change will not come from the food and diet companies. It will not come from restaurants or supermarkets. You and your family will drive this change, cooking together in your own kitchens. Spatulas and spoons are the first line of defense in the war against bad food. Change starts at home. The food industry, like any industry, must be responsive to its customers. If you don't buy it, they won't sell it.

We've lost an entire generation of cooks to our fast food culture. Cooking is a skill passed down from parent to child. If your mother doesn't teach you, where are you supposed to learn to chop onions, or cream butter, or make salad dressing? American high schools used to teach home economics, and that's gone too, in the name of education cutbacks and No Child Left Behind (which is really No Child Moving Forward and No Teacher Left Standing). The majority of kids growing up today have never boiled water, not even in a microwave. Kids create a dish from scratch? As they say in Brooklyn, my hometown, "Fuggedaboutit!"

If you don't know how to cook — and a 2011 survey found that nearly one-third of

Americans don't — fear not. These recipes do not require exotic spices or pricey equipment or hours of prep time. All of them can be made with basic kitchen tools, with nothing more exotic than a blender, in less than half an hour of active cooking time. They have to be: They were tested by Cindy and her high school students at Mount Diablo High School in Concord, California, where she teaches healthy cooking and responsible eating. If kids can make these recipes in less time than a school period, you can too! And if high school students, who are notorious for not eating anything healthier than Flamin' Hot Cheetos and a corn dog or drinking anything healthier than a Starbucks Frappuccino, can enthusiastically consume their own creations made by their own hands, you can too! In all honesty, your lives may depend upon it.

We're All Getting Fatter and Sicker

If you doubt the seriousness of this epidemic, consider these signs of the Dietary Apocalypse: Nearly 70 percent of Americans are overweight; 30 percent are obese. In 1980, only 5 percent of children scored above the 95th percentile in body mass index (BMI), the standard way of gauging healthy body weight. Today, a whopping 20 percent of kids score above the 95th percentile. In 1980, there were almost no adolescent type 2 diabetics. Today, there are 40,000. More than 8 percent, or approximately 25 million, Americans have diabetes today. By 2050, it is predicted that one-third of Americans will be diabetic.

This problem is not limited to rich, over-privileged countries like America. The World Health Organization has found that the percentage of obese humans worldwide has doubled in the last twenty-eight years. Globally, the obese now outnumber the undernourished by 30 percent. Fifteen years ago it was the other way around. Every country, even developing ones, has seen an uptick in obesity rates over the last decade. World authorities now consider obesity and its associated diseases to be a greater threat to human health than are smoking or infectious diseases.

Consider the magnitude of this change. And you know the really amazing thing? This massive, and I mean massive, upending of our food life has happened in just three decades.

It's Not Your Fault

Why do I care so much about getting people into their kitchens to cook healthy food?

I'm a pediatrician. It's my job to care. Specifically, I am a pediatric endocrinologist, which means that I care for children who have hormonal imbalances. Every day I see the misery that results when the body's systems for maintaining and storing energy go haywire. It's my job to take care of kids who have become obese because of brain tumors, hormone excesses or deficiencies, muscle weakness, or other problems. They are tragically overweight and develop chronic metabolic diseases at frighteningly early ages.

But it's not their fault. And it's not your fault. Everyone thinks that obesity is a matter of personal responsibility. That explanation just does not cut it. Here are six reasons why your fat is not your fault.

1. **Obesity Is Not a Choice.** The quality of life for obese children is the same as for children on cancer chemotherapy. Obesity is not something to which people, especially children, aspire.

2. **Diet and Exercise Don't Work.** Everyone can name a celebrity who has lost weight, but the overwhelming majority of us ordinary folk fail in our weight loss efforts. Even if

we are successful for a while, we gain it back in short order.

3. **The Obesity Epidemic Is Now a Pandemic.** This is not an American problem, an Australian problem, a British problem, or a Japanese problem. This is a global problem. Around the world, we are all eating the Industrial Global Diet.

4. **Even Animals Raised in Captivity Are Getting Fat.** Livestock animals drink the same water and breathe the same air that we do. We don't yet know why this is happening to these animals, but it argues in favor of some sort of environmental insult to which all life on the planet is now exposed.

5. **The Poor Pay More.** The poor often don't even have supermarkets, let alone access to healthy food. Can a person exercise personal responsibility if there's no healthy choice available?

6. **The Greatest Rate of Increase in Obesity Is in the Youngest Patients.** Children between the ages of two and five have experienced the greatest rate of weight increase in the last decade. It is impossible

to assign personal responsibility, or free choice, to this age group. We even have an epidemic of obese six-month-olds. Infants don't diet or exercise.

For various reasons, the complicated system that regulates energy in our bodies — the nerves, hormones, and brain structures that determine what we eat, how much we eat, and whether our body stores that energy as fat or uses it for the business of living — has gone haywire.

If We're All Dieting, Why Are We Still Fat and Sick?

You might say, "I don't have a disease. What does all this have to do with me?"

Well, people around the world are putting on the pounds almost as quickly as the kids in my clinic. They're gaining for similar reasons: The energy regulation systems in their bodies have been thrown out of balance. But in the case of the general public the cause is not brain tumors or other medical issues. The cause is bad food. It's a matter of what's in the processed food of the typical modern diet, and what isn't in that processed food.

Every item in the supermarket screams

that it's "low fat" or "low carb" or "low calorie." Everyone has a new, magic solution: Eat low carb! Don't eat fat! Eat lots of protein! Drink this powder! Fast every other day! Count food points! Buy prepared diet food! Eat wild food! Eat raw food! Juice your food! Eat only greens! Take this pill! Take that shot! Have your stomach stapled!

You might ask yourself why we think we have it right. Because we are not saying any of those things. We're not proposing a magical solution. We're proposing a sensible solution.

I ask you: Have you seen anyone suddenly shed pounds and keep them off for more than a year or two with any of these miracle weight loss systems? Aside from bariatric surgery (which only works in about two-thirds of patients), everyone else loses for the first six months, and then the weight slowly returns over the next six months.

Big Food's Not So Small Secrets

Here are some other things that the food and diet industries don't want you to know:

- **A calorie is *not* a calorie.** The Coca-Cola Company's 2013 video "Coming Together," states: "Beating obesity will take action by all of us, based on one simple common-sense fact: All calories count, no matter where they come from, including Coca-Cola and everything else with calories . . ." In other words, "a calorie is a calorie."

This is just not true.

The fact is that different calories are metabolized differently, and how those calories are metabolized and where they go have everything to do with what diseases you might develop. You cannot eat 1,500 calories of jelly beans each day, lose weight, and be healthy. Your body uses and stores fuel — calories — very differently depending on the quality of those calories.

Because: A calorie is *not* a calorie.

- **It's the insulin, stupid.** If you eat a steady diet of high-sugar, low-fiber, low-quality protein (burgers/chicken nuggets/pizza) and refined grains, you will jack up your insulin levels bigtime. That drives energy storage into fat cells, makes fat in your liver, and makes you feel very tired as your energy is diverted away from your muscles and your brain.
- **On the other hand, if you eat low-sugar, high-fiber, high-quality pro-**

tein **(eggs, fish, lean meats) and whole grains, your insulin response will be much lower.** You won't shunt energy into fat cells. Your body's energy systems will stay in balance. You will not only lose or maintain your weight, you will also feel better. In *Fat Chance,* I outlined the science behind these statements in great detail. I'll give you a quick summary of it below.

- **It's not about obesity.** The food industry would have you believe it's about obesity. Then they can blame your love handles on your lack of discipline, or automobiles, or television, or power lawnmowers, or the lack of sidewalks in our towns, or the lack of P.E. in our schools.

But guess what? Thin does not necessarily mean healthy. Someone who looks quite thin might have a lousy diet and have "visceral fat," that is, fat around the internal organs, putting him as much at risk for disease as someone who's obese. That's the case for as many as 40 percent of the normal-weight population. Sure, we should all strive to maintain a healthy weight. But focusing only on weight loss is the wrong approach to our problems.

- **We live in a toxic food environment.** Our bodies are hardwired to eat high-calorie food when it's available. And our brains are hardwired to like sugar. A lot. Studies show that you must introduce a savory food to an infant an average of thirteen times before he or she will accept it. But if it's a sweet food, you only have to introduce it once. Liking sugar is built into our DNA — because there are no foods in nature that are both sweet and acutely poisonous. This was the signal to our ancestors that a given foodstuff was safe to eat.

Today highly sweetened foods are immediately available everywhere you go. Plus sugar is addictive — weakly so, like alcohol, but addictive nonetheless. The food industry has hijacked these two phenomena for their own use. That's why more than 80 percent of the 600,000 food items in the American food supply are spiked with added sugar.

- **It's not your fault.** When you start to lose weight your body's starvation response kicks in and the hormone leptin drops. This makes you both hungrier and less energetic, defeating your best intentions. Our bodies are hard-wired to hang on to stores of fat for times of famine. But today, in most high- and middle-income nations, times of famine never come. The problem is that the Industrial Global Diet, by driving insulin higher, messes up the body's finely tuned system for regulating energy.

- **Your fat is not your fate, provided you don't surrender.** Not surrendering means we've got to start cooking, people. We need to completely rethink our relationship to food and to the food industry. We need to embrace food and yet be skeptical of the industry that supplies it. That's why we wrote this cookbook.

What It's Really About: "Metabolic Syndrome"

Though it sounds pretty grim, it's not hopeless. We just need to understand what we're doing to ourselves and what the food industry is doing to us. And to understand that it's necessary to outline just a bit of science. This is a cookbook, not a textbook. If you want to understand the science in detail, the complete picture is sketched out in *Fat Chance.*

This is what you need to know: Obesity is not a character flaw; obesity is not a behavior; obesity is not a disease (despite the American Medical Association declaring it one). Obesity is not a defect in energy *balance* (calories in/calories out). Rather, obesity is a defect in energy *deposition* — where excess energy is stored — that occurs because of changes in biochemistry and hormones that are caused by bad food.

Other downstream effects of obesity include sleep apnea, gallstones, and problems with your joints and feet. If you carry a lot of extra pounds, you put yourself at higher risk for all of these conditions. And, not surprisingly given the obesity rates, all of these medical problems have become more common in the last thirty years. They all increase the risk of early death.

This is not just a personal crisis for the people unlucky enough to carry lots of extra pounds. It's a financial and political crisis as well. All the diseases caused by excess body fat result in at least $192 billion in medical bills in the United States alone. The 2012 bills for diabetes and dementia in the United States were $245 billion and $200 billion respectively. The global cost runs into the trillions. That doesn't even take into account the lost productivity and the sheer human misery generated by these diseases. There's simply not enough money to pay for it all.

Those extra pounds may take a toll on our vanity, but even more serious are the medical conditions that "travel" with obesity. These diseases are known as "metabolic syndrome." They include, but are not limited to: type 2 diabetes, fatty liver disease, high blood pressure, lipid problems, heart disease, polycystic ovarian disease, cancer, and dementia. All of these are "chronic metabolic diseases" that occur due to ineffective energy processing, and can happen in normal weight people as well. Obesity is not the "cause" of these diseases; rather, obesity is a "marker" for these diseases. When we tackle the cause, toxic food, both the diseases *and* the obesity will get better, no matter what your weight.

Science for the Cookbook Crowd

Energy Storage and Insulin
Lloyd Blankfein, the president of Goldman Sachs, recently stated, "The *only* job of business is to make money." Not the primary job, the *only* job. Explains a lot, right?

The physiologic counterpart of this concept is "The *only* job of the pancreas is to store energy." The pancreas makes enzymes that break down food into smaller nutrient molecules. The pancreas also makes hormones like insulin, which escorts the energy from food into fat cells for storage.

It makes sense that the quest for, the regulation of, and the storage of energy — that is, calories — is one of the most important things that the body does. After all, if you don't store energy, none of the other processes of life can happen: no digestion, no breathing, no movement, no thought. None of it happens without calories. And insulin is the way the calories get where they need to go. Insulin shunts glucose and fatty acids to fat cells. It stores amino acids in muscle. It tops off the liver's glucose stores as "glycogen," or liver starch. Insulin shunts energy from the blood into fat cells.

Here's the key takeaway fact: Insulin makes fat. More insulin, more fat.

Calories come from various kinds of foodstuffs, from carrots to cheesecake to Coca-Cola. The calories arrive at the stomach and then the small intestine, where foodstuffs are broken down into smaller components. The liver has first dibs on all of these nutrients. Whatever the liver can't take up goes into general circulation in your bloodstream. When bloodstream glucose levels rise quickly, the pancreas releases the insulin to store the excess.

Energy Balance and Leptin

On top of the energy storage system is another complex system that's supposed to signal when you're hungry and when you're full. A structure at the base of your brain, the hypothalamus, acts like a traffic cop, monitoring what's going on and directing the various hormonal systems of your body.

The hypothalamus reads what's happening through the blood signals it gets: the hormones insulin and leptin. Insulin tells the hypothalamus when there are excess nutrients that need to be stored. Fat cells produce a different hormone, leptin, that tells the hypothalamus whether there are enough energy stores on board in the first place. In response to these signals, the hypothalamus tells your body whether you need more or less energy, whether you need to eat, or whether you need to push your chair from the table.

When these systems operate as they should, you feel hungry when your brain senses that you're running low on calories, and you feel full when you have had enough calories. When you need to expend energy, you have it on board. Things stay mostly in balance; you feel good and you maintain a stable weight.

Too Much, Too Fast

But what happens when you eat a meal of processed food, say, a Big Mac, super-size fries, and a full-sugar Coke? Or, what happens when you eat what may seem a "healthier" option, such as pasta with packaged tomato sauce, salad and croutons with bottled dressing, and ice cream for dessert? That's when your finely balanced energy system starts to run off the rails.

That fast food meal (or the home-cooked meal made with processed ingredients) delivers a huge burst of nutrients into your upper gut: boatloads of glucose, fructose, fats, and proteins. Because they've already been partly processed and because there is no fiber to slow down its absorption, these nutrients race through the stomach and small intestine. These organs absorb the nutrients very quickly, bringing everything to your liver all at once. There, your liver cells get overwhelmed, and turn the excess into liver fat. The pancreas gets the signal that the liver is sick and chugs out more insulin to make the liver do its job. This drives energy into fat cells for storage, making your body weight go up.

So what do you think happens if you eat processed or fast food regularly, day after day, year after year? Excess insulin means excess fat. Excess insulin also means that your brain can't tell if your leptin is working. If your brain can't see your leptin, your brain thinks it's starving, and that makes you feel hungrier. Now you are in a vicious cycle: The more you eat, the higher your insulin goes, and the more your brain thinks it's starving.

How Your Cells Get Sick

At the cellular level, the avalanche of energy and nutrients overwhelms your body's cellular power generators, called "mitochondria." When the mitochondria get overloaded they have no choice but to turn the extra energy into liver fat, making your liver even sicker. That makes you fatter, lazier, sicker, and you don't even know where all these problems came from. How can all this be happening when you're dieting, buying "low fat," and all the rest? Now you have "metabolic syndrome." Now you are losing years of your life as your cells and your body age more quickly.

What the science shows is that obesity is not the result of aberrant behaviors. Rather, obesity is the result of the nutritional alterations that drive our insulin levels higher. Gluttony and sloth are not the cause of the rapid global rise in obesity. Rather, they are the symptoms.

With a few rare individual exceptions, that's the biochemical and hormone situation for the 1.5 billion overweight and obese people on the planet. And it's a problem for a sizeable proportion of normal weight people too. The majority of people today, regardless of weight, produce twice as much insulin for the same dose of glucose as people produced thirty years ago. Even if they're eating about the same amount as the generation before them, they're making more fat in response. That means things are getting worse just by doing nothing. And that's what we're seeing on the streets, in our homes, and in my clinic.

The Not-So-Usual Suspects

Stress, environmental factors, lack of sleep, and many other things feed into the obesity pandemic by changing various biochemical pathways. And each person's insulin and leptin situation is slightly different. But really, the major cause of our ballooning waistlines worldwide boils down to two words: "toxic food."

The modern diet is larded with things that

upset our energy balance and our health. Here are just a few:

Fructose

Fructose is the Voldemort of the metabolic syndrome pandemic: stealthy, ever-present, and bad for the common good. The refined, white sugar that you put in your coffee or sprinkle on your cereal consists of molecules that have two halves: One half is "glucose," a minimally sweet substance (think molasses) that all your cells need for energy. The other half is "fructose."

Fructose is the sweet stuff. We like it. A lot. But the truth is that our bodies don't need fructose. There is not one biochemical reaction in the body that requires fructose. A technical way to say this is: Fructose *is* an energy source, but it is *not* a nutrition source. You can get along perfectly fine without fructose. Aside from its effects on the pleasure center of the brain, fructose has lost whatever value it might once have had to humankind. It's "vestigial" (a holdover, unnecessary). We don't need it. But boy, do we want it.

Does sugar cause weight gain? The data say yes, but not all that much. Is sugar a cause of obesity? In some people, probably so. Is sugar *the* cause of obesity? Not even close. What fructose does is cause metabolic syndrome, and that's what makes you sick, because your liver has a harder time metabolizing it. So, instead, the liver turns fructose into liver fat, and that leads to metabolic syndrome. This drives your insulin even higher, causing more weight gain. The reverse is also true: when metabolic syndrome improves, your weight will improve of its own accord.

Americans now consume an average of 22 teaspoons of sugar each day, up nearly 50 percent from a generation ago, according to the American Heart Association (AHA). We need to cut that in half, according to the AHA.

But just cutting out "high-fructose corn syrup" (HFCS) will not save you. HFCS, honey, molasses, agave syrup, brown sugar, organic demerara sugar, beet sugar — to your body, these are all the same thing, chemically.

Today, sugar is everywhere: A 2012 report by the magazine *Mother Jones* found that a generation ago, Americans spent 11.6 percent of their food dollars on processed foods and sweets; now, Americans spend 22.9 percent of food dollars on them. And sugar (the sweet stuff) is in all kinds of places you might not expect: yogurt, spaghetti sauce, crackers (check out Wheat Thins), ramen noodles, even hamburger meat!

Trans Fats

Patented in 1902 and introduced to our food supply as Crisco in 1911, trans fats are the single most dangerous item in our diet. They increase the shelf life of every item to which they are added. Bacteria don't have the machinery to digest trans fats, so foods with trans fats keep longer. And guess what? Your mitochondria, those cellular power plants, are just repurposed bacteria. They can't digest trans fats either. Rather than being converted into energy by the mitochondria, trans fats just stick around, literally: They line our arteries and our livers, causing disease.

Omega-6 Fatty Acids

These lead to the production of inflammatory compounds, the ones targeted by aspirin. We need some omega-6s to help our immune system function, but they're supposed to exist in balance with the omega-3 fatty acids that fight inflammation. We're supposed to have a 1:1 ratio between omega-6s and omega-3s. Today, most of us have twenty-five times more omega-6s on board than omega-3s. That leads to a pro-inflammatory state that drives heart disease, diabetes, and cancer.

Omega-6s are found in canola and corn oils, and in the meat from animals that are fed corn and soy. It makes a difference where you get your protein: Corn-fed beef, chickens fed commercial pellets, and corn-fed, farmed fish — all these feed into chronic inflammation in your body.

Alcohol

In small amounts, alcohol can be protective against disease, keeping your system on "alert," keeping your liver's detoxifying enzymes "ready to go," ready to process the toxic parts of your food. But in large amounts (more than two drinks per day for a man, one for a woman), alcohol over-whelms your mitochondria, gets turned into liver fat, and drives the development of metabolic syndrome. Just look at the "beer belly" of many adults today.

Branched-Chain Amino Acids

These compounds — leucine, isoleucine, valine — are the essential building blocks of protein. When you are building muscle, these compounds are good. That's why body builders take "protein powder." But when you're not building muscle, these amino acids go to the liver mitochondria to get turned into energy. And when the mitochondria get overwhelmed, they turn these branched-chain amino acids to liver fat. And liver fat, well, you get the punch line by now: Liver fat leads to metabolic syndrome. Branched-chain amino acids occur in many foods, but you find their highest levels in corn-fed beef, chicken, and farmed (corn-fed) fish.

What's Good for Big Food Is Bad for You

The packaged, processed foods that make up 80 percent of what's for sale at your local Kroger's, Piggly Wiggly, Walmart, or Safeway are great for the food companies: They're cheap. They're highly profitable. Even better, they keep forever, thus, the ten-year-old Twinkie, the Oreo that never spoils.

These processed foods have been engineered to make you crave them. They're full of sugar, fat, salt, and caffeine. Even worse, the ingredients in processed food make you overindulge once you get your mouth around them. Though there's still a robust academic debate about whether fast food can be addictive, doctors no longer dismiss the idea out of hand.

Nora Volkow, director of the National Institute of Drug Abuse, has gone on record supporting the concept of food addiction. Let me tell you this: After treating obese children for the last fifteen years, I can categorically say there are loads of kids who can't fend off a Big Mac Attack. The science says that sugar is addictive, though not in everyone, like alcohol. But it's addictive nonetheless. Combine sugar with another addictive substance, like caffeine, and now you've a truly addictive, toxic brew: It's called soda.

The food that's cheapest and most available may be good for the food companies. For us mere mortals, that food is a health disaster. It's toxic at high dose, and we're overdosed. Most of the food that surrounds you — in the coffee break room, at the meeting, in the supermarket, at the convenience store check-out, in the movie theater, at street-side stands, at sports events, and in your own cupboards — is processed and will make you fat or sick, or both.

Target the Biochemistry to Improve Your Health

So far, medical research has yet to find a pill or a shot that will really fix obesity, or metabolic syndrome for that matter. We can treat all the different diseases that travel with metabolic syndrome, but we can't stop the cellular damage. Based on how metabolic syndrome occurs (mitochondrial energy overload), there is no obvious drug target, so I wouldn't hold my breath waiting for the "magic bullet." But don't despair. There really is hope.

In order to reverse obesity and metabolic syndrome, we have to reverse the damaging biochemistry. That means we need to give the cellular power plants, the mitochondria, a break. We need to stop the liver overload in order to fix the insulin resistance. We need to get the insulin down in order to fix the leptin resistance, the reason we think we're hungry even though we're fat.

Calories are not the target. **INSULIN IS THE TARGET.**

As long as insulin stays high, the drive to eat and the drive to store energy cannot get better. *Get the insulin down.* That's what my clinic at UCSF does. That's what the recipes in this cookbook do. That's why this cookbook is different. And that's why this cookbook is necessary.

Until the food industry reformulates its fare to provide quality, not quantity, and until the U.S. government stops subsidizing the very foodstuffs that drive disease (corn, soy), the American foodscape is unlikely to change. In the meantime, how do we lower our insulin? We must start eating differently, more like our parents and grandparents did. We should be cooking food that has these things:

- **Fiber:** Everyone thinks that fiber is the throwaway nutrient. In fact, fiber is the stealth nutrient. It slows down the rate at which your body can convert food into energy. High-fiber food is like a timed-release capsule. It releases energy into your bloodstream at a slower rate. That way, your mitochondria, and thus your liver, your pancreas, and your brain — get the energy slower, so they don't get overwhelmed. Also, fiber reaches the end of the intestine faster. That sends a satiety, "I'm full," signal to your brain sooner, so you won't eat as much.

- **Omega-3 fatty acids:** These are anti-inflammatory compounds that we need to keep the omega-6s in check. You must eat them; your body can't make them. Omega-3s come from algae. Wild fish eat algae. We eat the wild fish. Yes, wild fish is more expensive than farmed fish, but many species of farmed fish eat corn. You might as well eat a steak. Another slightly cheaper source of omega-3s is flaxseed. You can also buy eggs from chickens that eat feed rich in omega-3s.

- **Micronutrients:** Some early research suggests that, as we've bred bigger and sweeter fruits and vegetables, that produce has become less nutritious. Some studies suggest that domestic produce has fewer healthy micronutrients and antioxidants, compounds that combat inflammation. That's what's behind all the calls to eat "wild food." You don't need to forage for your veggies, but you do need to eat lots of leafy greens like spinach and kale, and lots of fruits and vegetables, peels and all. Supermarket produce will do as well as the fancy organic kind for your general needs.

Eat "Real" Food

Food writer Michael Pollan has said, "Don't eat food that your grandmother wouldn't recognize as food." We don't need to go that far. After all, would Grandma recognize tempeh, tofu, or edamame? Pollan also has said, "Eat food. Not too much. Mostly plants." But when you eat "real" food, the not-too-much takes care of itself. And there are plenty of plants — corn, soy, refined wheat — that aren't all that good for you.

No, the science says that we need to get back to basics. We need real, whole food that we cook at home: whole grains, grass-fed meats, meat and eggs from free-range chickens, wild fish, whole vegetables and fruits, peels and all.

Sounds utopian to most. Indeed, the problem is that "real" food is expensive and considered "specialty" food. This cookbook takes that into account. These recipes are designed for everyone, including parents in low-income neighborhoods. You should be able to afford and find the ingredients in these recipes at most local supermarkets. If you can't, demand these ingredients. More on that later.

You aren't going to find these healthier ingredients in "diet" frozen dinners. You're not going to find them in packaged sauces, packaged cereals, packaged desserts, packaged snacks, or condiments, even those labeled "healthy." In fact, if products are labeled "low fat" that often means that the fat has been replaced with sugar instead.

You're not going to find this kind of real food at McDonald's, or at any other fast food chain. Witness what happened to the "McLean Deluxe," hamburger meat infused with seaweed. Even though it tasted pretty good, people would not purchase it. When people go to McDonald's, they are not going to be diet-conscious. Even if you eat a salad from the drive-thru, that salad is going to come with croutons and salad dressing dripping in sugars, trans fats, and omega-6s. In fact, a McDonald's salad (plus the dressing) may have more calories and sodium than does a Big Mac. The "healthy" chicken topping the salad will have been fed corn or soy, because that's cheaper. So the chicken will be full of branched-chain amino acids and omega-6s, which leads to — you've got it now — metabolic syndrome.

Dessert should be special, a once-a-week affair. Refined sugar should be a treat, something to look forward to. It should not be an everyday, every meal centerpiece. And if you're going to have dessert, make it fantastic, something to remember. If you can buy it at a supermarket, I promise you, it's *not* fantastic.

Yes, avoiding the sugar and other problem nutrients in processed food is a little more trouble. Cooking things from scratch may take a little more time. Some items — fresh berries or high-quality meats or fish — may cost a little more. Would you rather pay a couple extra bucks for good produce and spend a little more time cooking whole grains? Or would you rather end up with a lifelong, chronic condition that costs tens or even hundreds of thousands of dollars, and may even cost you your life? Think of it this way: it's your time or your health. Short-term gain for long-term pain.

The Inspiration for This Cookbook

I started synthesizing the science into these conclusions more than a decade ago. Long before I gave a lecture that turned into a four-million-plus-hit YouTube video explaining the science and the policy implications of sugar (youtube.com/watch?v=dBnn iua 6-oM), long before I wrote *Fat Chance,* long before I appeared on *60 Minutes, NPR Science Friday,* and *The Colbert Report,* I started speaking to the medical community about the obesity pandemic and the science behind it.

While giving a talk at John Muir Medical Center in 2006, I met Cindy Gershen. Cindy's husband, Lance, is a pediatrician, and he had let her know about the subject of the talk. She came armed for bear. At first, I thought she was a stalker. Then I realized, no, she was way worse! She practically held me down kicking and screaming while she extracted every scientific point I had made to date. Then she said, "Thank you. You have just scientifically validated everything I've learned through experience." We've been best friends ever since.

Cindy's Story

In 1981, when Cindy was in her mid-twenties and pregnant with her third child, she opened her first food business, Sunrise Bakery and Café in Walnut Creek, California, twenty miles east of San Francisco. After her son was born, his sleep patterns didn't let her rest much. So she stayed up with him through the night and baked pastries, quiches, and breads for her café. People lined up outside for a taste of that home cooking.

She soon outgrew the café's space and opened Sunrise Bistro, a block away from the café. She continued the homemade tradition there, and expanded it beyond breakfast and snacks to include lunch and dinner entrées.

Two decades later, the Bistro was still going strong and had added a catering department. Yet Cindy rarely made it out of the kitchen. Over the years, she had loaded 210 pounds onto her petite, 5-foot-3-inch frame. She had thought she was eating healthy food, but still, she had become obese.

Cindy felt tired, depressed, and ashamed.

She told me that, during her fat years, she had a constant negative feedback loop going in the back of her mind: "How could she have let her body get so out of whack? What was wrong with her?" She told me that she would have done anything — anything — to get rid of the weight.

Cindy had tried a million diets: Weight Watchers, fasting, diet shakes, you name it.

Although she had a wealth of knowledge, she realized she lacked commitment. One day, Cindy decided not to diet. Instead, she fundamentally changed her approach to food. She kept her portions to reasonable levels. She eliminated snacks. She cut refined flour and refined sugar out of her diet. She avoided sodas, alcohol, and juice. She ate small amounts of whole grains, added lean proteins and dairy, doubled her fruits and tripled her vegetables.

Over six months, Cindy lost one hundred pounds. She felt healthier, more clear-headed, and more energetic than she had in years. As of this writing, she has kept that weight off for fifteen years.

"Until I heard you talk, I didn't understand why what I did worked," she told me. "And it is so liberating to learn that my problem with weight did not have its roots in some character flaw."

In very simple terms, when Cindy cut out added sugar, she broke an addictive cycle with food and stopped a whole grab-bag of unhealthy processes in her body: insulin and leptin resistance, misfiring biochemical signals that meant she never felt full, over-loaded mitochondria, liver fat; in other words, "metabolic syndrome."

When Cindy ate real food rather than processed food, she felt less hungry because it took her body longer to process the fuel she was putting into it. That has helped her to stick with her new, healthier habits. By reducing her insulin, Cindy's positive feed-back loop (leptin resistance) regained its servo-mechanism (leptin sensitivity), and became a negative feedback loop once again, allowing her to lose the weight and keep it off.

Cindy still gets choked up when she talks about that day when we met. She under-stands better than most how painful it is to be severely overweight: the cycle of self-blame and shame and diet failure and hopelessness. She often says she can't believe how good she feels now. She brims with energy. Let me tell you, this grand-mother gets more done before 9 A.M. than most people do in an entire day. I'm an overachiever, and yet she puts me to shame.

She says she still marvels at the revelation of feeling so good about her body after decades of hating it.

Cindy finally reversed her obesity by reversing her biochemistry. She did it by cooking and eating "real food" — indeed, with many of the recipes you'll find in this book.

Rob and Cindy Go on the Road

Not long after our first meeting, Cindy and I started working together. We called our events "Eat and Learns." You can't just talk to people about the benefits of "real" food; you have to show them. That means feeding them.

We spoke at retirement communities and political gatherings and schools and conferences. I'd explain the science, Cindy would tell her story and the method behind the madness. Then we'd cook a healthy meal with the audience to show them that it's not difficult.

We do the same thing in my clinic: We hold a "teaching breakfast" with the patients and the parents. We've learned that you can't get kids to change until the parents change, and they won't change until you show them four things: 1) Their kid will eat the food; 2) Other people's kids will eat the

49

food; 3) They themselves like the food; and 4) They can afford the food.

Providing all that information offers the best chance of turning a family around; anything less than that is doomed to failure. And that's what we continue to see from all these healthy-eating programs nationwide. Most health and diet regimes don't work long-term. It's time for a change.

Changing Communities

Emboldened by her scientific understanding of her own story, Cindy revamped the menus of her restaurant and catering business, cutting down on sugar and refined flours, adding lots more beans, grains, vegetables, and fruits to her menus.

Gradually, Cindy became a public advocate for healthier food and healthier lifestyles. She sponsored a "Mayor-A-Thon" to get politicians involved, walking a mile a week with elders at a large retirement community to promote healthier lifestyles. She organized health festivals. She challenged other restaurants to serve healthier food to their customers. She started a nonprofit, Wellness City Challenge (wellnesscitychallenge.org), to promote healthier lifestyles. I agreed to serve on the board of Wellness City Challenge, and still do. I have also started my own nonprofit, The Institute for Responsible Nutrition (responsiblefoods .org), to provide the medical, nutrition, and legal know-how to take on the processed food industry. We work together to change communities. Today, the San Francisco Bay Area. Tomorrow, we're coming to your town.

As Cindy got more and more involved with promoting healthy lifestyles in local communities, she started to work more and more with schools. She saw kids like those who populate my medical practice at UCSF: preteens with diabetes, grossly obese teenagers, kids who have trouble focusing, kids who are hyperactive, kids with constant fatigue. Cindy felt that many of these problems could be solved if only kids had the knowledge and the power to change how they eat. Eventually, she decided that she needed to start teaching these kids about nutrition and how to cook healthy food.

Cindy got a part-time job as a teacher at Mount Diablo High School, an underserved, struggling school in the suburban town of Concord, about ten miles from affluent Walnut Creek, where she lives and operates her businesses. Cindy says she is blessed with the people who staff her businesses, so she could run the restaurant and catering operations while only checking in for a few hours each day. She was free to become a part-time high school teacher.

Think about this: Cindy gave up a lucrative day job that she loves to take on the biggest challenge in America: toxic food. Talk about being an overachiever!

Kids Will Eat This Food and Like It

During the 2011 to 2012 school year, Cindy taught one class of about twenty high school juniors how to cook healthy food. Together, they fed their entire class and offered free breakfast and lunch to all the teachers who wanted to participate. The kids ate food that everyone else says teenagers won't eat: whole foods low in sugar and high in fiber and nutrients. Dessert was fruit, not cakes and cookies. She has continued these efforts, adding more classes through the 2012 to 2013 calendar and into the current school year.

I have visited Cindy's classes many times, and what I've seen there gives me so much hope for the future. Some of Cindy's students have lost fifty, even a hundred pounds, eating the dishes you'll find in this cookbook. Teens who once had trouble focusing, who were once behavior problems, who once had no direction have become energized and ambitious. Cindy has changed their food and empowered her charges for the rest of their lives. The mantra of the class: "Change the Food, Change the Future."

When we were choosing the recipes for this book, Cindy enlisted students from her classes to help test the recipes at a scale more appropriate for a home kitchen, rather than for a restaurant or a school cafeteria. After they cook, the kids eat their creations: servings of shaved, roasted Brussels sprouts; kale chips; and quinoa. When I've visited Cindy's classes, I have witnessed it again and again.

Look, I'm a pediatrician. I get to see other people's kids all day. And I'm telling you this: You have never met a more positive, friendly, alert, and engaged group of young people. No attitudes or obsessing over smart phones or gang colors here. These kids are armed with survival skills, and they're not just surviving — they're thriving.

You Can Do It Too

When they see my videos on YouTube or read *Fat Chance,* people frequently e-mail me. The most common question, is, "So what do we do now?" Cutting out sugar and the bulk of refined flours, making things from scratch — all that sounds so difficult. It sounds so complicated. It sounds so bland. It sounds so un-fun.

Both the food and the diet industries would like you to believe just that. The reason Cindy and I decided to write this book together is that it's just not true. It's another misleading, corporate dogma to be debunked.

With new knowledge, a new approach to food, and a few basic cooking techniques and recipes, you can change your life based on the science I outlined in *Fat Chance.* The food you make can be delicious, it can be fast, and it can be fun.

The steps you need to take are not all that complicated, and it's our hope that this book will show you that's so. You don't need to diet. In fact, if you ever go on a diet again, I will have failed. You can lose weight and keep it off. Even more important, you can reverse the damage of metabolic syndrome. You can live a longer, happier, and healthier life. And ultimately, it's cheaper too. Let's get cooking!

■ ■ ■ ■

2

■ ■ ■ ■

CHAPTER 2
DEFENSIVE NUTRITION

We did not write this cookbook to tell you all the things that you can't have.

I do not count calories, and neither does Cindy. We do not diet. We stay active, but we have not become gym rats or prisoners to the treadmill. We have made peace with our bodies and with our food.

Some people espouse the concept of "caloric restriction," an extremely low-calorie diet, as the only way to lose weight and increase lifespan. The joke goes, "caloric restriction won't make you live longer, it will just feel that way."

You don't need to drastically cut your intake to 1,000 or 1,200 calories a day to live long and prosper. You need to eat real food. If you're feeling draggy, old, and tired, check out your food. I'll bet you 10-to-1 that toxic food's your culprit.

Both Cindy and I love to eat. We love to cook. We love the hunt for ingredients at their peak: in stores and in farmers' markets, and sometimes in our own gardens. We love the heavy round fuzz of a peach in August. We love the luxuriant delicacy of just-picked salad greens. We love pizza, the gooey mess of melted mozzarella cheese. We love the savory, fatty indulgence of a well-cooked, but reasonably-sized, piece of meat. We enjoy the (very) occasional sweet treat (see below).

We think that gathering around a table with friends is one of life's great pleasures. I love chopping and stirring in the kitchen with my wife, Julie, and our two daughters, Miriam, fourteen, and Meredith, eight. We're like any other family: we love barbecues, holiday dinners, and picnics. We love eating together. That's why we cook.

Cindy can whip up a brunch for thirty without breaking a sweat. It helps that she grew up in a big, boisterous Italian family. She brought three kids, and her husband Lance brought five kids, to their marriage. They've got loads of grandkids. Parties at Cindy and Lance's house feature amazing spreads: tables groaning with salads of all kinds, sliced fruit, rice and grain gratins and casseroles, grilled meats, poached fish. There's not a chip or a pretzel in sight, and no one ever complains.

Shopping, cooking, and eating should not be a guilty pleasure that makes you sick and threatens your life. Give us three weeks. Shop, cook, and eat in the spirit of this book for that period. That's about the same amount of time it takes most of my patients to detox off sugared soda. I'm willing to bet your health that you won't even miss the processed junk food. In fact, the processed food will not taste as good to you. I've seen it over and over. Once people taste "real" food again, they don't go back to the processed kind.

How Real Food Became Toxic Food

It seems like every day someone comes out with a new theory, or program, or cookbook, promising the solution to all our food woes. What we are proposing with these recipes is not magic — it is, rather, a complete reorientation of our food lives, based on the science of what is driving our obesity and diabetes epidemics.

This isn't as difficult as it sounds. What we are proposing is that you shop, cook, and eat more like your grandparents did. The food in this book is simple and straightforward. It's also delicious.

It's easy to forget how much our food lives have changed in the last fifty years: A couple of generations ago, "convenience food" didn't really exist. If food was "packaged" that probably meant that your mother or your aunt or your grandmother canned it. People shopped every two days and ate fresh, seasonal ingredients. There wasn't really a freezer section at the grocery store. People cooked dinner each night. It was a rarity when families went out to eat.

In the 1960s, packaged foods roared onto the market: Swanson TV dinners, Birds-Eye frozen vegetables, Hamburger Helper, Kraft Macaroni & Cheese, Chef Boyardee Beefaroni, Rice-A-Roni, Ore-Ida Golden Fries, and on and on. All these foods were seen as efficient and modern. People chowed down on them. Gradually, where once we'd had farmers and food, we had spawned a "food industry."

At the same time, families began to find it difficult to get by on one salary. Gradually, two-income households became the norm. In addition, the suburbs grew, and parents became glorified chauffeurs for their kids' endless activities aimed at getting them a leg up for college. Life got harried and busy. Feeling the chaos and the new frenetic pace, people stopped cooking. They started relying on meals out, usually at fast food outlets. Or they bought "ready-to-eat" processed foods from the supermarket. Along the way, food became an individual "commodity." The goal became, can I get the lowest price? instead of, am I getting the best I can?

Then, in the late 1970s, dietary saturated fat became the bogeyman. As Americans raced to cut fats out of their diet, the food companies raced to respond. But they had a problem: How could all these popular processed foods be made to taste good without the fat? Pretty quickly, they came upon a solution: Add sugar. And boy did they add sugar! Today, you find added, refined sugar in all kinds of places that you might not expect it: spaghetti sauce, Bloody Mary mix, taco seasoning, fast food french fries, sliced bread, every breakfast cereal, most yogurts, and pretty much anything in the freezer case or the snack and soda aisle. And excess sugar is the real bogeyman for both obesity and diabetes.

By the 1980s, families were eating several meals a week that, you guessed it, were not only fatty and full of refined carbohydrates, but positively loaded with sugar. Funny thing: This is exactly the same time that the obesity epidemic reared its ugly head. And it's gotten worse every decade since.

Why Is This Cookbook Different?

Remember that your body needs five classes of essential nutrients to remain healthy:

- **Protein:** The body's building blocks. Four calories per gram. Of the twenty amino acids, nine are essential; your body can't make them. You must eat them.
- **Fats:** Concentrated source of energy. Nine calories per gram. There are several essential fatty acids as well, such as oleic acid, DHA, and EPA. You can't make them. You must eat them.
- **Vitamins and other metabolic co-factors:** Drivers of various cell processes, such as energy metabolism, growth, and repair. There are two vitamins that you don't have to eat: vitamin D, provided you get enough sunlight (and we don't), and vitamin K, which is made by the bacteria in your intestine. The rest must be eaten.
- **Minerals:** Necessary catalysts of numerous body functions. Again, no options; you have to eat these.
- **Water:** Remember, our bodies are mostly water!

Wait — something's missing. . . . What

about carbohydrates, you say?

Carbohydrates are your body's "easy" fuel, at four calories per gram. In addition, glucose molecules are necessary to add to various proteins to change their characteristics (for instance, peptide hormones), a process called "glycosylation."

So why aren't carbohydrates essential? Because the only carbohydrate your body needs is glucose, and your liver is very efficient at making it from protein or fat when it needs to. So, while glucose is "essential," dietary carbohydrate is not. Worse yet, if you overconsume dietary carbohydrate, your liver will turn the excess into fat, driving disease. So carbohydrate is decidedly a good-news-bad-news deal. How do you make carbohydrates good news? Consume them with their inherent fiber! Eat them as whole grains, the way they came out of the ground. That slows absorption, and keeps the liver healthy. It is the fiber that's essential, not the carbohydrate!

Most diets and weight loss programs emphasize one or more of these essential nutrients, while discounting the others. What we're saying is that we all need to get "real." We need *all* these nutrients to live and function at our best. We just need to consume them from basic ingredients, in reasonable portions.

Though the media and my critics love to tag me as the "anti-sugar guy," I'm not. Like Berkeley restaurateur Alice Waters of Chez Panisse fame and food writer Michael Pollan of *The Omnivore's Dilemma* fame, I'm a "real food" guy.

You might say Alice Waters leads the "aesthetic school": real food for food's sake, because it looks and tastes better. Michael Pollan leads the "socio-ecological school": real food because the changes in our diet have hurt our economy and our environment. I'm in the "biochemical school": real food promotes healthy body biochemistry while a processed food diet is literally toxic — it causes chronic disease.

You may choose the school you prefer. Choose the issue that floats your boat. It doesn't matter. Real food is the answer to all of our eating problems. That's what makes this cookbook different. If you care about food, if you care about your environment, if you care about health, then this cookbook is for you.

Back to Basics

The food that we emphasize in this cookbook has a lot in common with the food your forebears used to enjoy:

- It includes meats and fats and cheese and eggs. Eaten in moderation, your body needs the proteins and fats in these foods. If you travel to remote areas of the world where people don't have enough fat in their diet, they look sick, with thin, brittle hair and dry, papery skin.
- It does not eliminate the sugar that occurs naturally in foods like milk, potatoes, and fruit. What it does eliminate is most of the refined sugar that is currently added to processed food by the bucket load.
- It emphasizes foods that provide lots of fiber: green food and brown food. Fiber is essential because it slows the digestion of food, delivering nutrients and energy to your liver and your bloodstream at a steady rate, avoiding the spikes in blood sugar that shunt calories to fat and cause myriad problems.
- It's full of whole grains: hulled barley, steel-cut oats, quinoa, farro, brown rice.
- It cuts out processed foods, sauces, and condiments.
- It provides delicious, healthy alternatives to prepared-food pitfalls that can

undercut even a home cook trying to be healthy: salad dressing, ketchup, jarred spaghetti sauce, and barbecue sauce.

- It offers no-sugar and low-sugar desserts. Where we've provided "full sugar" treats, the recipes still call for one-third less sugar than conventional recipes. We promise that you and your family won't even notice the difference.

Sugar: "A" Cause or "The" Cause?

Sometimes, when I meet someone at a party or a hospital function and tell them what I do, they exclaim, "Oh! You're the anti-sugar guy!" Well, yes and no. Sugar is a big part of the problem, but it's actually much more complicated.

People often ask, "Is sugar the cause of obesity?" Common sense would argue that sugar is clearly related to excess weight. But I don't believe in common sense, I believe in data. The data show that the two most "obesogenic" (obesity-causing) foodstuffs in our diet are potato chips and french fries (carbohydrate and fat together). Sugar comes in a distant third. Furthermore, the data actually show that sugar only accounts for a total of 0.8 extra BMI points, leaving us to account for an average increase of five to seven BMI points nationally. As I said in Chapter 1, sugar is *a* cause of obesity, not *the* cause.

It's not the calories in sugar that do the most damage, it's the way that excess added sugar is metabolized in the liver, which causes chronic disease and distorts brain and hormone signaling, leading people to feel increasingly hungry, even as they eat more and more.

Eating more calories than you burn may give you love handles or a bottom that's larger than you might want. But that fat is just under the skin, what doctors call "subcutaneous fat." It might make you depressed when you shop for bathing suits, but that kind of fat won't necessarily make you sick.

What makes you sick is inappropriate energy storage in organs not designed for energy storage. As I've outlined above, the spikes in blood sugar caused by eating processed food overwhelm your body's systems, and force it frantically to stash calories wherever it can, mostly in the liver, muscles, and other organs. This is what doctors call "visceral fat," and that kind of fat leads to the group of illnesses we call "metabolic syndrome."

Sugar may not provide all the calories that

are making us fat, but it's the carrot, the bait, the lure. Added sugar makes us crave more food, and makes our bodies store calories in the wrong places when we eat.

This allows the food industry to trumpet an excuse for the garbage diet they're foisting on the unsuspecting public:

- **We just give the public what it wants.** Well, as I've outlined above, if you give the public lots of added sugar, that makes people want ever more products with lots of added sugar. This way, Big Food can blame your extra fat on your bad habits and lack of discipline. If you didn't like Doritos and Hostess Fruit Pies, they wouldn't make them, right?

Again, it's not that simple, because processed food manufacturers have also discovered something they'd rather you not know:

- **If you build it, they will come.** In other words, if you add sugar to things, boy, do the consumers come. Thus far, all attempts to get people to eat less have met with failure. Why? Sugar interferes with our biochemical hunger and reward signals. Sugar tricks us into eating too much of the wrong things. Sugar makes us sick. And the food industry hides it in plain sight.

If It Has a Label, It's Processed

If you're going to avoid toxic food, you need to learn to read food labels.

If it's not processed, it doesn't need a label. When was the last time you saw a nutrition label on a bunch of scallions or a russet potato? Complete abstinence from processed food has become a major tenet of the Slow Food movement that's caught on in high-income cities like San Francisco, where we live, and in New York, Chicago, and Los Angeles.

I certainly don't want to be a food scold. But people need to realize that if it has a nutrition label, it's processed. In an ideal world, your family wouldn't eat anything from a package. But I'm realistic: I know that "zero processed food" is just not "real world" for most families. I'm not always perfect in this regard myself. Every Wednesday, I see patients all day in clinic, with no access to a refrigerator. I get about ten minutes for lunch on those days. My Wednesday lunch ritual has become Chinese food from the takeout place right on campus, which is hardly healthy.

By the same token, I realize that most people don't bake their own bread anymore. The bread most of us eat is processed. Ditto for pasta. Most families buy canned beans, and many brands have added sugar. Most of us eat cereal, 99 percent of which is processed and over-sugared. Some of us occasionally have a bag of pretzels or chips. That's *really* processed.

What to do? When you do buy bagged and boxed ingredients (even lightly processed foods), just do so with a healthy dose of skepticism.

With all the low-fat, low-carb, low-sugar, and low-calorie claims screaming from every jar, bag, and box, you'd think that most things in the supermarket are good for you. That's what the food companies want you to believe.

Alas, the opposite is true: As I've pointed out, 80 percent of the food in most markets is processed. And the vast majority of that food is just packed with sugar, fat, and refined carbs. Unfortunately, the food industry gives us our processed food with a sugar chaser. That's what makes it taste good. Take out the sugar, salt, and fat, and processed food tastes god-awful, like straw or sawdust. Journalist Michael Moss of *The New York Times* wrote a whole book about that called *Salt, Sugar, Fat: How the Food Giants Hooked Us.*

You think you can figure out what's healthy by reading nutrition labels? Think again. Not only is the American food safety regulation and labeling system deeply flawed, but Big Food hides the toxic ingredients, or disguises them. You really can't judge a food by its label, that is, unless you know what you're doing. The whole country, the whole world actually, needs a tutorial in what I like to call "Label Reading 101."

Hiding in Plain Sight

With my wife, Julie, I've written an e-book, *Sugar Has 56 Names: A Shopper's Guide.* In it, we explain these issues in detail and deconstruct the food labels of the most common processed foods. We hope you'll take this guide to the market with you on your smart phone or tablet. Just remember: You may think you're buying something that doesn't have sugar, but the food industry calls sugar by fifty-six different names.

Fifty-Six Names for Sugar:

Agave nectar*
Barbados sugar*
Barley malt
Beet sugar*
Blackstrap molasses*
Brown rice syrup*
Brown sugar*
Buttered syrup*
Cane juice crystals*
Cane sugar*
Caramel*
Carob syrup*
Castor sugar*
Confectioners' sugar*
Corn syrup
Corn syrup solids
Crystalline fructose*
Date sugar*
Demerara sugar*
Dextran
Dextrose
Diastatic malt
Diatase
Ethyl maltol
Evaporated cane juice*
Florida crystals*

* Contains fructose.

72

Fructose*
Fruit juice*
Fruit juice concentrate*
Galactose
Glucose
Glucose solids
Golden sugar*
Golden syrup*
Grape sugar*
High-fructose corn syrup*
Honey*
Icing sugar*
Invert sugar*
Lactose
Malt syrup
Maltose
Maple syrup*
Molasses*
Muscovado sugar*
Organic raw sugar*
Panocha*
Raw sugar*
Refiner's syrup*
Rice syrup
Sorghum syrup*
Sucrose*
Sugar*
Treacle*
Turbinado sugar*
Yellow sugar*

Here are a few main points to keep in mind as you navigate the nutritional minefield that is the average supermarket.

- The Food and Drug Administration (FDA), the agency charged with keeping our food supply safe, is mostly interested in "acute" toxins, things that make you keel over as soon as you consume them. The FDA is not set up to deal with foods that may cause serious health problems over time — things like sugar and refined carbs.
- The FDA keeps a list called "Generally Regarded as Safe" (GRAS), begun in 1958. The GRAS list is the enemy of anyone who eats. An ingredient may get the GRAS seal of approval simply because of experience or common use in foods. Or it may become GRAS because it's safe under "the conditions of its intended use." But in 1958, when the list started, no one foresaw our current sky-high levels of sugar, omega-6 fats, and trans fats.
- *Too bad.* Once something has been judged GRAS, it's almost impossible to get that designation removed. And what about new ingredients? All the food companies have to do is pay a

bunch of scientists to sit in a room and declare the ingredient GRAS. Of 10,000 items on the GRAS list, 3,000 have not even been reviewed. I don't know about you, but that doesn't make me feel very safe.

- The nutrition labels won't save you. The information you really need just isn't there. For instance, the label lists "total sugars" in your strawberry ice cream. But the natural sugars in the milk and the fruit won't hurt you; it's the "added sugar" you need to watch. Likewise, the label lists "total fat." But all fats are not created equal. Olive oil is good for you, whereas omega 6s are pro-inflammatory and will kill you over time. Both get lumped together on the nutrition label.

Frankly, Cindy and I both think all food is inherently good. It's what companies do to the food that's not. It would be far more useful if Big Food would tell us what they did to the food; that is, what they took out of each product and what they added in, rather than these nutrient totals. But I'm not holding my breath waiting for that to happen. Maybe, if enough consumers complain, if enough consumers send a message with their dollars and their votes, things will change. But that's a process that will take at least a decade, if not more. In the meantime, you and I need to be food samurai: We need to slash through all the labeling and processing subterfuge to defend the health of our families.

Defensive Food Shopping

My wife, Julie, and I go into much more detail in *Sugar Has 56 Names,* but here are some things to watch for as you make your way through the supermarket:

- **Serving Size.** Make sure to note how many servings are in each can or each bag. Who ever ate half a pack of ramen noodles, for instance? So, if the label says "two servings," remember that the nutrition numbers are misleading you by half. You may glance at it and think, *Wow, only 150 calories!* But if there are two servings in the pack, you're really consuming 300 calories.

- **Cholesterol Is Not the Bogeyman.** In the 1970s, we were told that eggs were bad for us because they have cholesterol. It turns out that if you're not part of a small minority of people with a genetic lipid disorder, eggs may be one of the healthiest foods you can eat.

- **A Calorie Is Not a Calorie.** As I've outlined above, your body metabolizes fat calories differently from sugar calories. It's the number of calories from refined carbohydrate that you need to watch. Carbohydrates and sugar create the blood sugar spikes that lead to metabolic syndrome. Here's your clue: Look at the "calories from fat." Subtract the fat calories from the total calories, and you'll get a rough idea of the calories from carbohydrate.

- **A Fat Is Not a Fat — 1.** Omega-3 fatty acids will save your life; trans fats will kill you. "Total fat" is just not a useful measure. And a food can be labeled "trans fat–free" if it has 0.49 grams or less of trans fats per serving. So if you eat four processed foods each day, even though they may be labeled "trans fat–free," you may still be eating as much as 2 grams of trans fat, enough to do real damage over time.

- **A Fat Is Not a Fat — 2.** Omega-6 fatty acids, which promote inflammation, come from plant oils such as corn oil and soybean oil. Eating corn-fed beef, chicken, or fish currently means high levels of omega-6s. Honestly, it's better for your health to eat a little less meat or pay a little more for grass-fed, free-range, or wild-caught animals.

- **A Protein Is Not a Protein.** Certain amino acids in protein are common while others are rare. If you are deficient in the rare amino acids (for example, tryptophan), you don't feel good, you are not happy, and you are hungry. It pays to eat the highest-quality protein, with the highest concentration of tryptophan. That's eggs.

- **A Carb Is Not a Carb.** The nutrition label lists "total carbohydrates." That includes the fiber plus the three types of carb, things that have glucose (starch), or fructose (sugar), or galactose (milk sugar). The body processes these different types of starch very differently. See *Fat Chance* for the science. Remember, carbs are not essential, and can be detrimental. Eating carbs along with their inherent fiber will help reduce your blood insulin and improve your health. But you can't assume, for example, that "whole-grain" bread really has that fiber, because the FDA has no definition for "whole grain." Look for granular crusts on bread and baked goods — those are more likely to contain intact whole grain. Don't buy any carbohydrate that doesn't have at least 3 grams of fiber per serving.

- **A Sugar Is Not a Sugar.** The "total sugar" listed on the label includes the natural sugars inherent in fruits, vegetables, and dairy. What you really need to worry about is "added sugar." It's not always easy to parse this out, but take the case of yogurt: A 6-ounce plain yogurt has 7 grams of sugar, all lactose. A pomegranate yogurt of the same size has 19 grams of sugar, so roughly 12 grams have been added. That's as much as a serving of Cap'n Crunch cereal. Maybe yogurt isn't always so healthy.

- **Ingredient Lists.** If it has more than five ingredients, it probably has fillers and chemicals that you don't need. If an ingredient has a name that doesn't sound like English, it's a filler, a preservative, or something else that makes it processed food, not "real food."

Six Rules to Shop By
As you can see, reading the current nutrition label and shopping in a modern super-

market is a lot like trying to navigate a road map in Japanese. Michael Pollan came up with a whole book of *"Food Rules."* As I push the grocery cart, I keep in mind these six:

1. Don't go to the store hungry.
2. Shop the edges of the supermarket. Stay out of the aisles.
3. If the food has a company logo you've heard of, it's been processed.
4. If it says "partially hydrogenated," the trans fats in that food will outlive you.
5. If it doesn't say "whole grain," it isn't. And even if it does say "whole grain," it might not be.
6. If sugar is any one of the first three ingredients, it's a dessert.

And don't forget: By my count, sugar has at least fifty-six names.

Thinking About Meals

As I've outlined in *Fat Chance,* we've got our food priorities dangerously off-kilter. You may think that the food pyramid that was in vogue when you were a kid is a good guide to a decent dinner for your family.

But the food pyramid was never based on solid science; it was more of a marketing campaign. During the last half-century, the USDA has had two food guides, a food wheel, two versions of the food pyramid that recommended more grains and cereals than fruits and vegetables, and most recently, "My Plate," which recommends that half of our calories should come from fruits and vegetables. Does any of this make sense? What should you do? Do you think Julia Child was worried about the food pyramid?

Think about what you consider a good, healthy meal. Is it meat, starch, and a vegetable? Is it a turkey hero sandwich grabbed from a deli? Is it Cheerios with a side of broccoli, an actual meal recently described to me by a UCSF med student?

Here's the deal: Whatever you may think constitutes a "healthy" meal, it probably doesn't have nearly enough fiber. It probably doesn't include enough whole grains. It probably makes meat the centerpiece rather than a bit of savory protein to accent the whole grains, vegetables, greens, and fruits. It probably includes dessert. It probably includes processed foods like pasta, or supermarket bread, or even an "artisanal" baguette. It's fine to eat that way occasionally, but a steady diet of those kinds of meals will zap your energy. It will age you, because it's putting extra pressure on your liver. It will make you sick — slowly, but surely.

Cindy's Plate

When she was trying to get control of her food and her body, Cindy came up with a formula that she calls Cindy's Plate. Until we have more rational, science-based guidance from the federal government, I think Cindy's formula makes a lot of sense. Remember, it's not about dieting. It's about eating real food in sensible portions.

Here's what Cindy eats in one day:

- Two 6-ounce portions of cooked vegetables (each about a cup)
- Two 6-ounce portions of salad and raw vegetables
- Three 6-ounce portions of fruit
- Two 4-ounce portions of lean protein: mostly chicken, turkey, fish, tofu, or eggs
- Four to six tablespoons of good fat: olive oil, rice bran oil, or safflower oil
- Three 1-cup portions of dairy: milk, cottage cheese, yogurt, or *unsweetened* alternative milks, such as soy, almond, rice, or hazelnut
- Two and a half cups of cooked whole

grains or starch, polenta, hulled barley, cracked wheat, quinoa, brown rice, sweet potato, yams, or potatoes (grilled, roasted, or baked)

Cindy almost never deviates from this guideline. She feels that if she did, she would return to her unhappy past of dieting and hating her body. And believe me: if you piled up 2 1/3 pounds of fruits and vegetables, 1 1/2 pounds of dairy, and 1/2 pound of protein, you'll see that Cindy's not going hungry. In terms of volume, she's probably eating more than my patients who struggle with obesity.

Cindy doesn't worry about calories. Instead, she has a food plan. When she goes out, or when she goes on vacation, she simply eats according to her guidelines. She seeks out restaurants that will give her what she needs. She tries to eat roughly the same amount of vegetables, fruits, grains, and protein wherever she is. She doesn't worry. She enjoys her food. She feels good every day.

Cindy doesn't believe in snacks. She believes that you need a period of fasting between meals to really taste your food, and to allow your blood insulin level to come down. Because of the way she eats, she's rarely hungry between meals. Sometimes, during a busy day in the clinic, I do grab for a snack to give me a boost of energy. When I do, I try to remember these guidelines: A snack should have no more than 150 to 200 calories. It should contain two food groups, such as dairy and vegetable, or meat and fruit. That rules out a 250-calorie bag of crackers, chips, or cookies!

When we're teaching classes, Cindy refers to her eating style as Cindy's Plate. I'm less controlled than Cindy. I admit it: I love a delicious meal in a restaurant or at home, and I'm just not going to measure out all my food exactly. I also carry more extra pounds than Cindy!

If you want to try Cindy's Plate, you can divide up each meal this way. When you eat in a restaurant, try to divide your plate up like this as well:

- 1/2 vegetables or fruit
- 1/4 meat or dairy protein
- 1/4 dairy or whole grains

When you think of it this way, it's obvious how completely backward the standard American diet has become. Instead of fruits and veggies taking up half the plate, fats, sugar, and processed food do. We're eating exactly the opposite of the way that we should eat. Shop, cook, and eat real food, and you'll be amazed how good you feel.

A Word About Dessert

Two generations ago, dessert was something that a family enjoyed after a special Sunday dinner. It did not accompany every meal. Ice cream was not a twice-a-day occurrence. School lunch did not come with cookies, cake, or candy.

Desserts are great. Of course they're great. Otherwise, why would it be so difficult to resist them? But they should be *treats,* not diet staples.

I'm on record: actor Alec Baldwin asked me if I eat dessert. When I'm in New York, I have a piece of Junior's cheesecake. When I'm in New Orleans, I enjoy bread pudding with whiskey sauce. Other than these kinds of dalliances, I'm pretty careful. When I do have a sweet dessert, I make it a really good one. Life's too short to eat bad dessert.

Dessert is not just ice cream, cakes, cookies, pies, and candy. The alcohol in a couple of glasses of wine are metabolized the same as the sugar in a piece of chocolate cake. That's dessert. Pancakes with maple syrup deliver *more* sugar than a slice of chocolate cake. That's dessert. If you have orange juice with those pancakes, that's two desserts. By all means, have a margarita when you go out to a Mexican place with friends. But remember, that's dessert. If it's processed, and it lists sugar in the first three ingredients, it's dessert.

If you go out for dinner, have the shrimp cocktail drenched in ketchup, two glasses of wine, steak with sugary teriyaki sauce, bread and butter, and potatoes au gratin — you've already had five desserts in one meal: the wine, the hors d'oeuvres, the potatoes, the white bread and butter, the teriyaki sauce. You've just had almost a week's worth of sugar- and carb-loaded treats, so don't feel particularly virtuous about splitting the apple tart or crème brulée with your dining partner.

My kids know that during the week, if they want something sweet after a meal, they can reach for a piece of fruit. Julie and I try to make sure we stock the fridge with seasonal fruits at their peak so that our kids can satisfy their sweet tooth in a healthy way.

When Cindy goes out into the community to teach healthy cooking to young kids, she always asks, "How many desserts a day to stay healthy?"

"One!" The students learn quickly.

The kids also learn that "dessert" is

anything with lots of added sugar or refined carbs: an iced fruit bar, one cookie (a normal-size cookie, not one of those disks the size of your hand), one or two pieces of hard candy. Dessert is not a whole bag of Fig Newtons nor a quart of ice cream. That's not dessert, that's diabetes in a container. Over time, that sort of overindulging will most definitely kill you.

For a big dessert, like that decadent piece of chocolate cake, an ice cream sundae, or strawberry shortcake with whipped cream, I think that once a week is a good guideline. We find that when we do allow ourselves to indulge, it feels like an incredible luxury. We linger over each bite, and when we're finished, we feel satisfied, not stuffed and guilty.

Dessert should be part of your life. And remember that dessert is not just cake: For instance, there's really very little difference, health wise, between whole-wheat pasta and regular pasta. Whole-wheat pasta is less processed and has more fiber, but it's still loaded with carbs that will cause an insulin spike. You'll find recipes for pasta in this book. Our feeling is that if you eat it in moderation, about a cup for a serving, and you eat it as part of a diet that is mostly whole grains, fruits, veggies, and good proteins, you'll be fine. The same goes for juice. Juice is bad for you, it's all sugar, but one small glass occasionally isn't going to kill you. Think of juice or pasta the way you'd think of a daiquiri cocktail: as a treat to be enjoyed occasionally.

And when you have dessert, it should be ethereal and sublime. Don't throw away your dessert experience on packaged cookies or fluorescent SpongeBob "ice cream" bars. Make it yourself. And make it special. There's nothing worse than wasting your dessert on a store-bought preparation with twenty-five ingredients in it. My wife Julie's cookies are legend; there's no store-bought cookie that can touch them.

■ ■ ■ ■ ■

3

■ ■ ■ ■

CHAPTER 3
WEAPONS IN THE WAR AGAINST TOXIC FOOD

BASIC COOKING TECHNIQUES

I grew up in Canarsie, Brooklyn, watching my mother cook. There was no fast food back then, and the only processed food was Swanson TV Dinners; the rest was all from scratch. Supper was all hands on deck when my father came home on the LL subway from working in Manhattan. My mother would always experiment on company — the more outlandish the menu, the better. The only time the family ate out was on Sunday evenings at the local Chinese restaurant. I still remember that place's broiled scallops with water chestnuts wrapped in bacon. Extended family dinners such as Jewish holidays meant Grandma's giblet soup, true nirvana. My greatest regret is that Grandma never wrote the recipe down. If she had, it would be in this cookbook! After Grandma passed away, nobody could make that soup as well as she had.

When I was in med school, I took a primary interest in cooking. A guy who cooked was a pleasant shock for a girl on the first date. Today, dinner still means all hands on deck: my wife, Julie; both daughters; and myself. They wait till I get home, even when I'm on call, no matter what the time. And there's no TV during dinner. *Jeopardy!* gets DVR'd. It's about the food, and being together.

Cindy grew up in the East Bay suburbs of San Francisco, where she still lives. Her grandparents owned a catering business in Emeryville, a town between Oakland and Berkeley. Cindy likes to say that she can't remember a time when her family wasn't congregated in the kitchen, laughing, teaching, dancing, and cooking, always cooking. Everything in her family happened in the kitchen.

Her grandmother and her aunts lived at the stove and around the family table. Cindy gravitated to them. They made the kitchen a safe haven, a place for nurturing. By age three, Cindy was helping to make Italian omelets, or "frittatas." By seven, she'd moved on to gnocchi, those amazing Italian pillows of semolina and ricotta cheese or potatoes (See our recipe, p. 383).

From these expansive, joyful women, her

Nana and her aunts, Cindy learned a casual style of cooking: a little bit of this, a little bit of that. Thank God she had a mother who didn't like to cook, but loved to eat. Cindy had a reason to cook, and an appreciative audience.

Her big, boisterous family followed certain themes — each dish had a base that didn't waiver — but her relatives weren't afraid to experiment. Everything was fresh and homemade. They all attempted to outdo each other, trying to serve up "the freshest" or "the best" in the most loving way. It was about the food, but also about the atmosphere. The way they lived communicated this message: "I give you my time, because you are worth it." Cindy says, "We cooked and ate as a family, and we felt loved."

We feel that, for many families, there's just not enough love coming from home kitchens, nor from restaurants. It's our hope that this book will give you the tools to enjoy cooking, eating, and experimenting in the same way that our families did. Food should foster family and community. It should be joyful. It should make you feel good. We want people to feel that food is worth their passion and their time. We want people to have more energy, to be happy and healthy. But remember — food is *not* love. Food is food. Love is love. Don't mistake the two. And kids need both.

Feeding your family should not be a chore. It should not be difficult. Strangely, with the advent of the Food Network and endless food reality shows — *Top Chef Masters, Barefoot Contessa, Chefography, Extreme Chef, Ace of Cakes, The Chew* — you'd think that Americans would all be gourmet cooks. But I think that actually the endless food programming puts off many people. Cooking seems something that celebrities and experts do, not normal Americans.

Trust us, you don't need to be able to do all those things you see on cooking shows or in food magazines. Cooking doesn't have to be complicated. After all, people have been doing it for 1.8 million or 400,000 or 12,000 years, depending on which archaeologist you believe. In this chapter, we'll give you the basics you need to get started. If you want to get fancy once you've mastered the basics, great. And if you don't, no one will notice; they'll only be too happy for a home-cooked meal.

Cooking Is Hands-On
We both think the best way to cook is to get in there and use your hands. Obviously,

wash your hands before you handle food. Cindy drills that into her students endlessly. Don't be afraid to toss salad ingredients with your hands before you add the dressing. Blending pastry or cookie ingredients with your hands works just as well as a pastry mixer or a food processor, sometimes it's even better. Feel those kale and chard greens, or those peaches and plums to see if they're fresh. Poke that chicken breast or pork cutlet to decide whether it's done. Tap the top of a frittata or a quick bread to see if it bounces back.

You've got to jump into cooking. It's about your body. So don't forget to use your body when you're feeding yourself. Feel. Poke. Test. Stir. Toss. Roll. Knead. Crumble. Rub.

Different Every Time

When you plan a meal, try to have all the elements of Cindy's Plate, as described in Chapter 2: one-half fruits or vegetables, one-quarter protein, one-quarter dairy and/or whole grains. Within this structure, there are infinite variations. That's what the recipes in this book are all about.

Here's how to think of a menu: Let's say you're planning a meal for a lot of kids. For the salad, you could do mixed greens, carrots, and tomatoes (see salad ideas, p. 287). Kids all like ranch dressing, so you can whip up a quick batch of our no-sugar dressing (p. 141). For the main course, you could do Stuffed Bell Peppers (p. 471) with polenta. Let's say you're out of the cornmeal used in that recipe, then you could forget about a grain on the side and just add frozen corn or corn cut off fresh cobs to the ricotta stuffing. Maybe you have some kale or some spinach in your crisper that needs to be used. You can layer that between the tomato sauce and the peppers. For dessert, you can slice some good apples and toss them in lemon juice.

We've made this menu many times for young kids, high school kids, at-risk kids, all kinds of kids. They all chow down with gusto.

Making Five Recipes from One
You'll also see that throughout this book we've included variations following each recipe.

Cindy likes to say that with one base recipe, you can travel around the world by just changing the herbs and seasonings. For instance, chicken may have descended from a Southeast Asian jungle fowl, but now every cuisine uses this bird. Tomatoes may come from South America, but they're used everywhere now, in East Asia, India, Europe, Australia. Everybody has onions.

So let's say you have a recipe that features Chicken Braised with Onions and Tomatoes (p. 417). You can make this simple and plain, and it will be delicious. Or, you can bring in cultural influences, styling this basic recipe in many different ways:

South America: Add oregano, cumin, chili powder, potatoes, and carrots. *¡Ahi Esto!* Chicken Colorado.

Italian: Add oregano, garlic, zucchini, and bell peppers. *Ecco!* Now it's Chicken Cacciatore.

India: Add curry powder, cumin, cayenne, potato, peas, and perhaps cauliflower or chickpeas. Sprinkle with chopped, fresh cilantro. *Dekha!* Feast on Chicken Curry.

China: Add a little brown sugar. Fry chicken with bell peppers and pineapple, onion, ginger, garlic, and cilantro. *Qiáo!* Now it's Chicken Stir Fry.

France: Add a splash of white wine, a couple tablespoons of cream, garlic, and tarragon. Voilà! Chicken Fricassee.

Each time, you're basically starting off with chicken, tomatoes, and onions. But you've got many different versions. Variety is the spice of life, and spice is the variety of food.

Or take the basic aromatic mix that the French call "mirepoix," chopped or diced onions, celery, and carrots. We use it as the base for many recipes in this book. In China, they add ginger to this mixture. In India, they leave out the celery and add curry powder; in South America, it's chili powder and cayenne. In Greece, they add dill; and in Scandinavia, they add dill and sour cream. From the same base comes many different dishes.

Don't be afraid to play around with these variations. It's what makes cooking fun!

Can You Make Other Recipes Healthier?

Face it — Southern fried chicken, cream biscuits, and sautéed collard greens with bacon are fantastic, but hardly staples of a healthy diet. Occasionally is fine, about once a week. Don't feel you always have to change what's good. That is real food too. Enjoy it.

In general, we don't recommend radically changing recipes from other cookbooks. Rather, change the food you're eating and choose recipes that reflect that change. However, there are a few things you can do to add fiber and cut sugar from conventional recipes.

- Substitute the white flour in any recipe with one-third whole-wheat flour. It will add a little fiber, and no one will notice.
- Try using Cindy's fiber-rich baking blend: one-half whole-wheat flour, one-fourth old-fashioned rolled oats, one-fourth unbleached all-purpose flour. You can use this in pancakes, cookies, brownies, piecrust and pizza crust, then proceed as usual.
- Cut the sugar in any recipe by one-third. Most recipes today call for way more sugar than they did a generation ago. As your family's palate changes, they will begin to notice other flavors, like the chocolate, the oats, the nuts. It's my bet they won't even miss the sugar.
- You can substitute applesauce or prune paste or pureed berries for refined sugar in some recipes. Just be aware that this will make the result a little more dense, and a little more moist. This tactic works best in quick breads, muffins, pancakes, and dense desserts like carrot cake. You can't add apple-

sauce or prune paste to white chiffon cake and expect it to taste even remotely like chiffon cake. Be realistic!

Shop Like You Mean It

As I travel around the country, I hear a lot of people tell me that it's difficult to find some of the healthy ingredients similar to the ones we call for in this book. If you shop the way you've always shopped, that very well may be true. Food deserts — areas without a decent grocery or produce store — remain a very real problem, especially in poorer towns and neighborhoods.

But remember, grocery stores want to sell products to you. It doesn't matter that much to them if it's food that will make you sick (like sugary breakfast cereal or frozen dinners) or food that will make you healthy. Give them the opportunity to change. Ask for what you want. Change your neighborhood. Remember, if you don't buy it, they won't sell it. And if you do buy it, they will sell it!

Get together with a couple of friends. Get your office or school involved. Get some people together and go to the store manager and ask for what you want. I'm betting the manager would be more than happy to stock the ingredients you desire. You don't have to wait for a Whole Foods or a Trader Joe's to come to town. Help your local stores to stock healthier choices by letting them know that's what you and your neighbors want.

Here are some other tips to help you eat healthy without breaking your budget:

- **Befriend your local butcher.** If you're worried about ground meat (remember pink slime?), pick out the roast you like and ask the butcher to grind it fresh for you. I promise they will be happy to do this for you; they want your business more than Walmart does. You can also do this with poultry like chicken or turkey. Make sure the market has a window into the butchering area, so you can see the butcher doing what you ask.

You can always ask the butcher to custom cut things for you. This is as true in a chain supermarket as it is in a "boutique" butcher shop in some trendy town. Butchers will cut up a whole chicken into pieces, butterfly a leg of lamb, cut up a turkey, or cut a roast into stew pieces. It's free. You just have to know to ask. Butchers will also give advice on how to cook various cuts of meat.

If they won't custom cut, and if they don't know enough to give you advice, find another butcher, or talk to the store manager.

- **Shop seasonally.** Buy what's coming out of the nearby fields now. It will always be cheaper. That means cherries in June or July (not in January) and hard squashes in December (not in July). Buying seasonal usually also means buying local and sustainable.
- **Buy from local produce markets.** Big supermarkets throw away produce that's not perfect. Most cities and towns have little vegetable marts, often run by immigrant families. These small, mom-and-pop stores sell that produce in a "half-off" section. Don't turn your nose up at slightly bruised fruits; they will make lovely fruit compote or applesauce. They can be mixed into whole-grain pancakes or muffins. Tomatoes with a little mold at one end can be trimmed and turned into sauce. Broccoli that's past its prime will do just fine in a quinoa casserole or in soup.
- **Buy in bulk from big box stores.** This is where we buy things like seasonal fruit, whole grains, nuts, raisins,

and other dried fruit, and canned staples like tomato sauce. The stock turns over quickly in these stores. You know the goods won't be old.

- **Don't be penny wise and pound foolish.** A 99-cent 1-pound bag of beans at a dollar store will likely be old and won't cook up as well. Splurge and spend the $1.50 a pound at a big box store or health food store.

Guess What? Real Food Is Cheaper

Cindy planned the following summer meal for a family of four:

- Salad of carrots, cucumbers, and romaine lettuce
    1 1/2 pounds of greens at about 75 cents a pound: $1.25
    1/2 pound each carrots and cucumbers, at 50 cents a pound: $1
- Barbecue chicken legs, or whole chicken or chicken parts
    1 pound of chicken at $2 a pound
    (Or ask the butcher to cut up a whole chicken, which is usually cheaper by the pound; that's enough for two meals plus soup into the bargain.)

- Roasted sweet potatoes
  1 pound at 75 cents a pound: 75 cents
- Roasted zucchini or summer squash
  1 pound at 69 cents a pound: 69 cents
- Sliced peaches, or another stone fruit such as plums or nectarines
  1 pound at 99 cents a pound: 99 cents.

So How Does This Add Up?

Salad	$2.25
Chicken	2.00
Sweet potato	0.75
Squash	0.69
Stone fruit	0.99
Yummy dinner for four:	$6.68

You can't go to McDonald's with a family for that low price, and you won't have leftovers after burgers and fries. Why do you think there's a "food industry" anyway? They make big money. Remember that for every dollar you spend on processed food, 19 cents is for the food and 81 cents is for the marketing. Real food is looking better and better . . .

How to Make Healthy "Fast Food"

We love to cook. Like most Americans, we don't always have the time. There are a few simple things you can do that will help you throw together a great meal in fifteen to thirty minutes on a busy weeknight.

- **Whenever you cook, make extra.** This goes for meats and fish of all kinds, veggies, beans, whole grains, soups, stews, chili. You can mix leftover fish with a bit of mayo and chopped scallions and have it the next day in a sandwich, or you can simply crumble it over salad.
- **Freeze the extras in one-meal portions in plastic bags.** Date and label! You may think you'll remember, but you won't. Chunky tomato soup and chili look amazingly similar when frozen.
- **Don't throw cooking water away.** When you cook beans or whole grains, the water they cook in will make soups and stews a little richer. Freeze in bags and use as needed.
- **Designate a "use me" shelf in your freezer.** Freeze leftover poultry backs and wing tips in bags until you have enough to make broth. Don't throw

away those leftovers: that one-half cup of cooked broccoli or that cup of uneaten pasta. Put it on the "use me" shelf and add to soups and stews, or whatever. Use things within three months. After that, freezer burn becomes a problem.

- **Get ready for real fast food in the morning.** When you know you're going to be in a rush, transfer a few "use me" bags from freezer to fridge before you leave for work. They will be ready to turn into a casserole, a pasta, an egg scramble, or a stew when you get home.

Basic Cooking Rules

Cindy posts these rules in her cooking classes, but I find they're a good reminder to home cooks as well.

- Always wash your hands and put your hair up.
- Read over the recipe before you start cooking.
- Preheat the oven, if baking or roasting.
- Use a timer to keep track of cooking times.
- Never leave food out for more than 2 hours.

- Be sure to wash counters and sinks with soap, water, bleach, or disinfectant.
- Scrub vegetables instead of peeling.
- Read the label, check for sugar and fiber. (See Label Reading 101, p. 71.)
- Taste before adding salt.
- When steaming vegetables, always finish by rinsing them in cold water. This will hold their color and flavor.
- Never rinse pasta. Don't put olive oil or butter on pasta to keep it from sticking. The starch on the noodles helps sauces to cling. It's OK to put a little oil in the water to prevent it from boiling over.
- Clean as you go!
- Compost and recycle = no waste! Good for the environment.

What You Need: Equipment

The cooking shows and magazines would love for you to buy every gadget and lovely platter in the Williams-Sonoma or the Dean & DeLuca catalogs. You don't need to do that. Here's what you need to make all the recipes in this book:

- Small, medium, and large mixing bowls

- At least three wooden spoons
- Whisk
- Set of liquid measuring cups, glass or plastic with spouts
- Set of dry measuring cups, metal or plastic with smooth rims
- Set of measuring spoons
- Three rimmed cookie sheets for roasting and baking
- Pyrex glass dishes in these sizes:
  - 8-by-8-inch
  - 9-by-13-inch
  - 5-by-9-inch
- A few platters, small, medium, and large, two of each
- Serving bowls, small, medium, and large, two to three of each
- 1 1/2-gallon stockpot
- 1-gallon stockpot
- 8-inch omelet pan, nonstick or stainless
- 10-inch frying pan
- 12-inch frying pan
- Heavy cast-iron skillet, preferably 12-inch
- Two saucepans, 1-quart and 2-quart sizes, with lids
- Small sieve
- Colander
- Paring knife

- 8-inch serrated knife, not pointed
- 8-inch chef's knife
- Two cutting boards, one for meat, one for everything else
- Pepper mill
- Peeler
- Grater
- Cheesecloth
- Spatula
- Potato masher (This is also good for other veggies!)
- Meat thermometer
- Blender
- Steamer insert
- Aluminum foil
- Parchment paper
- A metal rack for roasting and cooling

Extras (Not absolutely necessary, but nice to have):

- Food processor
- Hand mixer
- Food scale (Top of the line costs $100-plus, but you can get a perfectly serviceable scale at a big box store for about $15.)
- Electric knife sharpener (Again, the most expensive will set you back $100-

plus, but you can get an entry-level model for about $25.)

Don't worry about buying fancy pots and pans. Buy pots and pans that are heavy enough to be sturdy and to keep food from burning. You don't need "top of the line" kitchenware to cook the food in this book. Cast-iron skillets and sturdy stainless steel pots will do just fine. Cuisinart makes affordable stainless steel cookware. You can also find decent cookware at the big box stores. Just make sure the pots and pans are not too thin: Over-thin cookware means burned dinners. Pots should feel substantial in your hands, not feather-light.

What You Need: Knife Basics

When Cindy looks to hire kitchen staff at her restaurant, one of the first things she looks for is "knife skills." Face it — there are no knife skills if the knife is not sharp. Many people don't want to cook because they are afraid of their knives. And dull knives are something to be afraid of. Buy knives that feel good in your hand and keep them sharp with a honing steel, also called a sharpening steel. (You may want to buy an electric knife sharpener, but those are expensive.)

If you're going to cook, you must know how to handle a knife. Whole books have been written on knife technique. You don't have to know how to debone and butterfly a chicken, but you should be able to handle a chef's knife. Here are just a few basic tips:

- Hold the tip of the knife down. Use it as an anchor.
- Meanwhile, push down and forward with the hand on the handle.
- Curl the first two finger joints of your free hand under. Press your knuckles against the flat of the blade to guide it. Move your free hand back as you cut, keeping the flat of the blade against your knuckles.
- Don't cut with the front and tip of the knife. Cut with the part of the blade back toward the handle. This way you don't have to lift the knife up very far to cut, and you're less likely to cut your fingers.

What You Need: In Your Pantry
It's always easier to cook when you have a critical mass of ingredients in your kitchen. These are the things that we think are good to have on hand most of the time. These recommendations are good for a family of

four. Buy more if your family is larger, or less if your family is smaller.

Beans and Grains

If you're buying in bulk at a big box store, you'll have to buy at least four or five pounds of many of these items. Don't buy more than that. Always have at least one pound of each variety stored in airtight containers. Plastic works fine, but you can also reuse large jars for dry-goods storage. Label and date!

Use these staples — that's the whole point of changing your eating style, right? Because the whole grains contain fats in their hulls, bran, and germ, they will go bad after about six months. Old beans take longer to cook and don't taste as good.

- Barley, dehulled (unprocessed, takes a bit longer to cook) or pearled (hull and bran removed, cooks faster, still a good source of fiber)
- Brown rice
- Cornmeal
- Farro (A whole grain, often thought to be wheat, but actually a plant and grain all its own with a complex nutty taste, not as heavy as many other whole grains)

- Oats, steel cut (Whole-grain groats, the inner portion of the oat kernel, that have been cut)
- Oats, rolled (Oats that have been rolled into flat flakes, then steamed and lightly toasted. These cook faster than steel-cut oats. Most sold as "oat-meal" usually, but not always, have had the nutritious outer bran removed because the bran can make the grain spoil faster. If you want rolled oats with the bran, these are usually sold as "old-fashioned" oatmeal. "Quick" oat-meal is more highly processed, rolled, steamed, toasted, and cut into small pieces so that it will cook faster.)
- Quinoa (Not a true cereal because it does not come from a grass, but from a plant called goosefoot. A staple in Peru and Bolivia, quinoa provides healthy fats, calcium, and antioxidants. It has a texture similar to couscous.)
- Wheat, cracked (Crushed or steel-cut raw wheat, high in fiber)
- Wheat, bulgur (Wheat kernels partially steamed and toasted, then cracked)
- Whole-wheat flour (Whole grains of wheat, bran, germ, and endosperm, ground)
- White flour (Also called unbleached

all-purpose flour; only the endosperm of the wheat grains, ground)

- Chickpeas (Also called garbanzo beans)
- Kidney beans
- Lentils, any color, red, yellow, or green
- Pinto beans
- Split peas, yellow or green

Nuts, Seeds, and Dried Fruit

Buy nuts and seeds raw, store in the freezer. As you need them, toast in a 350°F oven for about 8 to 10 minutes; check them at 8 minutes. Nuts burn very fast, so use a timer! You can also toast nuts and seeds in a heavy skillet over medium heat for 3 to 5 minutes. (Toast a little extra each time, toss in salads or grain pilaf, or have a few as a healthy snack.)

- Almonds
- Coconut, unsweetened, the big wide strips, not the sugar-saturated shreds. You may have to go to a health food store to find these.
- Pecans
- Sunflower seeds
- Walnuts
- Raisins
- Dried fruit of your choice, apricots,

pears, whatever (For granola and salads)

Canned or Jarred Goods
- Canned beans in water, one or two
  cans each of the varieties above
- A few jars of tomato sauce or marinara sauce; look for brands that just
  use tomatoes and spices. There's no
  need to add sugar to tomatoes!
- At least three 28-ounce cans crushed
  tomatoes
- Three or four cans of tuna in water
  (dolphin-safe). Tuna has gotten a bad
  rap due to its mercury content. Chunk
  Light has less mercury than Solid
  White. So you can give your kids (over
  six years old) Chunk Light tuna sandwiches once a week, or Solid White
  sandwiches twice a month, and stay
  under the toxic threshold.

Seasonings
Herbs and spices are the keys to dynamite
cooking and big compliments. You'll see that
in many of this book's recipes, we used
dried herbs and fresh herbs interchangeably. We've done this because we know that
not everyone is inclined to keep a lot of
fresh herbs in their refrigerator. If that

means you, then just use dry herbs. The dishes will still be delicious. If you don't mind the extra expense, and space in your crisper, use fresh herbs, which will impart a clearer, more intense taste profile than their dried counterparts. Just remember that fresh herbs don't stand up to long cooking, and that you generally need three times the amount of fresh herbs. Add fresh herbs just before you finish cooking, or sprinkle them over finished dishes.

Keep dried herbs in small glass containers in a dark cupboard. Don't keep them for more than a year. Buy them at a health food store, or another market that sells them in bins. They are much, much cheaper in bulk. It often makes sense to designate a particular month to replace all your spices. If that's too much trouble, or too expensive, date the jars as you buy them.

- Allspice (Just a small jar, this is used in small amounts.)
- Basil
- Cardamom, ground
- Chinese five-spice powder
- Chives, dried
- Chili powder
- Cinnamon, ground
- Cloves, ground

116

- Coriander, ground
- Cumin, ground
- Curry powder
- Dill
- Garlic powder
- Garam masala (An Indian spice blend. Delish!)
- Ginger, ground
- Italian seasoning
- Mustard, powdered
- Mustard seed (Good in salads and whole-grain pilafs.)
- Nutmeg, ground
- Onion powder
- Oregano
- Paprika, smoked
- Paprika, sweet
- Pepper, cayenne
- Pepper, black
- Red pepper flakes
- Rosemary
- Sage
- Salt, celery (Good in salads and stews.)
- Salt, iodized (The regular kind)
- Salt, kosher (Salt flakes, which have a nice texture for salads)
- Salt, garlic
- Sesame seeds
- Thyme

After nine months, when dried herbs get close to the end of their peak flavor, combine them into herb blends to use them up quickly:

- Chinese blend: ginger, mustard, five-spice powder, salt
- Italian blend: oregano, basil, thyme, rosemary, red pepper flakes
- Indian blend: cumin, curry, coriander, cardamom
- Spanish blend: oregano, cumin, chili powder, cayenne, red chilies

Dry Storage

If you have enough space, keep these in a dark, dry cabinet. Don't buy huge bags of potatoes or onions unless you can use them up in a couple of weeks. Otherwise, they'll spoil. It's usually adequate to have four or so on hand.

- Garlic, one head
- Onions, yellow
- Potatoes, sweet. These come in many varieties: red, pink, orange, yellow, even violet and purple. They're all delicious. Sweet potatoes are also a better source of fiber, complex carbs, protein, iron, and calcium than other veg-

etables.

- Potatoes, russet
- Shallots (Smaller than onions, but sweeter, and with a little kick)

Baking

- Baking powder
- Baking soda
- Chocolate chips, good quality (Dessert should be worth it!)
- Honey, a medium-size jar (It crystallizes if kept too long), a good grade
- Sugar, brown
- Sugar, white, a small container
- Vanilla or vanilla extract
- Yeast, rapid-rise packets or a jar (In the fridge it will keep longer. Wet yeast can be cut into cubes and put in the freezer.)

Condiments and Vinegars

Everyone has their favorites, but these are the basics you should always have around:

- Hot sauce, such as Tabasco, Tampico, or Sriracha (Or all of them!)
- Mayonnaise, Best Foods (West Coast) or Hellmann's (East Coast)
- Mustard, Dijon
- Mustard, yellow

119

- Soy sauce, light salt
- Tamari sauce (Tamari is thicker, darker, and richer than soy sauce.)
- Worcestershire Sauce (Great for marinades and dressings, it has a very small amount of sugar.)
- Red wine vinegar
- White wine vinegar
- Balsamic vinegar
- Apple cider vinegar

Oils

Many oils have a "best before" date stamped on the label. If your brand doesn't, figure that nut oils or flavored oils will last about a year. Vegetable oils — olive, safflower, canola, peanut, and so on — last one to two years in the pantry. All oils will last a bit longer if you keep them in the refrigerator. I use most of these oils interchangeably. You can also substitute butter for oils in many cases — it just depends on the flavor you're after.

- Olive oil (makes your liver work better). Just know that its "smoke point" (when the oil begins to smoke and burn) is relatively low. Don't use olive oil if you're going to be cooking over very high heat.

- Rice bran oil. It has a higher smoke point than olive oil, making it good for frying. It does not have the unhealthy omega-6 fatty acids found in corn or canola oil.
- Coconut oil. Good for frying, good for baking.
- Safflower oil, organic, cold press. A neutral-flavored oil, it has been shown to increase a protein that regulates blood-glucose levels.
- Sesame oil. The primary oil for Chinese cooking, it's generally used for flavoring.
- Non-aerosol cooking spray. You can buy this, or just fill a spray bottle with neutral-flavored oil, such as olive oil or safflower oil.

Refrigerator Staples

In general, we eat fruits and veggies with the peels intact. Cindy swears by kiwi with the fuzzy skin — and her students eat it — but you don't have to go that far. Peel hard squashes, garlic, shallots, onions, citrus, bananas, melons, pineapple, and yes, kiwi. But your family probably won't even notice if you leave the fiber-rich peels on many other things: eggplant, potatoes, carrots, soft squashes, apples, peaches, pears, and plums.

- Apples
- Beans, green
- Beets (Buy with the tops, they're cheaper and you can sauté the tops as a green veggie.)
- Broccoli
- Brussels sprouts
- Butter, unsalted
- Carrots
- Cauliflower
- Celery
- Chicken breasts or thighs
- Kale
- Lemons
- Limes
- Milk, 2 percent, 1 gallon
- Oranges
- Pineapple
- Sparkling water, plain or flavored, such as raspberry or orange (This is a good substitute for soda. You can also make your own by chilling seltzer or plain water with a fruit of your choice: lemons, limes, and oranges, of course, but melons and strawberries also work well.)
- Swiss chard
- Tofu, firm
- Turkey, ground

- Yogurt, Greek, plain, unsweetened, no fat, no pectin

Freezer Staples
- Artichoke hearts
- Asparagus
- Beef, ground
- Berries, lots of berries: raspberries, blueberries, blackberries, mixed berries (Look for "individually quick frozen," no additives.)
- Chicken, ground
- Corn
- Green beans
- Kale
- Pineapple chunks
- Rice, brown, cooked (You can buy this at some markets, or make your own and freeze; excellent for "healthy fast food.")
- Spinach, chopped
- Shrimp or prawns
- Turkey, ground

Glossary of Cooking Terms

As we've relied more and more upon processed foods, many of us have forgotten the terminology of the kitchen. Some of us never learned it in the first place. You will no doubt know some of the terms below, but if you don't quite remember other terms in this book's recipes, please refer to this list.

AL DENTE. Italian expression used to describe pastas, vegetables, or grains that have been cooked until they offer a slight resistance to the bite.

BAKE. To cook with dry heat in an oven, usually at medium or low heat. Usually 350°F or lower.

BARBECUE. Generally refers to grilling done outdoors over an open charcoal, gas, or wood fire. More specifically, barbecue refers to long, slow direct-heat cooking that includes liberal basting with a barbecue sauce or spice rub.

BASTE. To moisten foods during cooking with pan drippings or a sauce to add flavor and prevent drying.

BATTER. A mixture containing flour and liquid, thin enough to pour.

BEAT. To mix rapidly in order to make a mixture smooth and light by incorporating as much air as possible.

BLANCH. To immerse in lightly salted, rapidly boiling water and allow to cook just briefly. This is usually followed by "refreshing," immediately plunging ingredients into ice water to stop the cooking process.

BLEND. To thoroughly mix two or more ingredients.

BOIL. To heat a liquid until bubbles break continually on the surface.

BROIL. To cook under strong, direct heat in an oven or a salamander (a restaurant-grade broiler).

CARAMELIZE. To heat sugar or ingredients with natural sugars (like onions or fruit) until they turn golden brown and have a caramel taste.

CHOP. To cut into pieces with a sharp knife or another chopping device.

CLARIFY. To separate and remove solids from a liquid, such as broth or melted butter, thus making it clear.

CREAM. To soften a fat, especially butter, by beating it at room temperature. Butter and sugar are often creamed together to make a soft paste that is used as a base for baked goods.

CURE. To preserve foodstuffs, especially meats, by drying and salting and/or smoking.

DEGLAZE. To dissolve the thin glaze of juices and brown bits on the surface of a pan in which food has been fried, sautéed, or roasted. To do this, add liquid and stir and scrape over high heat, thereby creating a liquid that can be used as a sauce.

DEGREASE. To skim fat from the surface of stews, soups, or stock. This may also be done by cooling in the refrigerator so that the fat hardens and can be easily peeled from the surface.

DICE. To cut food into cubes of uniform size and shape.

DISSOLVE. To become incorporated into a liquid, forming a solution.

DREDGE. To coat a food item in flour or bread crumbs before cooking it.

DRIZZLE. To drip a thin line of frosting, oil, or sauce back and forth over the top of the thing that you are baking or cooking.

DUST. Generally means to put a very light coating of some kind of powdered material on top of something, like dusting a banana bread with cinnamon or dusting a greased pan with flour.

FILLET. A boneless cut of meat or fish.

FLAKE. To break into small pieces.

FOLD. To incorporate a delicate substance, such as whipped cream or beaten egg whites, into another substance without releasing air bubbles. You cut down through the mixture with a spoon, whisk, or fork; go across the bottom of the bowl, up and over, close to surface. The process is repeated, while slowly rotating the bowl, until the ingredients are thoroughly blended.

FRY. To cook in hot fat.

1. To cook in a shallow layer of hot fat is called shallow-fat frying.
2. To cook in a deep layer of hot fat is called deep-fat frying.

GARNISH. To add elements, such as chopped herbs, lemon slices, or flowers, to make plated food look good.

GRATE. To rub on a grater to shred food in various sizes or bits.

GRATIN. From the French word for crust, gratin describes any dish that is baked in a shallow dish with a topping of seasoned bread crumbs and cheese.

GRILL. An open rack or grate with a heat source underneath. Depending on the type of grill, the heat source can be an open flame (either gas or charcoal) or electric.

GRIND. To crush, pulverize, or reduce to powder.

JULIENNE. To cut vegetables, fruits, or cheeses into thin strips.

KNEAD. To work and press dough to develop the gluten strands in the flour. This can be done with the palms of your hands or with a machine such as a standing mixer with a dough hook.

MARINATE. To flavor and moisturize pieces of meat, poultry, seafood, or vegetables by soaking them in or brushing them with a liquid mixture of oil, vinegar, and seasonings. Dry marinades (rubs), mixtures composed of herbs or spices, can be rubbed onto meat, poultry, or seafood.

MINCE. To cut or chop food into very small pieces.

MIREPOIX. A French term for a combination of chopped carrots, celery, and onions used to add flavor and aroma to stocks, sauces, and soups. Also referred to as "aromatics."

MISE EN PLACE. A French phrase that means "putting in place," as in a setup. It is used in professional kitchens to refer to organizing and arranging the ingredients that a cook will require during his or her shift. This also works well in a home kitchen. Collect and prepare all the things you need for a recipe before starting to cook.

MIX. To combine ingredients, usually by stirring.

PAN-BROIL. To cook (steak, for example) over direct heat in an uncovered, usually ungreased, skillet.

PANFRY. A form of frying characterized by the use of minimal cooking oil or fat (compared to shallow frying or deep frying); typically using just enough oil to keep what is being cooked from sticking to the pan.

PARBOIL. To cook food partially in advance so that its cooking time will be reduced when added to a recipe.

PEEL OR PARE. To remove the outermost skin of a fruit or vegetable. Whenever possible, don't do it! The fiber in most peels tastes good and is good for you.

PICKLE. To preserve meats, vegetables, or fruits in a mixture of salted water, vinegar, and spices.

PINCH. As much of an ingredient as you can pinch between your thumb and forefinger, about 1/8 teaspoon. Usually used with salt or sugar.

PLANKED. Cooked on a thick hardwood plank.

PLUMP. To soak dried fruits in liquid until they swell and soften.

POACH. To cook very gently in hot liquid kept just below the boiling point.

PUREE. To mash foods by hand, rub through a sieve or food mill, or whirl in a blender or food processor until very smooth.

REDUCE. To thicken and intensify the flavor of a liquid mixture by rapidly cooking the liquid uncovered and allowing the liquid to evaporate until the desired volume remains.

REFRESH. To run cold water over food that has been parboiled, to stop the cooking process quickly.

RENDER. To melt hard fat, such as lard.

ROAST. To cook by dry heat in an oven, usually at a high temperature, above 350°F.

SAUTÉ. To cook and/or brown food in a small amount of hot fat.

SCALD. To bring to a temperature just below the boiling point.

SCALLOPED. Baked, usually in a casserole, with sauce or another liquid such as milk or broth.

SCORE. To cut narrow grooves partway through the outer surface of food.

SEAR. To cook, usually meat, over very high heat, browning the surface. This locks in the juices.

SHRED. To cut or tear in small, long, narrow pieces.

SIFT. To put dry ingredients through a sieve or sifter.

SIMMER. To cook slowly in liquid over low heat at a temperature of about 180°F. The surface of the liquid should be barely moving, broken from time to time by slowly rising bubbles.

SKIM. To remove impurities, whether scum or fat, from the surface of a liquid during cooking, for a clear, cleaner-tasting result.

STEAM. To cook over boiling water in a steamer or double boiler.

STEEP. To extract color, flavor, or other qualities from a substance by leaving it in water just below the boiling point.

STERILIZE. To destroy microorganisms with heat.

STEW. To simmer slowly in a small amount of liquid for a long time.

STIR. To mix ingredients with a circular motion until well blended or of uniform consistency.

TOSS. To combine ingredients with a lifting motion.

TRUSS. To secure poultry with string or skewers, so that it holds its shape while cooking.

WHIP. To beat rapidly to incorporate air, as in heavy cream or egg whites.

If you work through the recipes in this

book, you'll discover how they reflect a style of shopping, cooking, and eating. It's our hope that the science behind these recipes will inspire you to care for your body by learning to cook. If you already know how to cook, we hope they'll help you to make your cooking style more healthy.

The recipes in this book form a "scaffolding," as they say in the education world. In other words, these dishes form a scaffold or foundation upon which you can build as your cooking skill increases. Cindy teaches her students to cook in this way: basics, then basic recipes, then variations.

A note on cooking times: The first time you make one of these recipes, give yourself twice as much time as we estimate. With practice, you'll become a speedier cook. Cindy can make these recipes in half the time noted. Over time, you will too.

The recipes in this book illustrate techniques and approaches. We hope they'll inspire you to cook for your family, to experiment once you've learned the base recipes, and to become an advocate for a less toxic food environment.

■ ■ ■ ■

4

■ ■ ■ ■

CHAPTER 4
THE BASICS: DRESSINGS, SAUCES, AND STAPLES

Commercial condiments are catastrophes because they are sugar apologists: salad dressings, sauces, even pickle juice. This is very much on purpose. In this chapter, you'll find easy alternatives to bottled and canned dressings, sauces, stocks, and staples. Want salt and crunch? Bypass the Ruffles and and try some Kale Chips (p. 181) or Roasted Chickpeas (p. 178). Think bread is too difficult to make? Our Whole-Wheat Sponge Bread (p. 188), with all the fiber you need and none of the added sugar of store-bought bread, requires only one bowl, one pan, one rise, and 20 minutes of active time.

It may sound really extreme to make your own ketchup and barbecue sauce. But they keep for quite a while, and you'll notice that many of the recipes in this chapter make large batches. That way, if you do get ambitious enough to make ketchup, you'll only have to do it every few weeks. Salad dressings can be used in other things besides salad: Marinate meats in them, or toss vegetables in them before roasting. A bonus: All of these things taste better when they're homemade. And they won't make you sick, the way conventional processed foods will.

None of these recipes is difficult, honest. They just take a little bit of planning and a little bit of time, in many cases just five to ten minutes.

Recipes:

Blue Cheese Dressing
Italian Vinaigrette Dressing
Ranch Dressing
Balsamic Vinaigrette
Caesar Dressing
Enchilada Sauce
Marinara Sauce
Barbecue Sauce
Ketchup
Cauliflower Béchamel Sauce
Stock — A Tutorial
Spinach and Ricotta Filling
Roasted Tomatoes
Fajita Seasoning Mix
Barbecue Rub
Roma Tomato Basil Salsa

Fresh Fruit Salsa
Marinated Olives
Roasted Chickpeas
Kale Chips
Edamame Spread
Basil Pesto
Whole-Wheat Sponge Bread

BLUE CHEESE DRESSING

= Makes: 1 quart

= Serving size:
2 tablespoons

= Total servings: 32

= Active time:
15 minutes

= Total time:
15 minutes

Cindy has made this recipe in her restaurant for more than thirty years. It came from an older chef she knew when she first started working in kitchens in the early 1970s. Sometimes simple is just better. Use a really good mayonnaise.

Ingredients
2 cups mayonnaise
1/2 cup buttermilk
5 ounces sour cream
5 ounces crumbled blue cheese
2 tablespoons chopped fresh parsley, or 2 teaspoons dried parsley
2 teaspoons Worcestershire sauce

1 1/2 teaspoons garlic salt

1 pinch (1/8 teaspoon) of ground black pepper

Place the mayonnaise, buttermilk, sour cream, blue cheese, parsley, Worcestershire sauce, garlic salt, and pepper in a large bowl and mix until smooth.

Stored in a sealed glass jar or another container in the refrigerator, this dressing will keep for two weeks.

VARIATIONS:
- Use Maytag blue cheese.
- Use Gorgonzola cheese.

GOES WELL WITH:
- Salads
- Carrot sticks, celery sticks, or other cold veggies
- Sandwich fillings — makes a great spread

Per serving: Calories 130, Calories from Fat 120, Total Fat 13g (20% DV), Saturated Fat 3g (15% DV), Trans Fat 0g, Cholesterol 10mg (3% DV), Sodium 160mg (7% DV), Carbohydrates < 1g (0% DV), Dietary Fiber 0g (0% DV),

Sugars 0g, **Added Sugars:** 0g, Protein 1g, Vitamin A 2%, Vitamin C 0%, Calcium 4%, Iron 0%.

ITALIAN VINAIGRETTE DRESSING

= Makes: 1 quart

= Serving size: 2 tablespoons

= Total servings: 32

= Active time: 10 minutes

= Total time: 10 minutes

This is the classic salad dressing, without all the high-fructose corn syrup in many bottled brands. Cindy's aunts and grandmother made this when she was growing up. It was the first salad dressing she served in her restaurant. Simple and flavorful, it's a keeper.

Ingredients

2 tablespoons chopped fresh parsley, or 2 teaspoons dried parsley

1 tablespoon Italian seasoning

1 teaspoon dried onion flakes, or 1 tablespoon fresh peeled and minced onion

1 teaspoon peeled and minced fresh garlic, or 1/3 teaspoon garlic powder

1 cup red wine vinegar

1 teaspoon Dijon mustard

1 teaspoon salt

1/2 teaspoon cracked black pepper
3 cups olive oil, or a blend of olive and safflower oils

STEP 1: Place the parsley, Italian seasoning, onion flakes or onion, garlic or garlic
powder, wine vinegar, mustard, salt, and
cracked pepper in a jar or bowl and mix
them together.

STEP 2: Slowly add the oil to the ingredients, whisking it constantly until the mixture
thickens slightly.

Stored in a sealed glass jar or another
container in the refrigerator, this dressing will keep for one month.

VARIATIONS:
- Add 1 pinch (1/8 teaspoon) of
  crushed red pepper flakes.
- Add 1/2 cup canned crushed tomatoes or 1/4 cup tomato paste.
- Use 1/4 cup finely chopped fresh
  cilantro or 1/4 cup finely chopped
  oregano, in place of Italian seasoning.
- Use 1/4 cup finely chopped basil, in
  place of Italian seasoning.

GOES WELL WITH:

- Raw or cold steamed vegetables
- Chicken and beef as a marinade
- Savory Watermelon and Feta Salad (p. 312)

Per serving: Calories 180, Calories from Fat 180, Total Fat 20g (31% DV), Saturated Fat 2g (10% DV), Trans Fat 0g, Cholesterol 0mg (0% DV), Sodium 80mg (3% DV), Carbohydrates 0g (0% DV), Dietary Fiber 0g (0% DV), Sugars 0g, **Added Sugars:** 0g, Protein 0g, Vitamin A 0%, Vitamin C 0%, Calcium 0%, Iron 0%.

RANCH DRESSING

= Makes: 2 cups   = Active time: 10 minutes

= Serving size: 2 tablespoons   = Total time: 10 minutes

=Total servings: 16

Packaged ranch dressing has loads of sugar and many other things that we're not sure we want to feed our children and grand-children. Homemade salad dressing beats the pants off store-bought, because you can control what's in it. This one has no sugar. The fat is not problematic in any way. Most important, it has minimal salt. Remember, you can always add salt, but you can't take it out. Kids love ranch dressing and this is a great recipe. Use a really good mayonnaise.

Ingredients
1 cup mayonnaise
1 cup buttermilk
1 tablespoon peeled and minced red onion or shallot
1 tablespoon fresh parsley, or 1 teaspoon dried parsley
1 tablespoon Dijon mustard
1/2 teaspoon garlic powder
1/2 teaspoon onion powder
3/4 teaspoon salt
1/4 teaspoon ground black pepper
1 pinch (1/8 teaspoon) of crushed red pepper flakes

Put the mayonnaise, buttermilk, onion or shallot, parsley, mustard, garlic powder, onion powder, salt, pepper, and crushed red pepper flakes in a bowl. Whisk until well combined.

Stored in a sealed glass jar or another container in the refrigerator, this dressing will keep for two weeks.

GOES WELL WITH:
- Any salad
- Dipping vegetables

Per serving: Calories 110, Calories from Fat 100, Total Fat 11g (17% DV), Saturated Fat 1.5g (8% DV), Trans Fat 0g, Cholesterol 5mg (2% DV), Sodium 240mg (10% DV), Carbohydrates 1g (0% DV), Dietary Fiber 0g (0% DV), Sugars < 1g, **Added Sugars:** 0g, Protein < 1g, Vitamin A 0%, Vitamin C 0%, Calcium 2%, Iron 0%.

BALSAMIC VINAIGRETTE

= Makes: 1 quart = Active time: 10 minutes

= Serving size: 2 tablespoons = Total time: 10 minutes

=Total servings: 32

You can't get any simpler than this dressing. And it's so good.

Ingredients

1 cup balsamic vinegar

1 tablespoon salt

1 teaspoon ground black pepper

4 cloves garlic or shallots, peeled and finely chopped

3 cups extra-virgin olive oil, or a blend of olive and safflower oils

STEP 1: Combine the balsamic vinegar, salt, ground pepper, and garlic or shallots in a bowl.

STEP 2: Slowly add the oil, blending until the ingredients are thoroughly combined.

Stored in a sealed glass jar in the refrigerator, this dressing will keep for one month.

VARIATION:
- Add 1/4 cup finely chopped fresh basil or parsley.

GOES WELL WITH:
- Salads
- Carrot and celery sticks, or other crudités
- Chicken and fish as a marinade

Per serving: Calories 190, Calories from Fat 180, Total Fat 20g (31% DV), Saturated Fat 3g (15% DV), Trans Fat 0g, Cholesterol 0mg (0% DV), Sodium 220mg (9% DV), Carbohydrates 2g (1% DV), Dietary Fiber 0g (0% DV), Sugars

1g, **Added Sugars:** 0g, Protein 0g, Vitamin A 0%, Vitamin C 0%, Calcium 0%, Iron 2%.

CAESAR DRESSING

= Makes: 2 cups

= Serving size:
2 tablespoons

= Total servings: 16

= Active time:
15 minutes

= Total time:
15 minutes

Caesar salad gets a bad rap. People worry about using the raw eggs called for in many recipes. Drenched in dressing and smothered in croutons and cheese, it can have as many calories as a Burger King Whopper. It doesn't have to be this way. With a moderate amount of dressing, croutons, and cheese, Caesar salad can be a healthy choice. Boiling the egg makes it safer to use. Plus, the dressing has many uses.

Ingredients
1 egg, boiled for 1 minute
1 ounce anchovy fillets (optional), chopped
5 tablespoons red wine vinegar
2 1/2 tablespoons lemon juice
1 clove garlic, peeled and minced
2 1/2 tablespoons Dijon mustard
1 tablespoon Worcestershire sauce

1 pinch (1/8 teaspoon) of ground black
  pepper
1 1/2 cups olive oil

STEP 1: Place the egg, anchovies, if using,
wine vinegar, lemon juice, garlic, mustard,
Worcestershire sauce, and pepper in a bowl.
Blend slowly until combined.

STEP 2: Slowly add the oil, blending until
smooth and creamy.

Stored in a sealed glass jar or another
container in the refrigerator, this dressing will keep for two weeks.

VARIATION:
• Add a 1/4 cup good-quality grated
  Parmesan cheese.

GOES WELL WITH:
• Romaine lettuce
• Chopped chicken
• Grilled salmon
• Shrimp
• Dipping vegetables

Per serving (Without Anchovies):
Calories 180, Calories from Fat 180,
Total Fat 20g (31% DV), Saturated Fat

3g (15% DV), Trans Fat 0g, Cholesterol 0mg (0% DV), Sodium 65mg (3% DV), Carbohydrates < 1g (0% DV), Dietary Fiber 0g (0% DV), Sugars 0g, **Added Sugars:** 0g, Protein 0g, Vitamin A 0%, Vitamin C 2%, Calcium 0%, Iron 2%.

ENCHILADA SAUCE

= Makes: 4 cups

= Serving size: 1/2 cup

= Total servings: 8

= Active time: 15 minutes

= Total time: 20 minutes

Canned enchilada sauce has all kinds of sugar and preservatives in it. Luckily, making your own couldn't be simpler. You can also use this to top eggs or breakfast burritos. It's lovely over polenta. Make the sauce ahead and freeze it. Then you can whip up a weekday Latin feast in no time.

Ingredients

3 tablespoons vegetable oil

1 tablespoon unbleached all-purpose flour

1/4 cup chili powder

2 cups Marinara Sauce (p. 149)

2 cups vegetable or chicken stock, or more if needed (optional)

1 teaspoon dried oregano, or 1 tablespoon

fresh oregano, if available
1 teaspoon ground cumin
Salt and ground black pepper

STEP 1: Heat the oil in a saucepan over medium heat. Add the flour and chili powder and stir until the flour begins to brown.

STEP 2: Add the Marinara Sauce, bring to a boil over medium heat, then reduce the heat to low and simmer uncovered until the sauce has reduced to 1 cup, 10 to 15 minutes.

STEP 3: Gradually stir in the stock, oregano, and cumin. Cook over medium heat until the sauce thickens, 10 minutes. If the sauce gets too thick, add a little more stock or some water. Taste for seasoning, adding salt and pepper to taste.

Stored in a sealed container in the refrigerator, this sauce will keep for seven days. The sauce can be multiplied and frozen for up to three months.

GOES WELL WITH:
- Quick Enchiladas (p. 400)
- Breakfast Burritos (p. 254)
- Mexican food of all kinds, including

tacos, burritos, and tostadas
- When mixed into browned ground meat, Mexican dishes or taco salad
- Eggs, drizzled on top
- Whole grains like polenta, as a topping
- Sautéed onions, peppers, and corn kernels

Per serving: Calories 110, Calories from Fat 60, Total Fat 7g (11% DV), Saturated Fat 0.5g (2% DV), Trans Fat 0g, Cholesterol 0mg (0% DV), Sodium 220mg (9% DV), Carbohydrates 12g (4% DV), Dietary Fiber 3g (12% DV), Sugars 5g, **Added Sugars:** 0g, Protein 4g, Vitamin A 30%, Vitamin C 10%, Calcium 4%, Iron 10%.

MARINARA SAUCE

= Makes: 2 quarts
= Active time: 15 minutes
= Serving size: 1/2 cup
= Total time: 1 hour 15 minutes
= Total servings: 16

Convincing people that they need to buy processed spaghetti sauce is one of the biggest cons ever. Jarred sauce has lots of added sugar, plus it's expensive. There's no reason to waste money on ready-made sauce.

Nothing could be easier than making a batch of marinara sauce. This recipe has no sugar, and the seasonings you want, not the ones they sell. Once the sauce is made, it's just as fast as Prego, Ragú, or Newman's Own. Its uses are endless. This makes a big batch. Freeze extra for later.

Ingredients
2 tablespoons olive oil
1 cup peeled and diced onion
2 tablespoons peeled and chopped garlic
3 cans (28 ounces each) crushed tomatoes
1/2 cup water
1 teaspoon salt
2 tablespoons Italian seasoning
1/2 teaspoon cayenne pepper
Salt and ground black pepper

STEP 1: Heat the oil in a saucepan over medium heat. Add the onion and garlic and cook until brown and tender, 3 to 5 minutes.

STEP 2: Add the crushed tomatoes, water, salt, Italian seasoning, and cayenne. Reduce the heat and simmer the sauce for 1 hour.

STEP 3: Taste for seasoning, adding more salt as necessary and black pepper to taste.

The sauce can be used immediately. Stored in a sealed container in the refrigerator this sauce will keep for four days. It also freezes well, for as long as three months.

VARIATIONS:
- Endless.
- Add chopped fresh basil, parsley, oregano, or rosemary, or all three, about 2 tablespoons each or to your taste.
- Eliminate Italian seasoning and add 1/3 cup chopped fresh mint, 1 tablespoon ground cumin, and 1/4 teaspoon cayenne pepper for a Middle Eastern spin.
- Add 1/4 cup chopped olives, 1/4 cup drained bottled capers, and 1 tablespoon of chopped anchovy, or anchovy paste.
- Add 1/2 cup cream or 1 cup of half-and-half.

GOES WELL WITH:
- Just about everything
- Pasta

- Polenta
- Roast meats, drizzled on top
- Scrambled eggs, mix it in

Per serving: Calories 60, Calories from Fat 15, Total Fat 1.5g (2% DV), Saturated Fat 0g (0% DV), Trans Fat 0g, Cholesterol 0mg (0% DV), Sodium 280mg (12% DV), Carbohydrates 10g (3% DV), Dietary Fiber 3g (12% DV), Sugars 0g, **Added Sugars:** 0g, Protein 2g, Vitamin A 15%, Vitamin C 20%, Calcium 4%, Iron 10%.

BARBECUE SAUCE

= Makes: 2 cups

= Active time: 20 minutes

= Serving size: 2 tablespoons

= Total time: 40 minutes

= Total servings: 16

Most commercial barbecue sauces are just loaded with sugar: 16 grams per serving, 30 grams per serving, even 44 grams (the equivalent of four cans of Coke) per serving. If you eat that stuff, you might as well put a melted Snickers candy bar on your grilled steak or chicken.

The thing in barbecue sauce that makes the

tang is the vinegar, not the sugar. So play up the vinegar! The meat has fat, which will soften the impact of the vinegar anyway. Also, making your own barbecue sauce means eating less salt, which is also good for you. This version avoids sugar-laden commercial ketchup, substituting tomato paste instead. The bacon lends a smoky flavor; the onion makes the sauce chunky. If you prefer smooth sauce, just puree everything in a blender or food processor.

Ingredients

2 thick strips of bacon, chopped fine, or 2 tablespoons olive oil

1 large yellow onion, peeled and finely chopped

4 cloves garlic, peeled and minced

1/3 cup apple cider vinegar

1 cup fresh Marinara Sauce (p. 149)

1 can (6 ounces) tomato paste

1 teaspoon ground cumin

1 teaspoon chili powder

1 pinch (1/8 teaspoon) of ground cloves

1/2 teaspoon cayenne pepper

1 pinch (1/8 teaspoon) of salt, or more to taste

Coarsely ground black pepper

STEP 1: Place the bacon, if using, in a

large saucepan over medium heat, and cook until it has rendered most of its fat and has begun to brown, 3 to 5 minutes. Or heat the oil over medium heat. Add the onion and cook, stirring frequently, until it begins to soften.

STEP 2: Reduce the heat to low and cook the onion until it turns a rich caramel brown, 20 to 30 minutes.

STEP 3: Increase the heat to medium. Make a space in the center of the saucepan, add the garlic, and cook, stirring, for 30 seconds.

STEP 4: Add the apple cider vinegar, Marinara Sauce, tomato paste, cumin, chili powder, cloves, cayenne, and salt. Bring the sauce to a boil, then reduce the heat to low. Simmer, uncovered, until the sauce thickens, about 30 minutes. Taste for seasoning, adding more salt as necessary and black pepper to taste.

Stored in a sealed container in the refrigerator, this will keep for one month. It does not freeze well.

GOES WELL WITH:

- You name it
- Sandwiches
- Grilled meats and fish
- Roasted potatoes or corn

Per serving (without bacon): Calories 20, Calories from Fat 0, Total Fat 0g (0% DV), Saturated Fat 0g (0% DV), Trans Fat 0g, Cholesterol 0mg (0% DV), Sodium 160mg (7% DV), Carbohydrates 4g (1% DV), Dietary Fiber < 1g (4% DV), Sugars 2g, **Added Sugars:** 0g, Protein < 1g, Vitamin A 4%, Vitamin C 6%, Calcium 2%, Iron 2%.

KETCHUP

= Makes: 1 cup

= Serving size: 2 tablespoons

= Total servings: 8

= Active time: 10 minutes

= Total time: 40 minutes

There's a big problem when the primary ingredient in ketchup is high-fructose corn syrup. Tomatoes already have lots of natural sugar in them. But the food companies add still more refined sugar to ketchup. Just 1 tablespoon of your average supermarket ketchup has as much added sugar as half a can of soda. And when have you ever eaten a burger, or anything else, with just 1 tablespoon of ketchup?

There are some sugar-free ketchups on the market, but not many. Making your own may sound like a major hassle. But you know, that's what great restaurants do. And it's one of the reasons they're great. Think about it. . . .

Ingredients

1 cup canned tomato sauce (Just tomatoes, nothing else!)
3 tablespoons red or white wine vinegar
1/2 teaspoon salt
1/4 teaspoon ground black pepper
1/4 teaspoon onion powder
1/4 teaspoon garlic powder
1 pinch of celery salt
1 pinch of mustard powder
1 pinch of ground allspice
1 pinch of ground cloves
1 pinch of ground cinnamon

STEP 1: Combine the tomato sauce, wine vinegar, salt, pepper, onion powder, garlic powder, celery salt, mustard powder, allspice, cloves, and cinnamon in a small saucepan over low heat. Cook, stirring frequently until ketchup thickens and the flavors meld, 30 minutes.

STEP 2: Let the ketchup cool in the refrigerator for at least 1 hour.

Stored in a sealed glass jar or another container in the refrigerator, the ketchup will keep for two weeks. It won't last that long; it's that good. This recipe can be doubled. It does not freeze well.

GOES WELL WITH:
- Just about everything!

Per serving: Calories 15, Calories from Fat 10, Total Fat 1g (2% DV), Saturated Fat 0g (0% DV), Trans Fat 0g, Cholesterol 0mg (0% DV), Sodium 190mg (8% DV), Carbohydrates 1g (0% DV), Dietary Fiber 0g (0% DV), Sugars < 1g, **Added Sugars:** 0g, Protein 0g, Vitamin A 4%, Vitamin C 6%, Calcium 0%, Iron 0%.

Cauliflower Béchamel Sauce

= Makes: 3 to 4 cups   = Active time:
                           10 minutes
= Serving size: = Total time:
  1/2 cup   20 minutes
= Total servings: 6-8

This is a great base, and a great alternative to fat- and sugar-laden commercial white sauces. I like to mix it with cooked barley and shredded chicken over a bed of wilted spinach and top it off with grated Parmesan cheese.

Ingredients
1 large head cauliflower, cut into small pieces
1/4 cup pine nuts
1/4 cup milk or a milk alternative like plain, unsweetened almond milk or soy milk
1/4 teaspoon ground nutmeg
1 1/2 teaspoons salt, or more to taste

STEP 1: In large pot, steam the cauliflower until tender, 10 to 12 minutes. Dry toast the pine nuts in a pan over medium heat until just golden brown, about 3 to 5 minutes.

STEP 2: Combine the cauliflower, pine

nuts, milk, nutmeg, and salt in a bowl or a food processor, if you have one. Mash or puree until creamy. Taste for seasoning and adjust as needed.

VARIATIONS:
- Use butternut squash in place of cauliflower.
- Add 2 tablespoons cheese (Parmesan, Reggiano, pecorino romano), olive oil, or nut oil. Add one or two herbs; dill, tarragon, or parsley would be nice here: 1 teaspoon dried, or 1 tablespoon fresh.
- Add a pinch (1/8 teaspoon) of cayenne pepper.

GOES WELL WITH:
- Soups, used in place of cream
- Roasted eggplant, layered with chopped cooked spinach, browned ground meat, and Parmesan cheese to make a quick moussaka
- Lasagna noodles, layered with meat sauce, cheese, and sautéed greens
- Chicken alfredo, as a sauce
- White pizza, as a base

Per serving: Calories 80, Calories from Fat 35, Total Fat 4.5g (7% DV), Saturated Fat 0g (0% DV), Trans Fat 0g, Cholesterol 0mg (0% DV), Sodium 640mg (27% DV), Carbohydrates 8g (3% DV), Dietary Fiber 3g (12% DV), Sugars 3g, **Added Sugars:** 0g, Protein 4g, Vitamin A 0%, Vitamin C 110%, Calcium 4%, Iron 6%.

Stock — a Tutorial

It's not hard to make stock. And it's the base for so many different dishes. Canned stock, stock packets, bouillon — they're full of sodium and sugar and who knows what. Any place a savory recipe calls for water, you can use your homemade stock. Try it. You'll find it gives the dish a whole different flavor. Stocks add very little in terms of calories or fat, but they add tons of flavor, nutrients, and minerals. All of the recipes that follow can be doubled.

VEGETABLE STOCK

= Makes: 6 cups = Total time:
1 hour 15 minutes
= Active time:
15 minutes

Ingredients
2 tablespoons rice bran oil
2 onions, peeled and chopped

4 celery ribs, chopped
2 carrots, scrubbed and chopped
1/2 cup halved cherry tomatoes
2 cloves garlic, peeled and minced
2 cups sliced white button mushrooms
1 teaspoon black peppercorns
1 teaspoon salt, or more to taste
8 cups water

STEP 1: Heat the rice bran oil in a large pot over medium heat. Add the onions, celery, carrots, and tomatoes. Cook, covered, stirring occasionally until the vegetables are soft and starting to brown just a bit, about 5 minutes.

STEP 2: Add the garlic and mushrooms and sauté for an additional 2 minutes. Add the peppercorns, salt, and water and bring to a gentle simmer. Cook gently until the stock tastes rich and full, about 1 hour. Strain the stock through a sieve, pushing on the veggies to extract as much flavor as possible. Discard the vegetable solids, wipe out the stockpot, and return the stock to the pot. Taste for seasoning, adding more salt as necessary.

If you are saving the stock for later, let it cool to room temperature, then refrigerate it in sealed containers for up to seven days. The stock can be frozen in sealed containers or freezer bags for up to three months.

BASIC CHICKEN STOCK

= Makes: 6 cups = Total time:
1 hour 15 minutes

= Active time:
15 minutes

Ingredients
Vegetable stock ingredients plus 1 chicken

Use a heavy knife to coarsely chop the bones from the chicken. Brown the chicken and its bones with the vegetables in Step 1 of the Vegetable Stock and then follow the recipe above.

BASIC BEEF STOCK

= Makes: 6 cups = Total time:
1 hour 15 minutes

= Active time:
15 minutes

Ingredients
Vegetable stock ingredients plus 1 pound of oxtail bones or beef marrow bones

Add the oxtail bones or beef marrow bones to the vegetables browning in Step 1 of the Vegetable Stock. Then continue with the Vegetable Stock recipe above.

VARIATIONS:
- Add 2 tablespoons of parsley after browning vegetables.
- Add 1 to 2 bay leaves to the water.
- Use water from cooking corn to make a sweeter broth.

GOES WELL WITH:
- As a base for all soups
- Instead of water when cooking grains

SPINACH AND RICOTTA FILLING

= Makes: 6 cups   = Active time: 10 minutes

= Serving size: 1/2 cup   = Total time: 10 minutes

= Total servings: 12

This is a staple at Cindy's restaurant. They use the spinach and ricotta mix to stuff peppers, zucchini, and mushrooms. They wrap it in housemade crepes to make cannelloni. They layer it with grilled eggplant to make vegetarian lasagna. It can be topped with tomato sauce. This needs to be part of your repertoire!

Ingredients
1 pound frozen chopped spinach, thawed
2 cups ricotta cheese
2 cups grated dry Monterey Jack cheese, or other mild white cheese
1 1/2 cups grated Parmesan cheese
Salt and pepper

STEP 1: Drain the thawed spinach and squeeze as much water as you can from it. You can do this by squeezing it handful by handful, or by draining it in a colander and pressing down on it to remove the liquid. Or, you can put all the spinach in a kitchen towel, twist the ends, and squeeze the spinach in the towel until most of the excess water has been removed.

STEP 2: Combine the ricotta, dry Jack, and 1 cup of the Parmesan in a large bowl. Mix with your hands, or with a spoon. Add the spinach. Mix until combined. Season with salt and pepper to taste. Sprinkle remaining 1/2 cup Parmesan over assembled dish.

Stored in a sealed container in the refrigerator, this spinach mixture will keep for five days. Don't freeze it.

VARIATIONS:
- Add 1 tablespoon minced or crushed garlic, sautéed.
- Add 1 tablespoon Italian herbs.
- Add 1 tablespoon chopped fresh herbs, basil, parsley, or tarragon.

GOES WELL WITH:
- Bell peppers, as a stuffing for pepper halves with seeds and ribs removed
- Zucchini, as a stuffing for squash cut lengthwise and hollowed out
- Small mushrooms; stuff and broil for an appetizer
- Portobello mushrooms; stuff and roast for dinner
- Grilled eggplant, layered with tomato sauce for eggplant lasagna
- Chicken breasts; stuff and bake
- Pasta shells; stuff and bake in a 400°F oven with Marinara Sauce (p. 149) or canned crushed tomatoes, 1/2 cup per serving. Cover pan with foil for 45 minutes, remove foil and continue to bake until brown and vegetables are fork tender. These baking instructions will also work for stuffed zucchini.

Per serving: Calories 210, Calories from Fat 130, Total Fat 15g (23% DV), Saturated Fat 9g (45% DV), Trans Fat 0g, Cholesterol 50mg (17% DV), Sodium 390mg (16% DV), Carbohydrates 4g (1% DV), Dietary Fiber 1g (4% DV), Sugars < 1g, **Added Sugars:** 0g, Protein 16g, Vitamin A 100%, Vitamin C 2%, Calcium 40%, Iron 6%.

ROASTED TOMATOES

= Makes: 2 cups

= Active time: 10 minutes

= Serving size: 1/2 cup

= Total time: 40 minutes

= Total servings: 4

Roasting caramelizes the natural sugars in tomatoes, making the flavor more intense and the fruit a little chewy.

Ingredients
6 large Roma tomatoes
2 tablespoons olive oil
1 teaspoon salt

STEP 1: Preheat the oven to 400°F.

STEP 2: Wash the tomatoes and chop them into large chunks.

STEP 3: Place tomatoes in a bowl with the oil and salt. Pour the tomato mixture in one layer on a greased baking pan. Roast the tomatoes until they are browned on top, about 20 minutes.

How to handle fresh tomatoes: A common mistake is keeping tomatoes in the refrigerator. Storing tomatoes in a refrigerator does not keep them fresher longer. Fact: Refrigeration makes them mealy after only a couple of days and diminishes their flavor. I keep mine on the counter in a bowl away from heat and sunlight.

Store the roasted tomatoes in an airtight container in the refrigerator for up to five days or freeze in freezer bags for up to three months. Be sure to date and label the bags. The recipe can be multiplied.

VARIATIONS:
- Use cherry tomatoes or any type of fresh, ripe tomatoes.
- Cut tomatoes into thick slices rather than chunks.
- Toss with capers and fresh chopped basil at the end of cooking.

- Layer raw skinless, boneless chicken breast and thigh meat cut into 1-inch pieces over raw tomatoes and roast them together. This also works with fish; bake until fish is flaky or firm (depending on whether fish is thick or thin).

GOES WELL WITH:
- Pasta
- Salad, when chilled
- Cheese, as an appetizer
- Sautéed zucchini and bell peppers

Per serving: Calories 80, Calories from Fat 60, Total Fat 7g (11% DV), Saturated Fat 1g (5% DV), Trans Fat 0g, Cholesterol 0mg (0% DV), Sodium 590mg (25% DV), Carbohydrates 4g (1% DV), Dietary Fiber 1g (4% DV), Sugars 2g, **Added Sugars:** 0g, Protein < 1g, Vitamin A 15%, Vitamin C 20%, Calcium 0%, Iron 2%.

Fajita Seasoning Mix

= Makes: 1 1/2 cups   = Active time:
                                                   10 minutes
= Serving size: = Total time:
   2 tablespoons   10 minutes
= Total servings: 6

Big Food needs to add sugar to packaged spice mixes to preserve freshness and taste, and also to cover up sour, bitter, or other unwanted flavors. I can't imagine why you'd spend $3 on a fajita seasoning packet when making your own is way cheaper and way healthier.

Remember to read the label on all spice blends when buying processed food. Check out the fifty-six names for sugar (p. 72). Here's a great substitute for taco seasoning. It's homemade, low salt, and no sugar.

Ingredients
1/2 cup chili powder
1/4 cup paprika
1/4 cup garlic powder
1 tablespoon ground cumin
1 tablespoon salt
2 teaspoons onion powder
1 teaspoon crushed red pepper flakes
1 teaspoon cayenne pepper

Mix the chili powder, paprika, garlic powder, cumin, salt, onion powder, pepper flakes, and cayenne together in a small bowl.

Stored in an airtight container in a dark, cool place, the seasoning mix will keep for three months.

VARIATION:
- Add crushed oregano.

GOES WELL WITH:
- Fish and meat
- Tacos
- Burritos

Per serving: Calories 35, Calories from Fat 10, Total Fat 1g (2% DV), Saturated Fat 0g (0% DV), Trans Fat 0g, Cholesterol 0mg (0% DV), Sodium 680mg (28% DV), Carbohydrates 6g (2% DV), Dietary Fiber 3g (12% DV), Sugars < 1g, **Added Sugars:** 0g, Protein 2g, Vitamin A 50%, Vitamin C 0%, Calcium 4%, Iron 10%.

BARBECUE RUB

- = Makes: 3/4 cup
- = Serving size: 1 teaspoon
- = Total servings: 36
- = Active time: 10 minutes
- = Total time: 10 minutes

This is the recipe that Cindy uses at her restaurant. People really appreciate not having their meat drenched in sugar. It's important to use this on a good cut of meat, so that you don't need to cover up any flavors that aren't the best.

Ingredients
1/4 cup kosher salt
2 tablespoons onion powder
1 tablespoon garlic powder
1 tablespoon smoked paprika
1 tablespoon ground cumin
1 tablespoon chili powder
1/2 tablespoon ground black pepper

Mix the salt, onion powder, garlic powder, paprika, cumin, chili powder, and pepper together in a small bowl.

Stored in an airtight container the rub will keep for three months. Do not refrigerate or freeze it, moisture will cause the mixture to clump up.

GOES WELL WITH:
- Chicken
- Beef
- Pork

Per serving: Calories 5, Calories from Fat 0, Total Fat 0g (0% DV), Saturated Fat 0g (0% DV), Trans Fat 0g, Cholesterol 0mg (0% DV), Sodium 400mg (17% DV), Carbohydrates 1g (0% DV), Dietary Fiber 0g (0% DV), Sugars 0g, **Added Sugars:** 0g, Protein 0g, Vitamin A 4%, Vitamin C 0%, Calcium 0%, Iron 2%.

ROMA TOMATO BASIL SALSA

= Makes: 2 cups = Active time: 10 minutes

= Serving size: 2 tablespoons = Total time: 10 minutes

= Total servings: 16

Use firm Roma tomatoes, they're less watery than other varieties. This can be used cold or hot.

Ingredients

1 pound Roma tomatoes, diced into 1/4-inch pieces

1 tablespoon garlic, peeled and minced

1/2 cup chopped fresh basil

1/2 cup extra-virgin olive oil

1/4 cup balsamic vinegar

1 tablespoon cracked black pepper

1 teaspoon salt

Mix the tomatoes, garlic, basil, oil, balsamic vinegar, pepper, and salt together in a bowl. The salsa is best when used immediately.

VARIATIONS:

- Add leftover salsa to marinara sauce for a little extra punch.
- Spread the salsa over salmon or white fish, adding capers and olives, and bake in a 400°F oven, for 20 to 30 minutes, or until the fish is firm (this will depend on the thickness of the fish).
- Roast eggplant, zucchini, or bell peppers, top with mozzarella or ricotta, and top with this salsa for a delicious main course or an appetizer.

GOES WELL WITH:

- Polenta
- Brown rice
- Barley
- Whole-grain pasta
- Grilled chicken
- Fish
- Tofu

Per serving: Calories 70, Calories from Fat 60, Total Fat 7g (11% DV), Saturated Fat 1g (5% DV), Trans Fat 0g, Cholesterol 0mg (0% DV), Sodium 150mg (6% DV), Carbohydrates 2g (1% DV), Dietary Fiber 0g (0% DV), Sugars 1g, **Added Sugars:** 0g, Protein 0g, Vitamin A 6%, Vitamin C 8%, Calcium 0%, Iron 2%.

FRESH FRUIT SALSA

= Makes: 2 cups

= Active time: 15 minutes

= Serving size: 2 tablespoons

= Total time: 15 minutes

= Total servings: 16

This is a great summertime salsa for grilled fish or chicken. If using yellow onions, be sure to seek out the sweet varieties, Walla

Walla or Vidalia. Regular yellow onions will overpower the fruit flavors.

Ingredients

1 cup peeled and diced mango or papaya

1/2 cup stemmed and diced fresh strawberries

1/2 cup finely chopped fresh cilantro

1/2 cup finely chopped sweet onion (Walla Walla or Vidalia) or red onion

1 tablespoon lemon or lime juice

1 teaspoon ground cumin

1/2 teaspoon salt

1 pinch (1/8 teaspoon) of red pepper flakes

STEP 1: Mix the mango or papaya, strawberries, cilantro, onion, lemon or lime juice, cumin, salt, and pepper flakes together in a bowl. Stir well.

STEP 2: Let the salsa sit for 30 minutes to marinate. Serve chilled or at room temperature. It can also be heated.

Stored in an airtight container, this keeps for two days in the refrigerator. It does not freeze well.

VARIATIONS:
• Add pineapple.

- Add kiwi.
- Add 2 tablespoons minced fresh mint.

GOES WELL WITH:
- Roasted or grilled chicken
- Roasted or grilled fish
- Tofu

Per serving: Calories 10, Calories from Fat 0, Total Fat 0g (0% DV), Saturated Fat 0g (0% DV), Trans Fat 0g, Cholesterol 0mg (0% DV), Sodium 75mg (3% DV), Carbohydrates 3g (1% DV), Dietary Fiber 0g (0% DV), Sugars 2g, **Added Sugars:** 0g, Protein 0g, Vitamin A 4%, Vitamin C 15%, Calcium 0%, Iron 0%.

MARINATED OLIVES

= Makes: 2 cups
= Active time: 10 minutes
= Serving size: 2 tablespoons
= Total time: 40 minutes
= Total servings: 16

Marinated olives are such a Mediterranean staple. Put these out for friends with cheese, fruit, and wine. Make sure the citrus zest is finely chopped or grated; big pieces will overwhelm.

Ingredients

2 cups mixed olives: green, black, Spanish, or kalamata
1 teaspoon fresh chopped oregano, basil, or thyme
1 teaspoon grated or minced fresh lemon or lime zest
1 teaspoon fresh lemon or lime juice
1 tablespoon extra-virgin olive oil

Mix the olives, oregano, lemon or lime zest and juice, and oil together in a bowl and let marinate for at least 2 hours, but 6 is better.

Stored covered in an airtight container in the refrigerator, the olives will keep for up to two weeks.

VARIATIONS:
- Add minced roasted garlic or small onions.
- Add cayenne pepper.
- Substitute walnut oil for the olive oil.

GOES WELL WITH:
- Mediterranean dishes with tomatoes

and fresh herbs
- Salad
- Roasted tomatoes
- Roasted chicken

Per serving: Calories 25, Calories from Fat 20, Total Fat 2.5g (4% DV), Saturated Fat 0g (0% DV), Trans Fat 0g, Cholesterol 0mg (0% DV), Sodium 125mg (5% DV), Carbohydrates 1g (0% DV), Dietary Fiber < 1g (2% DV), Sugars 0g, **Added Sugars:** 0g, Protein 0g, Vitamin A 2%, Vitamin C 0%, Calcium 2%, Iron 4%.

ROASTED CHICKPEAS

= Makes: 2 cups	= Active time: 5 minutes
= Serving size: 1/4 cup	= Total time: 30 minutes
= Total servings: 8	

The kids in Cindy's high school classes love these! You eat them as a snack or toss them into a salad, whole-grain pilaf, or pasta. These are better if you to start with dried chickpeas (also called garbanzo beans). Soak and cook them yourself. If you don't have time for that, use canned chickpeas.

Ingredients

2 cups cooked chickpeas, or 1 can (15 ounces) chickpeas, drained and rinsed

1 tablespoon olive oil

1/2 teaspoon salt, or more to taste

1/4 teaspoon cayenne pepper (optional)

STEP 1: Preheat the oven to 400°F.

STEP 2: Dry chickpeas with paper towels and place them in a bowl. Add the oil, salt, and cayenne, if using, and toss to coat.

STEP 3: Line a baking sheet with parchment or waxed paper and spread the chickpeas out into one even layer.

STEP 4: Bake the chickpeas until golden brown and crunchy, about 30 minutes, stirring halfway through so they cook evenly.

STEP 5: Remove the chickpeas from the oven and let cool. They can be eaten right away.

Stored in an airtight container in the refrigerator, the chickpeas will keep for about one day. If kept longer, the chickpeas will soften.

VARIATIONS:

- Toss the chickpeas with fresh herbs when they come out of the oven: parsley, oregano, thyme, or rosemary would all work.
- When you toss the chickpeas with salt and cayenne before baking, add 1 teaspoon dried spices: chili powder, ground cumin, curry powder, or garam masala (or a combination of chili, cumin, curry, and other spices).
- Vary the oil you use. Try sesame or walnut oil.

GOES WELL WITH:

- Soups, as a topping
- Salads
- Pasta dishes
- Curries, as a topping
- Roasted nuts, mixed together for a great appetizer

Per serving: Calories 80, Calories from Fat 20, Total Fat 2.5g (4% DV), Saturated Fat 0g (0% DV), Trans Fat 0g, Cholesterol 0mg (0% DV), Sodium 320mg (13% DV), Carbohydrates 13g (4% DV), Dietary Fiber 3g (12% DV), Sugars 0g, **Added Sugars:** 0g, Protein

3g, Vitamin A 0%, Vitamin C 4%, Calcium 2%, Iron 4%.

KALE CHIPS

= Serves: 4 to 6   = Active time: 10 minutes

= Serving size: 1/2 cup   = Total time: 30 minutes

Don't pay $6 for a small bag of kale chips. It's easy to make your own, and they taste better. It may take a while for kids to get used to these, but trust me: Before long, your kids will be scarfing these up as fast as you can make them.

Ingredients

1 tablespoon olive oil, plus oil for the sheet pans

1 bunch curly kale, washed and dried well

1 tablespoon fresh lemon juice

1/2 teaspoon salt

1/2 teaspoon fresh lemon zest

STEP 1: Preheat the oven to 300°F.

STEP 2: Lightly oil two baking sheets, using about 1 teaspoon per baking sheet, or use cooking spray.

STEP 3: Strip the curly leaves off of the kale by holding the bottom of each stem and pulling your hand up along it, stripping off the leaf part and leaving behind the tough stem. Tear the kale into large pieces and put them in a large bowl.

STEP 4: Add the lemon juice, oil, and salt to the bowl. Using your hands, mix so that the leaves are evenly coated. Caress the leaves as if you were putting moisturizer on them, making sure to get all the nooks and crannies.

STEP 5: Arrange the kale on the baking sheets in a single layer and put in the oven. Bake the kale until the leaves are dry and crisp, but before they start turning dark brown, about 20 minutes.

STEP 6: Sprinkle the grated lemon zest over the kale and serve warm or at room temperature.

Stored at room temperature on a covered plate, the chips will hold their crispness for one day.

VARIATIONS:
• Try adding cayenne and dill.

- Try using flavored salt, such as smoked or truffle salt.
- Use a flavored oil, or walnut oil.

GOES WELL WITH:
- Soups, chilis, and sandwiches
- Marinated olives, fruit, and cheese, as a snack or on an appetizer
- Sweet potato chips

Per serving: Calories 50, Calories from Fat 35, Total Fat 4g (6% DV), Saturated Fat 0.5g (2% DV), Trans Fat 0g, Cholesterol 0mg (0% DV), Sodium 310mg (13% DV), Carbohydrates 4g (1% DV), Dietary Fiber < 1g (3% DV), Sugars 0g, **Added Sugars:** 0g, Protein 1g, Vitamin A 130%, Vitamin C 80%, Calcium 6%, Iron 4%.

EDAMAME SPREAD

= Makes: 2 cups

= Active time: 8 minutes

= Serving size: 1/4 cup

= Total time: 10 minutes

= Total servings: 8

Edamame are simply boiled soybeans. You can usually find them frozen. This spread is high fiber and high protein. Kids love it.

Use it in place of hummus or bean dip.

Ingredients

1 pound frozen shelled edamame

1/4 cup lemon juice

1 teaspoon peeled and minced garlic, about 1 large clove

1 pinch (1/8 teaspoon) of ground black pepper

1/2 cup truffle oil, walnut oil, extra-virgin olive, or avocado oil

STEP 1: Boil the edamame in salted, boiling water for 1 minute.

STEP 2: Drain the edamame and put it in a blender, or food processor if you have one, with the lemon juice, garlic, pepper, and oil. Blend until smooth.

Stored in an airtight container in the refrigerator, this keeps for up to five days. It can be frozen for up to three months.

VARIATIONS:
- Substitute chickpeas for edamame.
- Substitute white beans for edamame.

GOES WELL WITH:

- Sliced bread, spread with olive oil and toasted, often called crostini
- Stuffed cherry tomatoes
- Bread
- Roasted vegetables in a wrap

Per serving: Calories 150, Calories from Fat 120, Total Fat 13g (20% DV), Saturated Fat 2g (10% DV), Trans Fat 0g, Cholesterol 0mg (0% DV), Sodium 0mg (0% DV), Carbohydrates 5g (2% DV), Dietary Fiber 2g (8% DV), Sugars 1g, **Added Sugars:** 0g, Protein 5g, Vitamin A 0%, Vitamin C 8%, Calcium 2%, Iron 6%.

BASIL PESTO

= Makes: 1 cup

= Serving size: 2 tablespoons

= Total servings: 8

= Active time: 10 minutes

= Total time: 10 minutes

Pesto is such a wonderful sauce. So versatile, you can use it in pasta, on pizza, to marinate meats and fish, and to mix into ricotta or sour cream to make a dip or a stuffing.

Ingredients

2 cups packed fresh basil leaves

2 cloves garlic, peeled

1/4 cup pine nuts or walnuts (optional)

2/3 cup extra-virgin olive oil

Kosher salt and cracked black pepper

1/2 cup grated Parmesan or pecorino romano cheese (optional)

STEP 1: Combine the basil, garlic, and nuts, if using, in a blender, or food processor if you have one, and pulse until coarsely chopped. Add 1/3 cup of the oil and process until fully incorporated and smooth. Season with salt and pepper to taste.

If you are using the pesto immediately, add the remaining 1/3 cup of oil and pulse until smooth. Transfer the pesto to a bowl and mix in the cheese, if using.

If you are freezing, transfer it to an airtight container, drizzle the remaining 1/3 cup of oil over the top, and freeze it for up to three months. Thaw the pesto in the refrigerator overnight. Stir in the cheese, if using, before serving.

VARIATIONS:
- Use half spinach, half basil.

- Use cilantro in place of basil.
- Add one red chili pepper.
- Play around with nut varieties: almonds and pecans also work.

GOES WELL WITH:
- Salad dressing
- Sandwiches, as a spread
- Fish, chicken, or meat; spread pesto over them, then roast, panfry, or grill
- Pasta
- Chopped tomatoes and cubed mozzarella
- Cold pasta, chopped cooked chicken or turkey, and chopped tomatoes for a wonderful pasta salad

Per serving: Calories 190, Calories from Fat 180, Total Fat 20g (31% DV), Saturated Fat 3.5g (18% DV), Trans Fat 0g, Cholesterol 5mg (2% DV), Sodium 135mg (6% DV), Carbohydrates < 1g (0% DV), Dietary Fiber 0g (0% DV), Sugars 0g, **Added Sugars:** 0g, Protein 5g, Vitamin A 10%, Vitamin C 3%, Calcium 8%, Iron 2%.

WHOLE-WHEAT SPONGE BREAD

= Makes: 1 loaf, about 14 slices

= Serving size: 2-ounce slice

= Active time: 20 minutes

= Total time: 2 hours 50 minutes (with rising and baking)

Yeast breads intimidate some, but this recipe is simpler than most. Rather than being kneaded, the batter is whisked vigorously. You can do this by hand. Or, use a hand mixer or standing mixer, if you have one. Rather than two rises, this bread rises only once. You don't have to worry about shaping the loaf. It rises in the baking pan.

This recipe yields a moist, satisfying bread. If you bake it in a loaf pan, you can slice this thin for sandwiches. Made in an 8-by-8-inch pan, and cut into squares, it's more like a hearty roll. This is sweet due to the honey, but 1/4 cup for a whole loaf is nothing. Still, the whole-wheat flour is still flour. So eat this as a sandwich or an accompaniment to soup or salad, not as a snack, or the whole loaf will be gone before you know it.

Ingredients

1/4 cup vegetable oil, plus more for the baking pan and for oiling the bread before baking

2 cups hot water

1/4 cup honey

2 envelopes, or 4 teaspoons, Fleischmann's Rapid Rise Yeast

1 cup old-fashioned rolled oats

4 cups whole-wheat flour

2 teaspoons salt

STEP 1: Preheat the oven to 350°F. Generously oil or butter an 8-by-8-inch baking pan.

STEP 2: Place the hot water (about the temperature of a hot bath), honey, and oil in a bowl. Mix well. Sprinkle the yeast on top and let sit until the mixture begins to bubble, 3 to 5 minutes. (That means the yeast has woken up. If it doesn't bubble, either your yeast is old, or not working, or the water is too hot and killed the yeast.)

STEP 3: Add the old-fashioned rolled oats, 1 cup of the flour, and salt. Mix until just combined. Add the remaining 3 cups of flour. Mix until just combined. (The more you mix, the tougher the bread gets.)

STEP 4: Oil your hands, and form it into a ball. Put the dough into the pan, press down, and cover the pan with a towel until the dough doubles in size, about 45 minutes in a warm place.

STEP 5: Bake until a cake tester or skewer inserted in the middle comes out cleanly, 45 minutes. Or you can tap the top of the bread; when you hear a hollow sound it will come out of the pan easily. Let the bread cool on a wire rack for 20 minutes, then cut and serve. Makes great toasted croutons (see p. 321).

VARIATION:
- Substitute molasses for the honey.

GOES WELL WITH:
- A pat of butter
- Low-sugar jam
- Soups, chilis, and stews
- Salad

Per serving: Calories 220, Calories from Fat 70, Total Fat 7g (11% DV), Saturated Fat 0.5g (2% DV), Trans Fat 0g, Cholesterol 0mg (0% DV), Sodium 360mg (15% DV), Carbohydrates 36g (12% DV), Dietary Fiber 5g (20% DV),

Sugars 5g, **Added Sugars:** 5g, Protein 6g, Vitamin A 0%, Vitamin C 0%, Calcium 2%, Iron 8%.

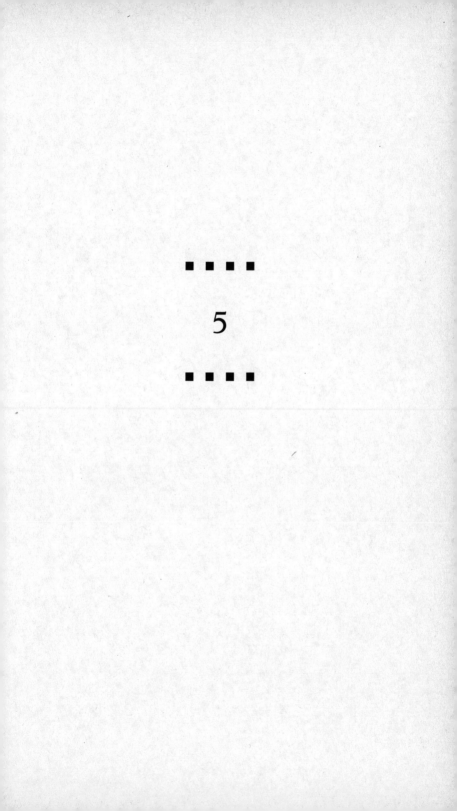

5

Chapter 5
Breakfast

In high-income and middle-income countries, breakfast is probably the most sugar-saturated meal of the day. Just think about it: sugary cereals; donuts; pastries; pancakes or French toast or waffles and syrup; jam; bagels; rolls of all kinds. Our usual choices, the sugary ones, are quick. They're easy since they're usually processed and ready-made. They give us a jolt of energy, temporarily. Ever feel like you've hit a wall at 10 A.M.? It's probably because of that sugar fest we call breakfast.

I get it: Mornings are busy, even chaotic, especially in a household with kids. How many people do you know who actually take time to sit at the table for breakfast? Not many, I'll bet. In this chapter, you'll find healthy breakfast alternatives. Most of these dishes can be made ahead so that you can just grab them in the morning. The things that need to be made fresh take only 5 to

10 minutes of active time.

Try these low-sugar, high-fiber breakfasts for a couple of weeks. I bet you'll find that you have energy *all morning,* no midmorning crash. You probably won't be hungry until lunch. And that's the idea.

Recipes:

Breakfast Grains — A Tutorial
Homemade Granola
Homemade Muesli
Nut Butter Bars
Tutti-frutti
Yogurt Parfait
Fruit Salad Twelve Ways
Berry Compote
Applesauce
Low-Sugar Blackberry Jam
Homemade "Sausage"
Almost Homemade Salsa
Power Muffins
Baked Fruit Oatmeal
Whole-Grain Yogurt Pancakes
Joe's Scrambles and Three Others
Polenta Patties with Sautéed Greens, Poached Eggs, Roma Tomatoes, and Basil Salsa
Lox and Egg Scramble

Veggie Brown Rice Frittata
Breakfast Burritos or Tacos

Breakfast Grains — A Tutorial

We've got half of it right: We often eat grains at breakfast. Unfortunately, we eat grains that are usually overprocessed and covered in sugar. Try whole grains instead. The fiber in them helps slow down the metabolism of nutrients, avoiding those insulin spikes that shunt calories to fat.

Top breakfast grains with a few chopped nuts, some yogurt or milk, some berries, compote, applesauce, or chopped fruit. That's a breakfast that will taste great and keep you going until lunch.

Cold Breakfast Cereals

Whole-grain, low-sugar cold cereals exist but you need to really read the label! Packaged granola or muesli often has as much sugar as a candy bar. Avoid it. Make your own instead.

Choose high-fiber cereals that have no added sweeteners. Look in the healthy food section at the supermarket, or try your local health food store.

Here are cold cereals that I recommend:
- Generic shredded wheat

- Puffed kamut
- Puffed barley
- Puffed whole wheat
- Homemade Granola (p. 205)
- Homemade Muesli (p. 208)

GOES WELL WITH:
- Milk, of course
- 1/4 cup berry compote or applesauce
- 1/4 cup fresh berries, 2 tablespoons plain yogurt, and 1 teaspoon chopped toasted nuts

Hot Breakfast Cereals

In America, we've got a very limited notion of what grains can be eaten for breakfast: We stick mostly to oatmeal (usually quick oatmeal packets, full of sugar), cream of wheat (overprocessed) or, in the South, corn grits. Expand your horizons! Barley, quinoa, polenta, even leftover brown rice or farro can make excellent breakfast choices. Top them with milk, fruit, compote, applesauce, or toasted nuts. After a while, your palate will change, and you'll begin to love the varied flavors and textures of these grains.

Whole grains do take longer to cook. See Chapter 7 (p. 339) for more information. You can cook the grains the night before, as you're making dinner. Or you can soak them overnight to speed things up in the morning. Freeze in one-serving sizes for up to one month.

STEEL-CUT OATMEAL

= Serves: 1   = Active time: 10 minutes

= Serving size: 1 cup   = Total time: 45 minutes

Old-fashioned rolled oats are better for you than sugary Cocoa Puffs, but steel-cut oatmeal has even more fiber. It also has a nutty, satisfying flavor. If you soak the grain overnight, as this recipe suggests, it takes no longer than rolled oats.

Ingredients
1 cup water
1/4 cup steel-cut oats
1/2 cup milk or unsweetened nondairy milk

STEP 1: Bring the water to a boil in a small pot. Add the steel-cut oats and cover the pot. Let the oats sit overnight in the pot.

STEP 2: In the morning, add the milk, or milk alternative, and bring to a boil. Cook the oats for 2 to 3 minutes, until soft and creamy.

VARIATION:

- For quick-cooking oatmeal, don't soak the oats overnight. Use 1/2 cup old-fashioned rolled oats, or quick oats, but make sure the quick oats are plain. The packets usually have loads of sugar. Cook according to package directions. Remember: The ratio of liquid to oats is always 2:1 for rolled oats and 4:1 for steel-cut oats.

Per serving: Calories 220, Calories from Fat 45, Total Fat 5g (8% DV), Saturated Fat 2g (10% DV), Trans Fat 0g, Cholesterol 10mg (3% DV), Sodium 75mg (3% DV), Carbohydrates 33g (11% DV), Dietary Fiber 4g (16% DV), Sugars 6g, **Added Sugars:** 0g, Protein 11g, Vitamin A 0%, Vitamin C 2%, Calcium 20%, Iron 10%.

BREAKFAST CORN MUSH (POLENTA)

- Makes: 4 cups
- Serving size: 1/2 cup
- Total servings: 8
- Active time: 10 minutes
- Total time: 40 minutes

In the southern United States, they call this

"corn grits," but in Italy, where Cindy's mother's parents were born, they call it "polenta." It's basically a grain mush or porridge that's been eaten since Roman times. Today it's most commonly made with cornmeal, but barley and other grains were used in the past.

Polenta is still a carb, but because it's ground coarsely, it maintains a lot of its original fiber. In other words, it's not refined. It's a much better choice than a standard refined carb like white rice or potatoes. If you buy the commercial versions instead of making it yourself, the sodium content will be significantly higher.

When served, fresh polenta has the homey consistency of mashed potatoes. Once it cools polenta hardens into the shape of whatever holds it. Then it can be sliced or fried and used in endless ways.

Ingredients
4 cups water
Salt to taste
1 cup corn grits or cornmeal

STEP 1: Bring the water and salt to a boil in a large pot over high heat.

STEP 2: Once the liquid is boiling, slowly add the grits or cornmeal, stirring constantly with a whisk to keep lumps from forming.

STEP 3: When the grain is mixed smoothly into the liquid, reduce the heat to low and simmer gently for 30 minutes until very thick. Stir occasionally to keep the polenta from sticking. Serve exactly as you would serve oatmeal: with milk, fresh fruit or nuts, raisins, and cinnamon.

Per serving: Calories 60, Calories from Fat 0, Total Fat 0.5g (1% DV), Saturated Fat 0g (0% DV), Trans Fat 0g, Cholesterol 0mg (0% DV), Sodium 45mg (2% DV), Carbohydrates 12g (4% DV), Dietary Fiber 1g (4% DV), Sugars 0g, **Added Sugars:** 0g, Protein 1g, Vitamin A 0%, Vitamin C 0%, Calcium 0%, Iron 2%.

BREAKFAST BARLEY

= Makes: 3 cups

= Serving size: 1/2 cup

= Total servings: 6

= Active time: 10 minutes

= Total time: 50 minutes

Grains like barley take a while to cook. Try

cooking them ahead and freezing them in small quantities in freezer bags. They will keep one month in the freezer.

Ingredients
1 cup hulled barley
3 cups water

Combine the barley and water in a pot and bring to a boil. Reduce the heat, cover the pot, and let simmer until the barley is tender, about 40 minutes. Serve like oatmeal or polenta, above. Or make it savory with 1/2 cup salsa and a poached egg on top.

Per serving: Calories 110, Calories from Fat 5, Total Fat 0.5g (1% DV), Saturated Fat 0g (0% DV), Trans Fat 0g, Cholesterol 0mg (0% DV), Sodium 0mg (0% DV), Carbohydrates 23g (8% DV), Dietary Fiber 5g (20% DV), Sugars 0g, **Added Sugars:** 0g, Protein 4g, Vitamin A 0%, Vitamin C 0%, Calcium 2%, Iron 6%.

BREAKFAST QUINOA

- Makes: 3 cups
- Serving size: 1/2 cup
- Total servings: 6
- Active time: 5 minutes
- Total time: 25 minutes

Quinoa is a staple grain in Peru and Bolivia. It has a springy, fine texture, like couscous, and a nutty taste.

Ingredients
1 cup quinoa, rinsed
2 cups water

Combine the quinoa and water in a pot and bring to a boil. Reduce the heat, cover the pot, and let the quinoa simmer until tender, about 20 minutes. Serve like oatmeal or polenta, above, or make it savory with 1/2 cup salsa and a poached egg on top.

Per serving: Calories 100, Calories from Fat 15, Total Fat 1.5g (2% DV), Saturated Fat 0g (0% DV), Trans Fat 0g, Cholesterol 0mg (0% DV), Sodium 0mg (0% DV), Carbohydrates 18g (6% DV), Dietary Fiber 2g (8% DV), Sugars 0g, **Added Sugars:** 0g, Protein 4g,

Vitamin A 0%, Vitamin C 0%, Calcium 2%, Iron 8%.

HOMEMADE GRANOLA

= Makes: 6 cups

= Serving size: 1/4 cup

= Total servings: 24

= Active time: 10 minutes

= Total time: 35 minutes

Commercial granola is the biggest rip-off ever. Healthy? Try again. All sugar, no fiber. Whether it's honey, or brown sugar, or agave, or "evaporated cane juice," it's all sugar to your body and it all has the same bad effects on your metabolism.

Thankfully, granola is ridiculously easy, and cheaper, to make at home. Homemade granola is low sugar, high fiber. Use rice bran oil or safflower oil to keep the omega-6s down.

Ingredients
1/2 cup rice bran oil or safflower oil
1/2 cup water
1/4 cup honey
1 tablespoon ground cinnamon
1 tablespoon vanilla extract
6 cups old-fashioned rolled oats

1 cup raw nuts, whatever you like: almonds, walnuts, pecans, cashews

1/2 cup unsweetened coconut (the wide strips, not the sugary shreds)

1/4 cup raw seeds, whatever you like: sunflower seeds, pepitas, sesame seeds

1 to 2 cups chopped dried fruit, whatever you like: raisins, currants, mango, apple, figs, apricots, pears, dates

STEP 1: Preheat the oven to 350°F.

STEP 2: Whisk the oil, water, honey, cinnamon, and vanilla extract together in a large bowl until mixed. Add the oatmeal and toss until all of the oatmeal is thoroughly coated.

STEP 3: Add the nuts, unsweetened coconut, and seeds.

STEP 4: Line a rimmed baking sheet with parchment paper. Spread the granola evenly over the baking sheet. Bake the granola, stirring occasionally, until it is brown and toasty, about 25 minutes.

STEP 5: Add 1 to 2 cups of chopped dried fruit. Don't add fruit until after baking the granola or it will become as hard as rocks.

Let the granola cool before serving. It will dry up as it cools.

Stored in an airtight container at room temperature, this granola will keep for as long as one month.

VARIATIONS:
Let your imagination go wild! Add whatever you like to this basic recipe.
- Add more vanilla extract.
- Substitute almond extract or maple extract for the vanilla, or add a bit of each in addition to vanilla.
- Add a teaspoon or so of ground ginger or cardamom.
- Add a 1/4 teaspoon of ground nutmeg.
- Use a different kind of sweetener: 1/4 cup maple syrup or agave or molasses.

GOES WELL WITH:
- Milk
- Plain yogurt
- Sliced seasonal fruit

Per serving: Calories 120, Calories from Fat 45, Total Fat 5g (8% DV), Saturated Fat 0g (0% DV), Trans Fat

0g, Cholesterol 0mg (0% DV), Sodium 0mg (0% DV), Carbohydrates 18g (6% DV), Dietary Fiber 3g (12% DV), Sugars 3g, **Added Sugars:** 3g, Protein 2g, Vitamin A 0%, Vitamin C 0%, Calcium 2%, Iron 4%.

HOMEMADE MUESLI

= Makes: 4 cups

= Serving size: 1/2 cup

= Total servings: 8

= Active time: 15 minutes

= Total time: 15 minutes

Stanford University has one of the best football programs in the United States. When Cindy read their breakfast recommendations to their athletes — raw rolled oats, nuts, and grains — she thought it sounded like muesli. Why spend a fortune on fancy cereal when you can make your own, and make it the way your family likes it? If it's good enough for Stanford football players, Cindy says it's good enough for her students at Mount Diablo High School.

Ingredients
2 cups old-fashioned rolled oats
1/4 cup sunflower seeds
1/4 cup chopped dried dates or apricots

1/4 cup unsweetened coconut
1/4 cup chopped almonds
1/4 cup raisins

Mix the oats, sunflower seeds, dates or apricots, coconut, almonds, and raisins together in a bowl.

Stored in an airtight container, the muesli will keep for up to two months.

VARIATIONS:
- For a hot cereal, combine 1/2 cup of muesli with 1 to 1 1/2 cups of milk or unsweetened soy, almond, or coconut milk in a saucepan. Bring to a boil, then lower the heat to a simmer, cover the saucepan, and cook for 5 minutes. Turn off the heat and let sit for 5 minutes before serving.
- Use the muesli mixture in oatmeal cookies; substitute the muesli for the old-fashioned rolled oats, raisins, and nuts.
- Use other rolled grains, barley, or 7-grain cereal along with rolled oats when making the muesli. (Note: Cracked grains and steel-cut oats will not work; they are too hard.)
- Add 1/2 cup muesli and 1 cup cold

milk or plain yogurt (see the Tutti-frutti recipe, p. 213).

GOES WELL WITH:
- Milk
- Plain yogurt
- Fruit compote or applesauce
- Fresh chopped fruit

Per serving: Calories 160, Calories from Fat 50, Total Fat 6g (9% DV), Saturated Fat 1.5g (8% DV), Trans Fat 0g, Cholesterol 0mg (0% DV), Sodium 0mg (0% DV), Carbohydrates 25g (8% DV), Dietary Fiber 4g (16% DV), Sugars 6g, **Added Sugars:** 0g, Protein 4g, Vitamin A 4%, Vitamin C 0%, Calcium 2%, Iron 8%.

NUT BUTTER BARS

= Makes: 8 bars (These can always be cut in half.)

= Serving size: 3 ounces

= Total servings: 8

= Active time: 15 minutes

= Total time: 30 minutes

These bars are great for a breakfast on the go. Use unsweetened puffed kamut or wheat found at natural food stores or large groceries. Feel free to use 2 tablespoons brown sugar instead of honey.

Ingredients
1 cup old-fashioned rolled oats
1 cup chopped almonds, walnuts, or pecans
1/4 cup raw sunflower seeds
1 tablespoon ground flaxseed (optional)
1 tablespoon sesame seeds
1 cup unsweetened puffed kamut or wheat
1/3 cup chopped dried apricots
1/3 cup raisins
1 cup creamy almond butter
2 tablespoons honey
1 teaspoon vanilla or almond extract

STEP 1: Preheat the oven to 350°F. Line an 8-inch square baking pan with waxed or parchment paper.

STEP 2: Spread the oats, almonds, sunflower seeds, flaxseed, if using, and sesame seeds on a large rimmed baking sheet. Bake until the oats and nuts are lightly toasted, about 10 minutes, shaking the baking sheet about halfway through. When toasted, remove from the oven, and transfer to large bowl. Add the puffed cereal, apricots, and raisins. Mix thoroughly.

STEP 3: Place the almond butter, honey, and vanilla or almond extract in a small saucepan and cook over medium heat until the mixture bubbles lightly, 2 to 5 minutes. Pour the almond butter mixture over the oats, almonds, sunflower seeds, dried apricots, raisins, and puffed cereal. Mix with a spatula until no dry spots remain.

STEP 4: Transfer the mixture to the prepared baking pan. Use parchment or waxed paper to press the mixture down firmly to make an even layer. Refrigerate until firm, about 30 minutes. Cut into 8 bars or 16 mini bars.

The bars can be wrapped individually in waxed paper. Stored in an airtight container or tin in the refrigerator, the bars will keep for up to a week or freeze them for up to one month. You can pack them in a lunch frozen. No need to defrost. They will be perfect by lunchtime.

TIP:
• Almond butter can be found at natural food stores or large grocery stores near the peanut butter.

VARIATIONS:
- Substitute dried peaches, plums, or apples for the dried apricots.
- Substitute peanut butter, or another creamy nut butter, for the almond butter.

GOES WELL WITH:
- Milk, or unsweetened milk alternative
- Sliced apples

Per serving: Calories 400, Calories from Fat 230, Total Fat 28g (43% DV), Saturated Fat 2g (10% DV), Trans Fat 0g, Cholesterol 0mg (0% DV), Sodium 70mg (3% DV), Carbohydrates 32g (11% DV), Dietary Fiber 8g (32% DV), Sugars 13g, **Added Sugars:** 3g, Protein 13g, Vitamin A 4%, Vitamin C 0%, Calcium 15%, Iron 15%.

TUTTI-FRUTTI

= Makes: 1 1/2 cups

= Active time: 15 minutes

= Serving size: 1 1/2 cups

= Total time: 15 minutes

= Total servings: 1

You will never find a dish that tastes sweeter

but has less sugar than this one. All the sugar is in the fruit, not added. This is a party in a bowl.

Ingredients
1/2 cup plain yogurt
1/4 cup Homemade Muesli (p. 208)
1/4 cup diced apple
1/4 cup peeled and diced banana
1/2 cup berries, fresh or individually quick frozen (IQF; this means the fruit has been frozen individually), with no added sugar

STEP 1: Stir the yogurt and muesli together in a bowl. Add the apple and banana and stir.

STEP 2: Gently stir in the berries.

This recipe can be multiplied. It can also be made the night before and stored in the refrigerator for two days in a covered container. But, if you are using frozen berries, add them just before you eat.

VARIATIONS:
- Vary the fruit; use fresh or frozen cherries, peaches, pears, even mangoes.
- Add sunflower seeds, flaxseed,

sesame seeds, chai seeds, or pumpkin seeds.

- Stir 1/4 teaspoon of vanilla extract into the yogurt.

Per serving: Calories 230, Calories from Fat 30, Total Fat 3.5g (5% DV), Saturated Fat 1.5g (8% DV), Trans Fat 0g, Cholesterol 5mg (2% DV), Sodium 135mg (6% DV), Carbohydrates 44g (15% DV), Dietary Fiber 5g (20% DV), Sugars 27g, **Added Sugars:** 0g, Protein 10g, Vitamin A 4%, Vitamin C 90%, Calcium 25%, Iron 15%.

YOGURT PARFAIT

= Makes: 1 Parfait   = Active time: 5 minutes

= Serving size: 2 1/2 cups   = Total time: 5 minutes

= Total servings: 1

This is Cindy's "go-to" breakfast. Make it the night before, or even two to three days ahead of time. You can carry it on a plane. Layered fruit, cereal, and yogurt will pass security; for some reason, plain yogurt will not. Children love it. It's a power meal. If you let it sit for at least 15 minutes, the yogurt softens the cereal. If you like it crunchy, then eat it right away.

Ingredients

1/2 cup shredded wheat or shredded wheat
and bran (check the label for no sweeteners added)

1 cup low- or nonfat plain yogurt (not
Greek, it's too thick)

1 cup chopped fruit or berries

Put the shredded wheat on the bottom of a
small cereal bowl or plastic container. If using mini shredded wheat, use whole. If using larger squares of shredded wheat, break
it up. Spread the yogurt over the cereal. Top
it with the fruit. That's it.

VARIATIONS:

- Use Greek yogurt instead of plain
  yogurt and eliminate the shredded
  wheat.
- Make Cindy's healthy cheesecake:
  Spread shredded wheat on a platter,
  cover it with two inches of plain
  Greek yogurt. Top it with mixed berries, chopped fruit, or fruit compote.

GOES WELL WITH:

- Salad, to make a lunch

Per serving: Calories 210, Calories from Fat 40, Total Fat 4.5g (7% DV), Saturated Fat 2.5g (12% DV), Trans Fat 0g, Cholesterol 15mg (5% DV), Sodium 170mg (7% DV), Carbohydrates 30g (10% DV), Dietary Fiber 3g (12% DV), Sugars 25g, **Added Sugars:** 0g, Protein 14g, Vitamin A 2%, Vitamin C 170%, Calcium 45%, Iron 4%.

Fruit Salad Twelve Ways

= Makes: 6 cups

= Serves: 6

= Serving size: 1 cup

= Active time: About 10 minutes for 2 to 4 pounds of fruit

= Total time: 10 minutes

If you have fruit with every meal, you'll satisfy your sweet tooth while also giving your body the fiber it needs to slow down the metabolism of fructose. This is real fruit. The key is fresh. You can buy a container of it at Trader Joe's or Safeway for $6, or you can buy twice as much whole fruit for the same price or less. It will be fresher, cheaper, and better, just not as fast.

Obviously, any combination of berries and/or sliced fruit can be called "fruit salad." Let your imagination run wild. Here are some combinations that I like:

1. Cubed watermelon, feta cheese, thinly sliced basil (p. 312).

Per serving: Calories 160, Calories from Fat 110, Total Fat 12g (18% DV), Saturated Fat 2.5g (12% DV), Trans Fat 0g, Cholesterol 5mg (2% DV), Sodium 135mg (6% DV), Carbohydrates 12g (4% DV), Dietary Fiber 1g (4% DV), Sugars 9g, **Added Sugars:** 0g, Protein 3g, Vitamin A 45%, Vitamin C 20%, Calcium 6%, Iron 6%.

2. Sliced apples with lemon juice or old-fashioned nut butters for dipping

1 cup sliced apples
1 teaspoon lemon juice
1 tablespoon nut butter

Per serving: Calories 60, Calories from Fat 0, Total Fat 0g (0% DV), Saturated Fat 0g (0% DV), Trans Fat 0g, Cholesterol 0mg (0% DV), Sodium 0mg (0% DV), Carbohydrates 15g (5% DV), Dietary Fiber 3g (12% DV), Sugars 11g, **Added Sugars:** 0g, Protein 0g, Vitamin

A 2%, Vitamin C 8%, Calcium 0%, Iron 0%.

3. Mexican papaya, peeled and tossed with lemon or lime juice.

The citrus mutes the sometimes funky smell of papaya.

1 cup chopped papaya
1 teaspoon lemon or lime juice

Per serving: Calories 60, Calories from Fat 0, Total Fat 0g (0% DV), Saturated Fat 0g (0% DV), Trans Fat 0g, Cholesterol 0mg (0% DV), Sodium 10mg (0% DV), Carbohydrates 16g (5% DV), Dietary Fiber 2g (8% DV), Sugars 11g, **Added Sugars:** 0g, Protein < 1g, Vitamin A 25%, Vitamin C 150%, Calcium 2%, Iron 2%.

4. Cantaloupe or honeydew melon, peeled and cubed, tossed with chopped fresh mint.

1 cup chopped cantaloupe or honeydew melon
1/2 teaspoon chopped fresh mint

Per serving: Calories 60, Calories from

Fat 0, Total Fat 0g (0% DV), Saturated
Fat 0g (0% DV), Trans Fat 0g, Choles-
terol 0mg (0% DV), Sodium 25mg (1%
DV), Carbohydrates 14g (5% DV),
Dietary Fiber 2g (8% DV), Sugars 13g,
Added Sugars: 0g, Protein 1g, Vitamin
A 110%, Vitamin C 110%, Calcium 2%,
Iron 2%.

5. Berry Compote (p. 225)

1/2 cup serving

Per serving: Calories 80, Calories from
Fat 0, Total Fat 0.5g (1% DV), Saturated
Fat 0g (0% DV), Trans Fat 0g, Choles-
terol 0mg (0% DV), Sodium 0mg (0%
DV), Carbohydrates 19g (6% DV),
Dietary Fiber 4g (16% DV), Sugars 13g,
Added Sugars: 0g, Protein < 1g, Vita-
min A 2%, Vitamin C 45%, Calcium
2%, Iron 4%.

6. Warm or cold Applesauce (p. 226)

1/2 cup serving

Per serving: Calories 110, Calories
from Fat 0, Total Fat 0g (0% DV),
Saturated Fat 0g (0% DV), Trans Fat

0g, Cholesterol 0mg (0% DV), Sodium 0mg (0% DV), Carbohydrates 30g (10% DV), Dietary Fiber 5g (20% DV), Sugars 22g, **Added Sugars:** 0g, Protein < 1g, Vitamin A 2%, Vitamin C 20%, Calcium 2%, Iron 2%.

7. Fruit kebabs

Peeled and cubed pineapple, honeydew, watermelon, cantaloupe. Cut fruit into 1 1/2-inch squares. Purchase 6-inch bamboo skewers at a housewares store. Thread four cubes of fruit onto each skewer. These work for any meal.

6 ounces pineapple
6 ounces honeydew melon
6 ounces watermelon
6 ounces cantaloupe

Per serving: Calories 60, Calories from Fat 0, Total Fat 0g (0% DV), Saturated Fat 0g (0% DV), Trans Fat 0g, Cholesterol 0mg (0% DV), Sodium 15mg (1% DV), Carbohydrates 15g (5% DV), Dietary Fiber < 1g (4% DV), Sugars 12g, **Added Sugars:** 0g, Protein 1g, Vitamin A 30%, Vitamin C 50%, Calcium 2%, Iron 2%.

8. Dried fruit and nuts

1/4 cup dried fruit
1 tablespoon almonds or walnuts

Per serving: Calories 200, Calories from Fat 70, Total Fat 8g (12% DV), Saturated Fat 0.5g (2% DV), Trans Fat 0g, Cholesterol 0mg (0% DV), Sodium 0mg (0% DV), Carbohydrates 32g (11% DV), Dietary Fiber 3g (12% DV), Sugars 22g, **Added Sugars:** 0g, Protein 4g, Vitamin A 0%, Vitamin C 2%, Calcium 6%, Iron 6%.

9. Grapes, cherries, and strawberries

1 cup grapes, pitted cherries, and hulled strawberries, mixed

Per serving: Calories 70, Calories from Fat 0, Total Fat 0g (0% DV), Saturated Fat 0g (0% DV), Trans Fat 0g, Cholesterol 0mg (0% DV), Sodium 0mg (0% DV), Carbohydrates 17g (6% DV), Dietary Fiber 2g (8% DV), Sugars 14g, **Added Sugars:** 0g, Protein 1g, Vitamin A 2%, Vitamin C 60%, Calcium 2%, Iron 2%.

10. Sliced and peeled oranges, grapefruit, and avocado with chopped fresh mint

1/2 orange, sliced
1/4 grapefruit, sliced
1/4 ripe avocado, sliced
1/2 teaspoon chopped fresh mint

Per serving: Calories 120, Calories from Fat 45, Total Fat 6g (9% DV), Saturated Fat 1g (5% DV), Trans Fat 0g, Cholesterol 0mg (0% DV), Sodium 0mg (0% DV), Carbohydrates 19g (6% DV), Dietary Fiber 5g (20% DV), Sugars 9g, **Added Sugars:** 0g, Protein 2g, Vitamin A 8%, Vitamin C 130%, Calcium 6%, Iron 2%.

11. Grilled stone fruit: peaches, apricots, nectarines

Grilling fruit is quick: Halve fruit, then take out the pits. If wanted, cut in half again. Spray with olive oil. Grill in a heavy pan on the stove over high heat or over a gas grill until brown, 2 1/2 minutes on each side.

1 medium peach or 1 medium nectarine, sliced or halved, or 2 small halved apricots

Per serving: Calories 70, Calories from Fat 0, Total Fat 0g (0% DV), Saturated Fat 0g (0% DV), Trans Fat 0g, Cholesterol 0mg (0% DV), Sodium 0mg (0% DV), Carbohydrates 16g (5% DV), Dietary Fiber 3g (12% DV), Sugars 13g, **Added Sugars:** 0g, Protein 2g, Vitamin A 30%, Vitamin C 20%, Calcium 2%, Iron 2%.

12. Grilled figs or pineapple served chilled or warm

4 medium-size figs or 1/8 pineapple

Per serving: Calories 150, Calories from Fat 5, Total Fat 0.5g (1% DV), Saturated Fat 0g (0% DV), Trans Fat 0g, Cholesterol 0mg (0% DV), Sodium 0mg (0% DV), Carbohydrates 38g (13% DV), Dietary Fiber 6g (24% DV), Sugars 33g, **Added Sugars:** 0g, Protein 2g, Vitamin A 6%, Vitamin C 6%, Calcium 8%, Iron 4%.

BERRY COMPOTE

= Makes: 2 cups   = Active time:
                     10 minutes
= Serving size: = Total time:
  1/2 cup   10 minutes
= Total servings: 4

This is wonderful cold or hot. Use cold over Greek yogurt, or hot over oatmeal or whole-grain pancakes.

Ingredients
1 pound mixed frozen berries individually quick frozen
1/2 cup Applesauce (p. 226)

Combine the frozen berries and applesauce. Let the compote sit in the fridge for 15 minutes, then serve lukewarm or chilled.

Stored in an airtight container in the refrigerator, the compote will keep for up to one week.

VARIATIONS:
- Use frozen peaches or apricots in place of berries.
- Use fresh berries or stone fruit in place of frozen.

GOES WELL WITH:
- Pancakes; warm it up and use it like syrup
- Yogurt or ice cream

Per serving: Calories 80, Calories from Fat 0, Total Fat 0.5g (1% DV), Saturated Fat 0g (0% DV), Trans Fat 0g, Cholesterol 0mg (0% DV), Sodium 0mg (0% DV), Carbohydrates 19g (6% DV), Dietary Fiber 4g (16% DV), Sugars 13g, **Added Sugars:** 0g, Protein < 1g, Vitamin A 2%, Vitamin C 45%, Calcium 2%, Iron 4%.

APPLESAUCE

= Makes: 3 cups

= Active time: 15 minutes

= Serving size: 1/2 cup

= Total time: 30 minutes

Packaged applesauce usually has a lot of added sugar, and it never has the fresh, snappy taste of homemade applesauce. Luckily, making your own applesauce couldn't be simpler. Honestly, it takes about 10 minutes.

Cindy serves this applesauce as a side dish in her restaurant, where she likes to make this recipe with fresh, tart apples. The quality and taste of the apples determine the flavor of the sauce. Fuji or Granny Smith apples make good choices here, or you can use a combination of your favorites. Don't peel the apples. If you slice the apples thinly, the peels are barely noticeable in the finished sauce, and they provide essential fiber.

When apples get expensive in the late spring and summer, you can use frozen apples in this recipe. You can buy these at the store, or slice your own during the autumn apple harvest, and freeze them in plastic bags to use later.

Ingredients
6 large apples
Juice of 1 lemon
1/2 teaspoon ground cinnamon
2 tablespoons water

STEP 1: Core and chop the apples and toss them with the lemon juice and cinnamon.

STEP 2: Place a medium-size pot over low heat. Add the water and heat until the liquid begins to steam.

STEP 3: Add the apple mixture to the pot

and cover it. Steam the apples until tender, about 15 minutes.

STEP 4: Using a potato masher, mash the apples to whatever texture you desire. Some people like a smooth sauce, others prefer chunky. Let the applesauce cool before serving.

Stored in a covered container in the refrigerator, the applesauce will keep for seven days.

VARIATION:
- You can also make the applesauce in a microwave; cook it on the high setting for 10 minutes.

GOES WELL WITH:
- Pork roast or pork chops
- Yogurt
- Pancakes
- French toast

Per serving: Calories 110, Calories from Fat 0, Total Fat 0g (0% DV), Saturated Fat 0g (0% DV), Trans Fat 0g, Cholesterol 0mg (0% DV), Sodium 0mg (0% DV), Carbohydrates 30g (10% DV), Dietary Fiber 5g (20% DV), Sug-

ars 22g, **Added Sugars:** 0g, Protein
< 1g, Vitamin A 2%, Vitamin C 20%,
Calcium 2%, Iron 2%.

LOW-SUGAR BLACKBERRY JAM

= Makes: 1 quart = Active time:
5 minutes

= Serving size: = Total time:
1 tablespoon 1 hour

You don't need to sterilize jars and go
through a complicated canning process if
you're going to use the jam immediately.
This quick jam will keep for two weeks in
the fridge. It won't last that long. Kids will
love it.

It's about the fruit, not the sugar. Two
tablespoons of sugar never killed anybody.
And for two pounds of berries? This is a
great way to reset your palette without giving up taste. Make a batch and give some
away to friends. They'll love you for it.

Ingredients
2 pounds blackberries or mixed berries,
fresh or thawed, if frozen
Half of a 1.75-ounce box of pectin, a
thickening agent found next to the sugar

in most grocery stores
2 tablespoons sugar

STEP 1: Place the berries in a 2-quart pot with a lid. Bring to a boil.

STEP 2: Mix in the pectin and sugar. Simmer for 10 minutes. If the jam seems thin, simmer a few minutes longer. Let cool. Spoon the jam into small containers and put it in the fridge to chill.

Stored in glass jars, or in plastic containers with a firm lid, the jam will keep for two weeks in the refrigerator or three months in the freezer. This recipe can be multiplied.

VARIATION:
- Use raspberries or strawberries.

GOES WELL WITH:
- Yogurt
- Toast
- Pancakes
- A PBJ

Per serving: Calories 20, Calories from Fat 0, Total Fat 0g (0% DV), Saturated Fat 0g (0% DV), Trans Fat 0g, Cholesterol 0mg (0% DV), Sodium 0mg (0% DV), Carbohydrates 5g (2% DV), Dietary Fiber 1g (4% DV), Sugars 4g, **Added Sugars:** > 1g, Protein 0g, Vitamin A 0%, Vitamin C 2%, Calcium 0%, Iron 2%.

HOMEMADE "SAUSAGE"

= Serves: 6	= Active time: 10 minutes
= Serving size: 3 ounces	= Total time: 25 minutes

This isn't technically "sausage," because it does not have a casing. But it tastes like breakfast sausage. Even better, it has no "mystery meat," no preservatives, no added sugar, no chemicals. It's quick, simple, and delicious. You can slice it, freeze the slices on a cookie sheet, then pop them into a plastic bag to fry up as needed.

Substituting turkey in savory foods is always a dicey proposition, because ground turkey doesn't have the fat of other meats, and therefore it has less flavor. So it's all about the seasoning. Season it right, and nobody cares: the more complex the flavors, the better. And fennel is a fantastic seasoning to extend a savory dish.

Ingredients

1 pound ground meat: beef, pork, chicken, or turkey, or a mixture

1 tablespoon red wine vinegar or a vinegar of your choice

2 teaspoons chopped fresh parsley

1 teaspoon dried basil, or 1 tablespoon fresh basil

2 teaspoons onion powder, or 2 tablespoons peeled and chopped fresh onions

1 teaspoon garlic powder

1 teaspoon salt

1 teaspoon cracked black pepper

1 teaspoon paprika

1 teaspoon dried pepper flakes or cayenne

1/2 teaspoon whole or ground fennel seeds

1/2 teaspoon ground oregano

1 pinch (1/8 teaspoon) of thyme

1 teaspoon oil, if frying the sausage

STEP 1: Place the meat in a medium-size bowl and add the wine vinegar, parsley, basil, onion powder, garlic powder, salt, cracked pepper, paprika, pepper flakes or cayenne, fennel, oregano, and thyme.

STEP 2: Knead the meat and seasonings with your hands until well combined.

STEP 3: Divide the meat into three portions and roll each into a log 1 to 2 inches in diameter. Refrigerate the logs for 1 hour.

STEP 4: Cut the logs into 1/4-inch-thick slices and fry them in the oil in a heavy skillet over medium heat until cooked through, 5 to 7 minutes. Or preheat the oven to 350°F and bake the slices until cooked through, 15 to 20 minutes. Serve.

VARIATIONS:
- If you don't want to wait, you can just crumble the meat mixture and fry it without chilling the logs first.
- Play with the herbs. Substitute cilantro and chili powder for the basil and paprika to make a Latin version.
- Add 1 or 2 cloves of garlic, peeled and chopped, or to taste.

GOES WELL WITH:
- Scrambled eggs
- An omelet or breakfast burrito
- Sandwiches as a filling

Per serving: Calories 210, Calories from Fat 140, Total Fat 16g (25% DV), Saturated Fat 6g (30% DV), Trans Fat 1g, Cholesterol 55mg (18% DV), Sodium 460mg (19% DV), Carbohydrates

1g (0% DV), Dietary Fiber < 1g (2% DV), Sugars 0g, **Added Sugars:** 0g, Protein 14g, Vitamin A 8%, Vitamin C 2%, Calcium 2%, Iron 10%.

ALMOST HOMEMADE SALSA

= Makes: 4 cups

= Active time: 10 minutes

= Serving size: 1/4 cup

= Total time: 10 minutes

= Total servings: 16

Check the prepared salsa label! Pace Picante or Ortega salsa brands have no added sugar. To them, I add chopped tomatoes, cilantro, onions, and cayenne pepper. This is a quick and healthy salsa. It's marvelous over eggs, or topping breakfast grains.

Ingredients
2 cups store-bought mild salsa
2 cups diced fresh tomatoes
1/2 cup chopped fresh cilantro
1/2 cup peeled and chopped red or yellow onion
1/2 teaspoon cayenne pepper
A squeeze of lemon or lime juice

Mix the salsa, tomatoes, cilantro, onion, cayenne, and lemon or lime juice together in a medium-size bowl.

This recipe can be multiplied. It will keep in the refrigerator in a plastic or glass container for up to a week.

VARIATIONS:
- Use a 15-ounce can of chopped fire-roasted stewed tomatoes in place of fresh.
- Add some chopped chipotle peppers in adobo, if you like your salsa spicy.
- Add 1/2 teaspoon of dried cumin or coriander.

GOES WELL WITH:
- Eggs
- Salad, as a dressing
- Meat
- Polenta, heated and spread with Parmesan cheese
- Warm breakfast grains and a poached egg and fresh or frozen greens

Per serving: Calories 15, Calories from Fat 0, Total Fat 0g (0% DV), Saturated Fat 0g (0% DV), Trans Fat 0g, Cholesterol 0mg (0% DV), Sodium 220mg (9% DV), Carbohydrates 3g (1% DV), Dietary Fiber < 1g (4% DV), Sugars 2g,

Added Sugars: 0g, Protein < 1g, Vitamin A 6%, Vitamin C 6%, Calcium 2%, Iron 2%.

POWER MUFFINS

= Makes: 20 muffins

= Serving size: One 4-ounce muffin

= Active time: 20 minutes

= Total time: 1 hour

The whole grains and fruit make these a power breakfast. When I can't have a yogurt parfait, I like to have a muffin. They freeze well and are great for a snack.

Ingredients

1 1/2 cups rolled oats

2 1/2 cups oat bran

4 teaspoons baking powder

4 teaspoons ground cinnamon

4 cups nonfat plain yogurt

3/4 cup eggs, beaten, or egg whites, or Egg Beaters

2 red apples, grated

2 cups blueberries, fresh or frozen, unthawed, no sugar added

Non-aerosol cooking spray

STEP 1: Preheat the oven to 325°F.

STEP 2: Place the rolled oats, oat bran, baking powder, cinnamon, yogurt, eggs (or egg whites or Egg Beaters) and apples in a bowl and stir until well blended. Gently fold in 1 1/2 cups blueberries. Reserve 1/2 cup blueberries.

STEP 3: Spray a muffin pan with non-aerosol cooking spray. Scoop the muffin dough into the muffin cups and lightly press down on the tops. Top each muffin with four of the reserved blueberries.

STEP 4: Bake the muffins until they are firm and just slightly golden brown on top, 25 to 35 minutes.

VARIATION:
- Substitute dried fruit, almonds, raisins, peaches, or other berries for the blueberries.

GOES WELL WITH:
- Salad or soup at lunch
- Eggs at breakfast
- Snacks, midmorning or afternoon
- Low-Sugar Blackberry Jam (p. 229)

Per serving: Calories 130, Calories from Fat 20, Total Fat 2.5g (4% DV),

Saturated Fat 1g (5% DV), Trans Fat 0g, Cholesterol < 5mg (1% DV), Sodium 50mg (2% DV), Carbohydrates 24g (8% DV), Dietary Fiber 4g (16% DV), Sugars 6g, **Added Sugars:** 0g, Protein 8g, Vitamin A 0%, Vitamin C 4%, Calcium 15%, Iron 8%.

BAKED FRUIT OATMEAL

- Serves: 10 to 12
- Serving size: One 4-ounce square
- Active time: 10 minutes
- Total time: 55 minutes to 1 hour

Oatmeal is terrific for you. It has lots of fiber, that unsung nutrient that slows down your body's metabolism of sugar. But on some mornings spending 15 minutes preparing rolled oats, or 1 hour preparing steel-cut oats, seems a bridge too far. This recipe offers a solution: You can make the oatmeal the night before. All you need to do in the morning is cut a slice, and enjoy!

Ingredients
3 cups old-fashioned rolled oats
2 teaspoons ground cinnamon
2 teaspoons baking powder

2 tablespoons brown sugar or honey (optional)

1 teaspoon salt

1 1/4 cups unsweetened soy milk (2 percent milk is also OK)

1 pound sweet apples, diced

2 tablespoons rice bran, coconut, or safflower oil

2 large eggs, or 4 large egg whites (save the yolks for another use)

1 tablespoon vanilla extract

STEP 1: Preheat the oven to 350°F.

STEP 2: Spray a 9-by-9-inch baking pan with cooking oil.

STEP 3: Combine the rolled oats, cinnamon, baking powder, brown sugar, if using, and salt in a medium-size bowl.

STEP 4: Combine the soy milk, apples, oil, eggs, vanilla, and honey, if using, in a large bowl. Add the oat mixture and mix well. Pour the oatmeal batter into the prepared baking pan.

STEP 5: Bake the oatmeal on the middle rack until the center is set and firm to the touch, 45 minutes.

Cool for 10 minutes, cut and serve. Can be served at room temperature. Covered, it will keep in the refrigerator for up to three days.

VARIATIONS:
- Make muffins using a nonstick muffin pan that makes 12. The baking time will be 25 minutes.
- Use fresh or frozen chopped peaches, about 2 fresh peaches or 1 cup frozen, in place of the apples.

GOES WELL WITH:
- Scrambled eggs
- A glass of milk
- A midmorning snack

Per serving (with added honey): Calories 170, Calories from Fat 40, Total Fat 4.5g (7% DV), Saturated Fat 1g (5% DV), Trans Fat 0g, Cholesterol 35mg (12% DV), Sodium 250mg (10% DV), Carbohydrates 28g (9% DV), Dietary Fiber 4g (16% DV), Sugars 9g, **Added Sugars:** 3g, Protein 5g, Vitamin A 2%, Vitamin C 4%, Calcium 10%, Iron 6%.

WHOLE-GRAIN YOGURT PANCAKES

= Makes:
  12 to 16 pancakes
= Serving size:
  2 medium-size
  pancakes

= Active time:
  15 minutes
= Total time:
  25 minutes

These pancakes are light and fluffy, not heavy like regular pancakes. They also have more flavor than regular pancakes. Top them with the Berry Compote (p. 225) and you've got a power meal.

Ingredients

1 1/2 cups oat bran
1 1/2 cups whole-wheat flour
1 cup rolled oats
1 1/2 tablespoons baking soda
1 cup eggs, beaten, or egg whites, or Egg Beaters
1/4 cup prune paste *
1/2 cup Applesauce (p. 226)
1 red apple, grated

* Prune paste: Boil pitted prunes in water for approximately 2 minutes. Drain the prunes and grind them into a paste in a blender or food processor. You can also sometimes find this in supermarkets, in the baking aisle labeled prune lekvar (prune butter).

241

2 1/4 cups nonfat plain yogurt
1/4 cup nonfat milk

STEP 1: Mix the oat bran, whole-wheat flour, oats, and baking soda together in a mixing bowl.

STEP 2: Mix the eggs (or egg whites or Egg Beaters), prune paste, Applesauce, apple, yogurt, and milk together in large bowl. Add the oat mixture and stir to mix (don't overmix the batter). This batter will keep in an airtight container in the refrigerator for 2 days.

STEP 3: Cook the pancakes on a lightly oiled preheated griddle or frying pan. Add 1/4 cup batter to the griddle. Cook over medium heat until the batter bubbles, and edges start to get solid. Flip and cook the other side.

This recipe can be multiplied. The pancakes can be cooked and frozen for a quick breakfast. To defrost, pop them in the microwave for 90 seconds.

VARIATIONS:
- Use unsweetened nut or soy milk in place of the nonfat milk.
- Use unsweetened soy yogurt in place of the nonfat yogurt.

GOES WELL WITH:
- Berry Compote (p. 130)
- Warm Applesauce (p. 131)
- Roasted or grilled peaches

Per serving: Calories 170, Calories from Fat 20, Total Fat 2g (3% DV), Saturated Fat 0.5g (2% DV), Trans Fat 0g, Cholesterol < 5mg (1% DV), Sodium 230mg (10% DV), Carbohydrates 35g (12% DV), Dietary Fiber 5g (20% DV), Sugars 9g, **Added Sugars:** 0g, Protein 10g, Vitamin A 4%, Vitamin C 4%, Calcium 10%, Iron 10%.

JOE'S SCRAMBLE AND THREE OTHERS

= Makes: 1 scramble = Active time: 20 minutes

= Serving size: half of recipe = Total time: 20 minutes

= Total servings: 2

This is Cindy's son Joe's favorite meal.

Ingredients
1 tablespoon olive oil
3 ounces Homemade "Sausage" (p. 231)
1/4 cup chopped green onions
1/2 cup chopped or sliced mushrooms
1 cup chopped fresh spinach
3 large eggs, beaten

243

1 ounce grated Parmesan cheese

STEP 1: Heat the oil in a medium-size frying pan over medium-high heat. Add the sausage and green onions and cook until done, about 5 minutes. Add the mushrooms and spinach and cook another 2 minutes. Add the eggs, scramble and cook until firm, about 5 minutes.

STEP 2: Transfer the scramble to a plate and top it with the Parmesan cheese.

Three More Scramble Ideas:
- Ben's: Add green chilies, Jack cheese, sour cream, and fresh tomatoes.
- Nana's: Add zucchini, broccoli, mushrooms, and Jack cheese.
- Alex's: Add ham, Jack cheese, guacamole, and salsa.

VARIATIONS:
- Add beaten eggs to the pan, scramble the eggs with spinach, mushrooms, and green onions. Turn off the heat, cover. The heat from the pan will firm up the eggs. Let it sit 1 minute for soft eggs, 3 to 5 minutes if you want it firm. Serve.
- Use 6 egg whites, in place of 3 whole eggs.

- Scramble 1 cup soft tofu instead of eggs.
- Add 1/2 cup zucchini and 1/2 cup bell pepper.
- Use 3 ounces bacon instead of sausage.

GOES WELL WITH:
- Brown rice or grilled sweet potatoes
- Fresh fruit
- Steamed or roasted vegetables

Per serving: Calories 340, Calories from Fat 230, Total Fat 26g (40% DV), Saturated Fat 9g (45% DV), Trans Fat 0g, Cholesterol 320mg (107% DV), Sodium 570mg (24% DV), Carbohydrates 4g (1% DV), Dietary Fiber < 1g (4% DV), Sugars 1g, **Added Sugars:** 0g, Protein 23g, Vitamin A 50%, Vitamin C 10%, Calcium 25%, Iron 15%.

POLENTA PATTIES WITH SAUTÉED GREENS, POACHED EGGS, ROMA TOMATOES, AND BASIL SALSA

= Serves: 6

= Active time: 30 minutes

= Serving size: 1/6 of recipe

= Total time: 30 minutes

Polenta is corn, but coarse and unrefined.

Team it with some vegetables and you can get kids to eat veggies for breakfast.

This is a favorite brunch dish at Cindy's restaurant. The polenta and the salsa take a bit more time than most of the recipes in this book, but it's worth the trouble and good enough to serve to guests. You could also use hollandaise sauce for the salsa. Everyone always thought hollandaise sauce (egg yolk, butter, lemon juice) was a heart attack waiting to happen, but it is nothing of the sort. Remember, the fat hypothesis has been debunked! One suggestion: add three drops of Tabasco sauce to the hollandaise to give it the kick that lemon juice can't.

Ingredients
1 batch polenta (see p. 200), cooled in an oiled 8-by-8-inch pan until firm
2 tablespoons olive oil
6 cups greens: spinach, chard, or kale, rinsed
6 eggs
1 teaspoon distilled white vinegar
1/2 cup Roma Tomato Basil Salsa (p. 172)

STEP 1: Remove the polenta from the loaf pan and cut into 6 slices, each 1/4 inch thick.

STEP 2: Heat 1 tablespoon olive oil in a large pan over medium-high heat. Add the polenta slices and fry until golden brown on both sides, about 3 minutes per side. Transfer the polenta slices to a plate and keep warm.

STEP 3: Add the remaining 1 tablespoon of oil to the pan and sauté the greens until wilted and tender.

STEP 4: Heat 2 inches of water just to a boil in a separate medium-size frying pan, add the white vinegar, then reduce the heat to low. Crack the eggs into the water and poach them until desired doneness, 2 to 3 minutes for soft yolks. Using a slotted spoon, remove the eggs from the water, being careful not to break the yolks. Transfer the eggs to a plate.

STEP 5: Place a polenta patty on each of six plates. Top each patty with greens and a poached egg. Pour salsa over all. Or, place all the polenta slices on a platter, top with greens, poached eggs, and salsa.

VARIATIONS:
- In place of polenta patties, use a Corn Cake (p. 492) and top with

Almost Homemade Salsa (p. 234).

- Place the polenta patties in a baking dish and top them with slices of tomato and mozzarella and fresh basil leaves. Sprinkle Parmesan cheese over all and bake in a 350°F oven for 15 minutes, until warm. Top with the eggs.
- In place of poached eggs, use scrambled eggs.
- In place of poached eggs, use 1 1/2 cups soft tofu.
- In place of poached eggs, use 1 1/2 cups black beans.
- Use hollandaise sauce instead of salsa.

GOES WELL WITH:
- Breakfast potatoes
- Green salad
- Fresh fruit

Per serving: Calories 450, Calories from Fat 160, Total Fat 18g (28% DV), Saturated Fat 3.5g (18% DV), Trans Fat 0g, Cholesterol 165mg (55% DV), Sodium 330mg (14% DV), Carbohydrates 61g (20% DV), Dietary Fiber 3g (12% DV), Sugars 2g, **Added Sugars:** 0g, Protein 14g, Vitamin A 90%, Vitamin C

50%, Calcium 8%, Iron 20%.

Lox and Egg Scramble

= Serving size:
1 recipe
= Total servings: 1

= Active time:
15 minutes
= Total time:
15 minutes

This is so yummy. Lox is cured salmon. Nova is salt-cured, lightly smoked salmon. Gravlax is cured with dill. They all taste great in this recipe. Dill gives it a distinctive flavor.

Ingredients

1 teaspoon olive oil
1/4 cup chopped or thinly sliced peeled red or yellow onion
1/4 cup thinly sliced bell pepper, any color
1 ounce salmon: lox, nova, or gravlax
1/4 cup chopped tomatoes (I like Roma or cherry)
2 eggs, or 1/4 cup egg whites
2 scallions, chopped (both white and green ends, too!)
Cracked black pepper

STEP 1: Heat the oil in a nonstick 8-inch omelet pan over medium-high heat. Add the onion and bell peppers. Sauté for 2 minutes.

Add the salmon and tomatoes and cook an additional 2 minutes for crisp veggies, 4 to 6 minutes for more tender veggies. The salmon flavor will spread to the veggies.

STEP 2: Whip the eggs. Pour the eggs into the salmon mixture. Add the scallions. Cook, stirring, 2 minutes for soft eggs, or 4 minutes for firm. Season with black pepper to taste.

Per serving: Calories 220, Calories from Fat 130, Total Fat 14g (22% DV), Saturated Fat 3.5g (18% DV), Trans Fat 0g, Cholesterol 335mg (112% DV), Sodium 700mg (29% DV), Carbohydrates 6g (2% DV), Dietary Fiber 1g (4% DV), Sugars 2g, **Added Sugars:** 0g, Protein 17g, Vitamin A 25%, Vitamin C 50%, Calcium 8%, Iron 15%.

VEGGIE BROWN RICE FRITTATA

= Serves: 6   = Active time: 15 minutes

= Serving size: 1 cup   = Total time: 30 minutes

A frittata is an Italian egg dish. Think of it as a quiche without the crust, or an omelet without the hassle. This *Fat Chance* version adds a bit of cooked whole grain. This increases the fiber content and makes it a whole meal.

Like quiches or omelets, frittatas can be endlessly varied, using whatever ingredients you have at hand. This is also good cold, in a lunch box, or cut into squares for hors d'oeuvres.

Ingredients

1 to 2 tablespoons olive oil, plus more for greasing the baking dish

10 eggs

6 cups packed fresh spinach, chopped

3 cups cooked brown rice

Salt and ground black pepper to taste

1/4 cup grated Parmesan cheese

2 tablespoons fresh dill, or 2 teaspoons dried dill

4 Roma tomatoes (This variety is best because they're not too watery.)

6 ounces crumbled goat cheese or feta cheese

STEP 1: Place a rack in the middle of the oven, and preheat the oven to 400°F.

STEP 2: Oil a 9-inch round or 9-inch

square baking dish with olive oil, or use cooking spray.

STEP 3: Beat the eggs. Mix the eggs with the spinach and brown rice in a large bowl. Add the salt, pepper, Parmesan cheese, and dill. Pour the egg mixture into the prepared baking dish.

STEP 4: Toss the chopped tomatoes with the 1 tablespoon of olive oil and layer them on top of the egg mixture in the dish. Sprinkle the goat cheese or feta on top.

STEP 5: Transfer the baking dish to the middle rack of the oven. Cook the eggs until they have puffed up and the top is brown, about 25 minutes. Remove the frittata from the oven, cut as desired, and serve.

VARIATIONS:
- This whole recipe can be done as a scramble. After mixing ingredients in Step 3, pour into a 10-inch skillet and scramble everything, about 8 minutes. Sauté tomatoes in a separate skillet over high heat until slightly browned, about 3 minutes. Sprinkle tomatoes over eggs. Top all with feta or goat cheese. Cover pan, and let sit

for 5 minutes. Serve right out of the pan.

- Change the vegetable: Shredded zucchini, sautéed diced bell peppers, cooked broccoli or cauliflower, cubed and sautéed eggplant, unpeeled, all work well here.
- Add a peeled chopped yellow onion or a couple of cloves of garlic, peeled and minced and sautéed.
- Change up the cheese: 6 ounces mozzarella, Swiss, cheddar, or Jack all work well.
- Vary the herbs: Substitute basil, parsley, or cilantro for the dill.
- Use 2 1/2 cups soft tofu instead of eggs.

GOES WELL WITH:
- Tossed salad
- Whole-grain bread
- Sliced fruit
- Brown rice
- Applesauce (p. 226)

Per serving: Calories 400, Calories from Fat 190, Total Fat 21g (32% DV), Saturated Fat 10g (50% DV), Trans Fat 0g, Cholesterol 300mg (100% DV), Sodium 400mg (17% DV), Carbohydrates 31g (10% DV), Dietary Fiber 5g (20% DV), Sugars 4g, **Added Sugars:** 0g, Protein 23g, Vitamin A 210%, Vitamin C 25%, Calcium 30%, Iron 20%.

BREAKFAST BURRITOS OR TACOS

= Serves: 8

= Serving size: 1 burrito or 2 small tacos

= Active time: 20 minutes

= Total time: 30 minutes

These are a great way to use up little bits of this and that. My kids won't eat leftovers. They have a passionate objection: They think leftovers are old food. But disguise leftovers in these burritos and voilà! A yummy breakfast. No sugar, and more important, no leftovers!

These burritos and tacos are always different, and they're always delicious. Kids drop by Cindy's classroom in the morning and scoop these up.

If you have a lot of ingredients that you need to use up, make extra burritos, cool them, wrap them individually in aluminum foil, and freeze them, label and date. Then, on that morning when you're rushed, unwrap and microwave the burritos for 2 minutes on high heat. You can do this for as many burritos as you need. That's fast food I can get behind!

Ingredients

2 cups chopped leftover veggies: bell peppers, onions, broccoli, and spinach work well. Stay away from ratatouille and stir-fry leftovers; their flavors will be too strong.

2 cups beans, potatoes, rice, or a bit of all of them

1 1/2 teaspoons butter or vegetable oil

8 eggs, beaten

8 whole-grain tortillas; the 10-inch size works best, or 16 6-inch corn tortillas

1 cup or 8 ounces grated cheese: cheddar, Jack, or pepper Jack work well

1 cup Almost Homemade Salsa (p. 234)

Salt and ground black pepper

STEP 1: Place the leftover veggies in a mixing bowl. Add the beans, potatoes, and/or rice and stir to mix.

STEP 2: Heat a large skillet over medium heat and add the butter or oil. Add the vegetable mixture and cook until heated through, 2 to 3 minutes. Add the eggs and cook, stirring using a spatula until done to taste, another 3 to 5 minutes.

STEP 3: If you are making burritos, spoon 1 cup of the egg-veggie-starch scramble in the center of each whole-grain tortilla. Sprinkle with the cheese, fold the sides of the tortilla toward the center, and roll it up. Top with the salsa and season with salt and pepper to taste.

If you are making tacos, spoon 1/2 cup of the egg-veggie-starch scramble in each corn tortilla, sprinkle with the cheese, and fold the tortilla over. Top with the salsa and season with salt and pepper to taste.

VARIATIONS:
- Add some chopped green onions or fresh chopped cilantro to the vegetable mixture; using 1/2 cup for every 8 servings works well. Use more if you want.
- Use leftover chili in place of the veggies.
- Add Mexican spices like oregano, cumin, coriander, or chili powder to the veggies; a total of 1 tablespoon of spices per 8 servings works well.

- Roll enough burritos to fill a baking pan, cover them with tomato sauce or enchilada sauce, sprinkle a little cheese on top, and heat them in a 400°F oven for 5 minutes.

GOES WELL WITH:
- Salsa
- Fruit and yogurt
- Sliced radishes and jicama

Per serving (burrito): Calories 440, Calories from Fat 130, Total Fat 15g (23% DV), Saturated Fat 6g (30% DV), Trans Fat 0g, Cholesterol 180mg (60% DV), Sodium 640mg (27% DV), Carbohydrates 57g (19% DV), Dietary Fiber 5g (20% DV), Sugars 2g, **Added Sugars:** 0g, Protein 17g, Vitamin A 120%, Vitamin C 6%, Calcium 20%, Iron 20%.

6

Chapter 6
Lunch: Soups, Salads, and Sandwiches

Lunch can be another food minefield, especially because you can be so pressed for time. Do you accompany colleagues to the burger joint? Do you brave the school cafeteria? Do you try the sandwiches or bagels offered at the meeting or conference?

This chapter gives you some simple, easy-to-pack alternatives. Many of these recipes call for beans or legumes like lentils. See Chapter 7 (p. 339) for more information on how to prepare these healthy ingredients.

Paired with a salad, some of these soups and stews would make great weeknight dinners. Also, they freeze well, so make extra and freeze the leftovers for times when life gets frantic.

Recipes:

Spicy Yellow Split Pea Soup with Tempeh
Lentil Stew

SPICY YELLOW SPLIT PEA SOUP
WITH TEMPEH

= Makes: 8 cups	= Active time: 20 minutes
= Serving size: 2 cups for a main meal, 1 cup as a starter	= Total time: 1 hour 5 minutes

This soup is substantial, warming, and delicious. It's also a fiber double whammy, containing both yellow split peas and tempeh. Many non-vegetarians may not be familiar with tempeh. Originally from Indonesia, it's a block of fermented whole soybeans, usually sold in the refrigerator sections of most supermarkets. It has a chewy, almost meaty texture, and a nutty flavor. It contains high-quality protein and more fiber in one serving than most people eat in a day. In this soup, the tempeh melds with the other ingredients, giving the soup more heft as the squash makes a nice thick broth. Tempeh absorbs liquid, so in this recipe parboil it to soften it and then sauté. Or roast it in the oven if you'd like a crispy, crouton-like texture. This step can be done a day ahead, and the tempeh can be refrigerated for one to two days.

Ingredients
1/4 cup olive oil
1 medium-size onion, peeled and chopped
1 rib celery, chopped
2 to 3 medium-size carrots, scrubbed and chopped
3 cloves garlic, peeled and minced
1 1/2 cups peeled and diced winter squash (butternut or kabocha varieties work well here)
8 ounces tempeh, chopped, boiled in 2 cups water, 3 to 5 minutes, and drained
8 cups water, or more as necessary
2 cups yellow split peas
1 teaspoon dried ginger or 1 tablespoon

grated fresh ginger
1 1/2 teaspoons hot Madras curry powder
1 1/2 teaspoons salt
1 1/2 teaspoons ground black pepper

STEP 1: Heat the olive oil in a large stockpot over medium heat. Add the onion, celery, carrots, and garlic, reduce heat to low, cover the pot, and sweat the vegetables for about 10 minutes.

STEP 2: Uncover the pot. Add the winter squash and tempeh. Sauté over medium heat until the vegetables begin to brown, about 5 minutes.

STEP 3: Add the water, split peas, ginger, curry powder, salt, and pepper. Bring to a boil, then reduce the heat. Simmer until the split peas are tender and the flavors have married, about 45 minutes. Thin with additional water to desired consistency.

VARIATIONS:
- Substitute ham for the tempeh. You'll lose some of the fiber benefit, but you may win over picky eaters.
- Use regular curry powder if your family doesn't like spicy dishes.

- Serve the soup topped with chopped cilantro and/or Greek yogurt.

GOES WELL WITH:
- Green salad
- Warmed corn tortillas
- Roti (also called *chapati* or *kolcha*), Indian-style flatbread made from stone-ground, whole-meal flour, available in some supermarkets and specialty stores
- Sliced mangoes

Per serving: Calories 300, Calories from Fat 90, Total Fat 11g (17% DV), Saturated Fat 1.5g (8% DV), Trans Fat 0g, Cholesterol 0mg (0% DV), Sodium 480mg (20% DV), Carbohydrates 37g (12% DV), Dietary Fiber 14g (56% DV), Sugars 5g, **Added Sugars:** 0g, Protein 18g, Vitamin A 60%, Vitamin C 8%, Calcium 8%, Iron 20%.

LENTIL STEW

= Makes: 10 cups = Active time:
20 minutes
= Serving size: = Total time:
2 cups as a main meal, 40 minutes
1 cup as a starter

This is a very simple recipe that can be a base for many variations. It's filled with vegetables and lentils, a great source of fiber.

Ingredients
1 cup peeled and diced onion
1 cup scrubbed and diced carrots
1 cup diced celery
1/4 cup olive oil
4 cloves garlic, or 1 large shallot, peeled and chopped
4 cups chopped tomatoes
1 teaspoon dried sage, or 1 tablespoon chopped fresh sage
2 teaspoons salt, or more to taste
1 teaspoon cracked black pepper
1 teaspoon ground cumin
Cayenne pepper (optional): 1 pinch (1/8 teaspoon) for flavor, 1 teaspoon for heat
3 to 4 cups vegetable broth, more if you want a soup, less for a stew
2 cups cooked lentils (see p. 341)

1 cup chopped fresh cilantro
4 cups chopped fresh kale or spinach

STEP 1: In a large skillet, sauté the onion, carrots, and celery in the olive oil over medium heat until the vegetables become tender, 5 minutes. Add the garlic or shallot and cook for an additional 2 minutes.

STEP 2: Add the tomatoes, sage, salt, pepper, cumin, and cayenne, if using. Simmer until the tomatoes and vegetables are soft and beginning to brown, about 10 minutes.

STEP 3: Add the vegetable broth and lentils. Cook, covered, for 20 minutes over low heat, simmering. Add the spinach or kale and cook until wilted, about 5 minutes.

This can be kept in the refrigerator for up to three days or frozen in small packages for up to three months. This recipe can be multiplied.

VARIATIONS:
- Add 2 cups cooked barley.
- Add 1 pound ground turkey meat or ground beef, browned.

- Add chopped zucchini or butternut squash.

GOES WELL WITH:
- Tossed green salad
- Sliced fresh fruit
- Poached or grilled fish

Per serving: Calories 310, Calories from Fat 100, Total Fat 11g (17% DV), Saturated Fat 2.5g (12% DV), Trans Fat 0g, Cholesterol < 5mg (2% DV), Sodium 950mg (40% DV), Carbohydrates 40g (13% DV), Dietary Fiber 15g (60% DV), Sugars 9g, **Added Sugars:** 0g, Protein 15g, Vitamin A 100%, Vitamin C 50%, Calcium 15%, Iron 25%.

VEGETARIAN LENTIL OR SPLIT PEA SOUP

= Makes: 3 quarts

= Serves: 6 as a meal

= Active time: 30 minutes

= Total time: 1 hour 30 minutes

= Serving size:
  2 cups for a main course,
  1 cup for a starter

Lentils are legumes, with amylose (slow-absorbing starch) and lots of fiber. This is my kids' favorite vegetarian soup! And mine too! It's fine to substitute chicken or beef broth for the vegetable broth.

Ingredients

1/2 pound lentils (green, red, or brown) or split peas (green or yellow)

1/4 cup good-quality olive oil

2 cups peeled and chopped yellow onions, finely diced

1 medium-size leek, rinsed, about 1 cup (substitute 4 scallions or 1 large shallot if leeks aren't available)

1 tablespoon peeled and minced garlic

1 cup diced carrots

1 cup diced celery

1/2 cup finely diced red bell pepper

1 tablespoon kosher salt, or 1 1/2 teaspoons table salt, or more to taste

1 teaspoon ground black pepper, or more to taste

1 teaspoon dried thyme, or 1 tablespoon fresh thyme

2 quarts vegetable stock or water

1 can (6 ounces) tomato paste

2 bay leaves

2 tablespoons red wine vinegar

Parmesan cheese, for garnish

STEP 1: In a large bowl, cover the lentils with boiling water. Let sit for 15 minutes. Drain and set aside.

STEP 2: In a large stockpot, heat the olive oil over medium heat. Add the onions and leek and sauté for 5 minutes, or until tender. Add the garlic and sauté an additional 2 minutes. Add carrots, celery, bell peppers, salt, black pepper, and thyme and cook, until the vegetables are translucent and browned, about 6 to 8 more minutes.

STEP 3: Add the vegetable stock, tomato paste, lentils, and bay leaves. Cover and bring to a boil. Reduce the heat and simmer uncovered for 1 hour, or until the lentils are tender.

STEP 4: Taste for seasoning, adding more salt or black pepper as necessary. Add the red wine vinegar. Serve hot and top it with grated Parmesan cheese.

This recipe can be doubled. The soup can be refrigerated for three days or frozen, in freezer bags or glass or plastic containers, for three months.

VARIATIONS:

- Add 2 tablespoons of curry powder. At serving, sprinkle with chopped cilantro rather than Parmesan cheese.
- Substitute lemon juice for the red wine vinegar just before serving.

GOES WELL WITH:

- Tossed salad
- Whole-Wheat Sponge Bread (p. 188)
- Grilled cheese sandwiches on whole-wheat bread

Per serving: Calories 220, Calories from Fat 100, Total Fat 11g (17% DV), Saturated Fat 2.5g (12% DV), Trans Fat 0g, Cholesterol < 5mg (2% DV), Sodium 950mg (40% DV), Carbohydrates 25g (8% DV), Dietary Fiber 7g (28% DV), Sugars 9g, **Added Sugars:** 0g, Protein 8g, Vitamin A 100%, Vitamin C 50%, Calcium 15%, Iron 15%.

VEGETARIAN BEAN CHILI

= Makes: 8 cups

= Serving size: 2 cups for a main course, 1 cup for a starter

= Active time: 15 minutes

= Total time: 30 minutes

Ingredients

1/4 cup olive oil

2 cups peeled and chopped onions

2 medium-size red bell peppers, diced

6 garlic cloves, peeled and minced

2 tablespoons chili powder

1 teaspoon dried ground cumin

1 teaspoon dried oregano, or 1 tablespoon chopped fresh oregano

2 teaspoons cayenne pepper

2 cups crushed tomatoes

1 cup reserved liquid from cooking beans

6 cups cooked beans

2 cups cooked kale or spinach

Salt and pepper

Chopped cilantro, sour cream, grated cheese, and chopped green onion, for garnish

STEP 1: Heat the oil in a large, heavy pot over medium-high heat. Add the onions and bell peppers. Sauté until soft, about 5 minutes. Add the garlic and sauté an additional minute.

STEP 2: Add the chili powder, cumin, oregano, and cayenne and stir for about 2 minutes.

STEP 3: Mix in the crushed tomatoes and

1 cup of reserved liquid from the beans. Cook for 10 minutes.

STEP 4: Add the beans, bring to a boil, stir, reduce the heat, and simmer for 20 minutes, until the flavors blend and the chili thickens. Add the kale or spinach, stir, and cook until wilted, about 5 minutes.

STEP 5: Season with salt and pepper to taste. Garnish and serve!

VARIATIONS:
- Add 1 1/2 teaspoons ground cinnamon.
- Add 1 cup of beer.

GOES WELL WITH:
- Brown rice
- Sliced apples
- Sliced tomatoes
- Yogurt
- Avocado

Per serving: Calories 600, Calories from Fat 160, Total Fat 18g (28% DV), Saturated Fat 3g (15% DV), Trans Fat 0g, Cholesterol 0mg (0% DV), Sodium 1440mg (60% DV), Carbohydrates 94g (31% DV), Dietary Fiber 28g (112%

DV), Sugars 9g, **Added Sugars:** 0g,
Protein 26g, Vitamin A 480%, Vitamin
C 230%, Calcium 35%, Iron 60%.

ROASTED CHICKEN SOUP
WITH VEGETABLES

= Makes: 2 quarts

= Serving size:
2 cups for a main dish,
1 cup for a side dish

= Active time:
20 minutes

= Total time:
1 hour
10 minutes

Your grandmother knew about the healing
powers of chicken soup. The peptones,
amino acids, and micronutrients in chicken
soup are as close to a magic elixir as modern
medicine gets. But commercial chicken
soup can sometimes have added sugar (to
cut the acidity), and rarely has any vegetables (except for the occasional bit of
mushy celery). Another knock against
canned soup: It's overloaded with salt. It is
much easier to add salt than it is to take it
away. The hardest part of this recipe is cutting up the chicken and the vegetables. After
you've done that, the rest is as easy as soup.
It's also a thrifty way to use leftovers.

Ingredients

1 cooked roasted chicken, or the bones and leftover meat from roasted chicken (about 2 cups)

1 to 2 tablespoons vegetable oil or olive oil

1 cup chopped yellow onion

2 carrots, chopped

2 ribs celery, chopped

10 cups boiling water

2 cups assorted chopped vegetables: spinach, chard, zucchini, green beans, butternut squash, kabocha squash, and/or carrots

1 1/2 to 2 cups cooked barley, cooked noodles, or raw cubed potatoes

Salt and ground black pepper

STEP 1: Remove the meat from the chicken, dice, and set aside. Using a cleaver, or kitchen knife, break the bones of the chicken carcass into pieces.

STEP 2: Heat the oil in a large stockpot over medium-high heat. Add the onions and sauté for 5 minutes, or until tender. Add the carrots and celery and brown over medium heat for 3 to 5 minutes. Add the chicken bones. Reduce the heat to low, cover the pot, and sweat everything for 20 minutes. Add the water, bring to a boil, reduce the heat, and simmer for 20 minutes, skimming any foam that may rise to the top.

STEP 3: Strain the broth through a fine mesh strainer, pushing on the bones, carrots, and celery to extract as much of their flavor as possible. Discard the remains in the strainer, wipe out the soup pot, and return the stock to the pot.

STEP 4: Add the chopped vegetables and the potatoes to the stock. Bring to a boil, then reduce heat and simmer covered for 10 minutes.

STEP 5: Add the reserved diced chicken and barley or noodles to the broth and simmer until just warmed through, 3 to 5 minutes. Serve.

VARIATIONS:
- Add a pinch of cayenne or 1 teaspoon of dried thyme when you add the boiling water to the bones.
- Toss in finely chopped fresh parsley, or chopped fresh thyme leaves, or a couple squirts of Tabasco sauce or Sriracha sauce just before serving.

GOES WELL WITH:

- Whole-grain bread
- Salad

Per serving: Calories 430, Calories from Fat 90, Total Fat 10g (15% DV), Saturated Fat 2g (10% DV), Trans Fat 0g, Cholesterol 155mg (52% DV), Sodium 290mg (12% DV), Carbohydrates 29g (10% DV), Dietary Fiber 6g (24% DV), Sugars 5g, **Added Sugars:** 0g, Protein 52g, Vitamin A 270%, Vitamin C 15%, Calcium 8%, Iron 20%.

SUMMER GARDEN AND BEAN SOUP

= Makes: 1 gallon

= Serving size: 2 cups for a main dish, 1 cup for a side dish

= Active time: 30 minutes

= Total time: 1 hour

I love a summer garden: zucchini, green beans, tomato, basil, and Swiss chard. There's nothing like fresh picked vegetables that you've grown yourself. Cindy, who lives in a warmer microclimate than my family, shares her garden vegetables with friends and neighbors along with recipes and containers of soup. This recipe makes for a great meal and freezes well.

Ingredients

4 slices bacon (optional), cut crosswise into 1/2-inch strips

1/4 cup olive oil

3 cups peeled and chopped yellow onion

2 cups chopped celery, including tops

3 cloves garlic, peeled and minced

Cracked black pepper

4 cups chopped Swiss chard, including leaves and stalks

1 cup diced zucchini or yellow squash

1 cup green beans, cut in thirds and then measured

2 cups shredded or chopped cabbage

2 cups sliced carrots

1/2 cup chopped fresh parsley, plus chopped parsley for garnish

1/4 cup fresh basil

8 cups chicken or vegetable broth

4 cups pureed white beans (any variety: cannellini, navy, or white northern), or 1 can (28 ounces) cannellini beans, drained and pureed

2 cups Marinara Sauce (p. 149)

Freshly grated Parmesan cheese

STEP 1: In a large stockpot, sauté the bacon, if using, until just browned. Remove

278

the bacon from the pot and set aside. Drain off the bacon fat and replace it with the olive oil.

STEP 2: Add the onion, celery, and garlic and sauté over medium-high heat until tender. Add the pepper and stir in the Swiss chard, zucchini, green beans, cabbage, carrots, 1/4 cup of parsley, and basil. Cook for about 5 minutes.

STEP 3: Add the chicken broth, beans, bacon, and Marinara Sauce and simmer until all of the flavors have come together, 30 minutes. Serve hot, garnished with chopped fresh parsley and a sprinkle of freshly grated Parmesan.

This recipe can be doubled. It can be kept in the refrigerator for up to one week or frozen in small packages for up to three months.

VARIATIONS:
- Add 2 cups cooked barley or brown rice in the last 10 minutes of cooking.
- Add spinach or kale in place of Swiss chard or cabbage.
- Add 2 cups cooked chopped chicken

or turkey.
- Substitute 1/2 pound Homemade "Sausage" (p. 231) for the bacon.

GOES WELL WITH:
- Savory Watermelon and Feta Salad (p. 312)
- Polenta croutons
- Whole-grain pizza dough, spread with Basil Pesto (p. 185) and dotted with Marinated Olives (p. 176)

Per serving: Calories 430, Calories from Fat 90, Total Fat 10g (15% DV), Saturated Fat 2g (10% DV), Trans Fat 0g, Cholesterol 155mg (52% DV), Sodium 290mg (12% DV), Carbohydrates 29g (10% DV), Dietary Fiber 6g (24% DV), Sugars 5g, **Added Sugars:** 0g, Protein 52g, Vitamin A 270%, Vitamin C 15%, Calcium 8%, Iron 20%.

SPLIT PEA AND VEGETABLE SOUP

= Makes: 1 gallon

= Serving size: 2 cups for a main dish, 1 cup for a side dish

= Active time: 15 minutes

= Total time: 1 hour

This is one of those recipes where mise en place, getting everything ready before you cook, really saves time. This soup will get thick as it cools; you can add water to thin it as desired. You can also add leftovers to this wonderful soup base. Be creative.

Ingredients
1/4 cup olive oil or safflower oil
2 cups scrubbed and diced carrots
1 cup diced celery
1 cup peeled and diced onion
2 cloves garlic, peeled and minced
1 1/2 pounds russet potatoes (about 3 medium-size), scrubbed and cut into 1/2-inch pieces
3 cups dried split peas (yellow or green), rinsed and picked over
1 teaspoon dried thyme
Salt and ground black pepper
16 cups water

STEP 1: Heat the oil in a large stockpot over medium heat. Add the carrots, celery, and onion and sauté until tender, about 5 minutes. Add the garlic. Cook for 2 more minutes.

STEP 2: Add the potatoes and split peas. Cook for 3 minutes. Add the thyme and season with 1 teaspoon salt and 1 teaspoon pepper, or to taste.

STEP 3: Add the 16 cups (1 gallon) water. Bring to a boil, uncovered. Reduce the heat to medium. Cover and cook until the split peas are tender and the flavors have blended, 45 minutes to 1 hour. Season with salt and pepper to taste.

This recipe can be multiplied. It can be kept in the refrigerator for up to three days or frozen in small packages for up to three months. Make sure to date and label!

VARIATIONS:
- Add more water if you want the soup to be thinner.
- Use sweet potatoes in place of russet potatoes.
- Add 2 cups diced butternut squash.
- Add 2 tablespoons chopped fresh sage when sautéing the carrots, celery, and onion.

GOES WELL WITH:
- Roasted pork loin
- Green salad
- Applesauce (p. 226) or sliced apples

Per serving: Calories 400, Calories from Fat 70, Total Fat 8g (12% DV), Saturated Fat 1g (5% DV), Trans Fat 0g, Cholesterol 0mg (0% DV), Sodium 85mg (4% DV), Carbohydrates 66g (22% DV), Dietary Fiber 21g (84% DV), Sugars 9g, **Added Sugars:** 0g, Protein 21g, Vitamin A 110%, Vitamin C 15%, Calcium 8%, Iron 25%.

ITALIAN WEDDING SOUP

= Makes: 5 quarts

= Serving size: 2 cups for a main course, 1 cup for a side

= Active time: 20 minutes

= Total time: 1 hour

This recipe makes soup for a crowd, like the crowd at a wedding. It was a comforting staple in Cindy's grandmother's kitchen. It's perfect as a starter to a dinner party. No sugar, loads of fiber, even in a soup. Just takes a while. Soups are better with chicken broth or stock instead of water: richer, more flavorful. The more seasonings you add, the less salt you need!

Ingredients

1 small turkey, about 10 to 12 pounds
1 tablespoon dried sage
2 teaspoons salt
1 tablespoon ground black pepper
3 cups peeled and chopped yellow onion
3 cups chopped carrots
3 cups chopped celery
4 cloves garlic, peeled and minced
1 pound fresh spinach or kale, chopped
4 cups chopped zucchini

STEP 1: Preheat the oven to 350°F.

STEP 2: First, roast the turkey. Rub with the sage, 1 teaspoon of salt, and 1 teaspoon of pepper. Place the turkey on a roasting rack set in a roasting pan. Bake for 2 1/2 to 3 hours (or until a meat thermometer registers 165°F). Let the turkey rest until cool enough to handle. This can be done one or two days before, or you can use leftover turkey. Remove the breast meat and use it for sandwiches. Break the turkey into pieces, and remove as much meat off the bones as possible; chop and reserve. You will need at least 5 cups of diced meat.

STEP 3: Transfer the turkey pieces (but not the back) to a 2-gallon stockpot. Fill the pot with water until it's two-thirds full, 24 cups. Bring the water to a boil, then reduce the heat and simmer for 1 hour. Skim any scum that rises to the top. Remove the turkey bones from the stock with a slotted spoon.

STEP 4: In a 2-quart saucepan, sauté the onion, carrots, and celery until tender, about 5 minutes. Add the garlic and cook for an additional 2 minutes. Add the onion mixture to the stockpot. Cook for 20 minutes so all the flavors can get into the broth.

STEP 5: Add the spinach or kale and zucchini. Bring the soup back to a boil, reduce the heat, and let simmer for an additional 20 minutes, stirring occasionally, until the greens have wilted and the zucchini is tender.

STEP 6: Add the 5 cups reserved turkey meat to the soup. Simmer until the turkey is just warmed through, 3 to 5 minutes. Serve.

This soup can be refrigerated for up to three days or frozen for up to three months.

VARIATIONS:
- Use chicken stock in place of the water.
- Add cooked sweet potatoes, rice, or barley.
- If you want to make a smaller batch, halve all the vegetable amounts and use a turkey or chicken leg. Reserve the meat, as in the main recipe.

GOES WELL WITH:
- Tossed green salad
- Multi-Grain Flatbread Pizza (p. 387)

Per serving: Calories 410, Calories from Fat 60, Total Fat 7g (11% DV), Saturated Fat 2g (10% DV), Trans Fat 0g, Cholesterol 220mg (73% DV), Sodium 950mg (40% DV), Carbohydrates 14g (5% DV), Dietary Fiber 4g (16% DV), Sugars 5g, **Added Sugars:** 0g, Protein 70g, Vitamin A 270%, Vitamin C 120%, Calcium 15%, Iron 30%.

TOSSED SALAD
TWENTY-THREE WAYS

So you're on the run and want to pack something the night before for lunch. Gotta be healthy; gotta be tasty; gotta be filling.

Fill me with energy and keep me from snacking!

1. Melon, Berry, and Chicken Salad

Ingredients
2 cups mixed greens
1/2 cup Cracked Wheat Salad (p. 307)
1/2 cup chopped grilled or roasted chicken (see p. 425)
2 tablespoons Italian Vinaigrette Dressing (p. 139)
1 cup cubed or sliced cantaloupe or other melon
1/2 cup fresh blueberries, blackberries, or raspberries

Place mixed greens on a plate. Top with Cracked Wheat Salad in the center. Add chicken and drizzle with Italian Vinaigrette Dressing. Garnish with sliced melons and berries.

Per serving: Calories 540, Calories from Fat 360, Total Fat 41g (63% DV), Saturated Fat 6g (30% DV), Trans Fat 0g, Cholesterol 40mg (13% DV), Sodium 780mg (32% DV), Carbohydrates 32g (11% DV), Dietary Fiber 7g (28% DV), Sugars 18g, **Added Sugars:** 0g,

Protein 15g, Vitamin A 210%, Vitamin C 200%, Calcium 8%, Iron 15%.

2. Cantaloupe Stuffed Chicken Salad

Ingredients
2 lettuce leaves
1/2 cantaloupe, halved and seeded, used as a bowl
1/2 cup Chicken Salad (p. 314)
1 slice Whole-Wheat Banana-Veggie Bread (p. 495)

Put lettuce on a plate and top with cantaloupe. Stuff with Chicken Salad and serve with bread.

Per serving: Calories 661, Calories from Fat 290, Total Fat 33g (51% DV), Saturated Fat 4.5g (22% DV), Trans Fat 0g, Cholesterol 45mg (15% DV), Sodium 920mg (38% DV), Carbohydrates 71g (24% DV), Dietary Fiber 9g (36% DV), Sugars 35g, **Added Sugars:** 0g, Protein 25g, Vitamin A 230%, Vitamin C 180%, Calcium 10%, Iron 20%.

3. Burrito Bowl Salad

Ingredients
1 large whole-grain 10-inch tortilla
2 cups mixed greens
1 cup Quinoa and Black Bean Burrito Bowl (p. 358)
2 tablespoons Almost Homemade Salsa (p. 234)
1 tablespoon shredded cheddar cheese or Monterey Jack cheese

Place warmed tortilla in a soup bowl or rimmed plate. Top with greens. Place 1 cup of burrito bowl mixture on top. Drizzle with Almost Homemade Salsa and sprinkle shredded cheese over all.

Per serving: Calories 600, Calories from Fat 120, Total Fat 14g (22% DV), Saturated Fat 3.5g (18% DV), Trans Fat 0g, Cholesterol 5mg (2% DV), Sodium 1150mg (48% DV), Carbohydrates 95g (32% DV), Dietary Fiber 15g (60% DV), Sugars 2g, **Added Sugars:** 0g, Protein 24g, Vitamin A 150%, Vitamin C 25%, Calcium 15%, Iron 40%.

4. Roasted Veggie and Grilled Chicken Salad

Ingredients
1 whole-grain tortilla
2 cups mixed greens
2 tablespoons Italian Vinaigrette Dressing
  (p. 139)
1/2 cup chopped chicken or turkey
1 cup roasted veggies

Place warmed tortilla in a soup bowl or on a rimmed plate. Place greens on the tortilla and drizzle with Italian Vinaigrette Dressing. Top with chicken or turkey and roasted veggies.

Per serving: Calories 660, Calories from Fat 330, Total Fat 38g (58% DV), Saturated Fat 5g (25% DV), Trans Fat 0g, Cholesterol 60mg (20% DV), Sodium 860mg (36% DV), Carbohydrates 50g (17% DV), Dietary Fiber 5g (20% DV), Sugars 3g, **Added Sugars:** 0g, Protein 31g, Vitamin A 110%, Vitamin C 200%, Calcium 8%, Iron 25%.

5. Steak Salad

Ingredients
2 cups mixed greens
4 ounces cooked steak (see p. 409), sliced
1/4 cup chopped tomatoes
1/4 cup chopped cucumber
1/2 cup roasted sweet potato or russet potato wedges
2 tablespoons Ranch Dressing (p. 141)
1 ounce blue cheese, crumbled

Place greens on a plate. Place the steak in the center. Sprinkle with tomatoes and cucumber. Arrange potatoes around edges. Drizzle Ranch Dressing over meat. Crumble cheese over all.

Per serving: Calories 520, Calories from Fat 260, Total Fat 29g (45% DV), Saturated Fat 11g (55% DV), Trans Fat 0g, Cholesterol 115mg (38% DV), Sodium 740mg (31% DV), Carbohydrates 25g (8% DV), Dietary Fiber 4g (16% DV), Sugars 4g, **Added Sugars:** 0g, Protein 41g, Vitamin A 120%, Vitamin C 35%, Calcium 25%, Iron 20%.

6. Barbecued Chicken Salad

Ingredients
2 cups mixed greens
1 Corn Cake (p. 492)
1/2 cup chopped leftover barbecued chicken
2 tablespoons Ranch Dressing (p. 141)
1/2 cup peeled and chopped jicama
1/2 cup chopped tomatoes

Place greens on a plate. Place a Corn Cake in the middle. Put the barbecued chicken over corn cake and drizzle with Ranch Dressing. Top with chopped jicama and tomato.

Per serving: Calories 570, Calories from Fat 160, Total Fat 18g (28% DV), Saturated Fat 3.5g (18% DV), Trans Fat 0g, Cholesterol 105mg (35% DV), Sodium 600mg (25% DV), Carbohydrates 69g (23% DV), Dietary Fiber 10g (40% DV), Sugars 7g, **Added Sugars:** 0g, Protein 34g, Vitamin A 130%, Vitamin C 50%, Calcium 15%, Iron 25%.

7. Salad Sampler

Ingredients
2 cups mixed greens
1/4 cup Pickled Beets (p. 458)
1/2 cup chopped roasted vegetables
1/2 cup chopped tomato
1 hard-boiled egg, halved
1/2 cup Cracked Wheat Salad (p. 307)
1 ounce cheese, such as sharp cheddar or mozzarella, shredded
2 tablespoons Italian Vinaigrette Dressing (p. 139)

Place greens on a plate. Place the following ingredients in little piles arranged in a circle: Pickled Beets, then roasted veggies, tomato, hard-boiled egg, Cracked Wheat Salad, and cheese. Drizzle Italian Vinaigrette Dressing over all.

Per serving: Calories 630, Calories from Fat 440, Total Fat 50g (77% DV), Saturated Fat 12g (60% DV), Trans Fat 0g, Cholesterol 215mg (72% DV), Sodium 1190mg (50% DV), Carbohydrates 30g (10% DV), Dietary Fiber 8g (32% DV), Sugars 11g, **Added Sugars:** 0g, Protein 20g, Vitamin A 150%, Vitamin C 180%, Calcium 30%, Iron 20%.

8. Another Salad Sampler

Ingredients
2 cups mixed greens
1 tablespoon Italian Vinaigrette Dressing
   (p. 139)
1/4 cup Newell Dual (p. 317)
1/4 cup Edamame Spread (p. 183)
6 Triscuits (Whole-grain crackers; these
   have no added sugar but have lots of fiber.)

Place greens on a plate and drizzle with Italian Vinaigrette Dressing. Arrange Newell Dual on one third of the plate, Edamame Spread on another third, and Triscuits on the last third.

Per serving: Calories 500, Calories from Fat 300, Total Fat 34g (52% DV), Saturated Fat 5g (25% DV), Trans Fat 0g, Cholesterol 115mg (38% DV), Sodium 310mg (13% DV), Carbohydrates 31g (10% DV), Dietary Fiber 7g (28% DV), Sugars 6g, **Added Sugars:** 0g, Protein 23g, Vitamin A 130%, Vitamin C 45%, Calcium 10%, Iron 20%.

9. Chopped Marinated Vegetable Salad (Vegan)

Marinate the vegetables in salad dressing overnight.

Ingredients

2 cups mixed greens

1/4 cup each: diced or chopped (choose any four)

    Carrots, scrubbed

    Jicama, peeled

    Celery

    Cucumbers

    Broccoli

    Cauliflower

    Red onion, peeled

    Cabbage

1/2 cup cooked chickpeas, or canned chickpeas, drained and rinsed

1/2 cup cooked cracked wheat or barley

3 tablespoons Italian Vinaigrette Dressing (p. 139)

1/4 cup chopped fresh parsley, cilantro, or basil

1 teaspoon chopped fresh oregano (optional)

1 pinch (1/8 teaspoon) of cayenne pepper (optional)

Place greens on a plate. Toss with four

vegetables of your choice, chickpeas, and cracked wheat. Drizzle with Italian Vinaigrette Dressing and sprinkle chopped herbs and cayenne pepper, if using, over all.

Per serving: Calories 630, Calories from Fat 400, Total Fat 45g (69% DV), Saturated Fat 5g (25% DV), Trans Fat 0g, Cholesterol 0mg (0% DV), Sodium 770mg (32% DV), Carbohydrates 49g (16% DV), Dietary Fiber 12g (48% DV), Sugars 5g, **Added Sugars:** 0g, Protein 10g, Vitamin A 250%, Vitamin C 90%, Calcium 15%, Iron 25%.

10. Salmon, Roasted Tomato, and Polenta Squares Salad

Ingredients
2 cups mixed greens
2 tablespoons Italian Vinaigrette Dressing (p. 139) or Balsamic Vinaigrette (p. 143)
4 ounces cold polenta, cubed and pan toasted, if desired
4 ounces grilled or poached salmon
1/4 cup chopped tomatoes

Place greens on a plate. Drizzle 1 tablespoon of dressing over greens. Place polenta in the center of the plate and top with salmon.

Top salmon with tomatoes; drizzle the remaining tablespoon of dressing over all.

Per serving: Calories 640, Calories from Fat 310, Total Fat 35g (54% DV), Saturated Fat 4g (20% DV), Trans Fat 0g, Cholesterol 80mg (27% DV), Sodium 270mg (11% DV), Carbohydrates 46g (15% DV), Dietary Fiber 3g (12% DV), Sugars 2g, **Added Sugars:** 0g, Protein 35g, Vitamin A 120%, Vitamin C 20%, Calcium 6%, Iron 20%.

11. Flank Steak, Grilled Onion, and Stone Fruit Salad

Ingredients
2 cups mixed greens
2 tablespoons Italian Vinaigrette Dressing (p. 139)
4 ounces grilled flank steak
1/2 cup chopped grilled onions
1/2 cup grilled stone fruit (see p. 223): plums, peaches, or nectarines

Place mixed greens on a plate and drizzle with 1 tablespoon of Italian Vinaigrette Dressing. Top with steak. Sprinkle with onions. Garnish with stone fruit around the edge of the plate.

Per serving: Calories 500, Calories from Fat 280, Total Fat 32g (49% DV), Saturated Fat 6g (30% DV), Trans Fat 0g, Cholesterol 90mg (30% DV), Sodium 180mg (8% DV), Carbohydrates 19g (6% DV), Dietary Fiber 4g (16% DV), Sugars 12g, **Added Sugars:** 0g, Protein 34g, Vitamin A 110%, Vitamin C 35%, Calcium 8%, Iron 15%.

12. Healthy Chef's Salad

Ingredients
2 cups shredded butter lettuce
2 tablespoons Ranch Dressing (p. 141)
2 ounces turkey or chicken
1/4 cup chopped tomatoes
1/4 cup radish slices
1/4 cup carrot slices
1/4 avocado, peeled and diced
1 hard-boiled egg, peeled and chopped
2 tablespoons grated Monterey Jack or Swiss cheese

Place butter lettuce on a plate and drizzle with 1 tablespoon of Ranch Dressing. Arrange other ingredients in little piles in a circle: chopped turkey or chicken, tomatoes, radishes, carrots, avocado, and hard-boiled egg. Drizzle the remaining tablespoon of dressing over all.

Per serving: Calories 470, Calories from Fat 290, Total Fat 33g (51% DV), Saturated Fat 8g (40% DV), Trans Fat 0g, Cholesterol 250mg (83% DV), Sodium 460mg (19% DV), Carbohydrates 14g (5% DV), Dietary Fiber 6g (24% DV), Sugars 6g, **Added Sugars:** 0g, Protein 30g, Vitamin A 190%, Vitamin C 35%, Calcium 25%, Iron 20%.

13. Caprese Salad

Ingredients
1 romaine lettuce leaf
1 cup Whole-Grain Vegetable Pilaf (p. 371)
1 eggplant, marinated, sliced in 1/2-inch slices, and grilled
2 ounces sliced mozzarella cheese
2 slices tomato
Fresh basil leaves
1 tablespoon balsamic vinegar

Place lettuce leaf on one side of a plate and top with Whole-Grain Vegetable Pilaf. On the other side of the plate, alternate slices of eggplant, mozzarella, and tomato. Top with basil and drizzle balsamic vinegar over all.

Per serving: Calories 470, Calories from Fat 220, Total Fat 24g (37% DV), Saturated Fat 4.5g (22% DV), Trans Fat 0g, Cholesterol 0mg (0% DV), Sodium 720mg (30% DV), Carbohydrates 55g (18% DV), Dietary Fiber 10g (40% DV), Sugars 24g, **Added Sugars:** 0g, Protein 12g, Vitamin A 30%, Vitamin C 20%, Calcium 40%, Iron 10%.

14. Grilled Chicken Salad with Steamed Green Beans and Slivered Almonds

Ingredients

2 cups mixed herbs and greens: baby greens, basil leaf, parsley, cilantro

4 ounces grilled herbed chicken breast, thinly sliced or shredded

1/2 cup cubed roasted potatoes

2 tablespoons Marinated Olives (p. 176)

1/2 cup chopped steamed green beans

1/2 cup Roma Tomato Basil Salsa (p. 172)

2 tablespoons slivered almonds, toasted, if desired

Place greens on a plate. Top with chicken. Arrange potatoes, olives, and green beans in little piles in a circle. Top with Roma Tomato Basil Salsa. Sprinkle with slivered almonds.

Per serving: Calories 630, Calories from Fat 250, Total Fat 29g (45% DV), Saturated Fat 4g (20% DV), Trans Fat 0g, Cholesterol 95mg (32% DV), Sodium 740mg (31% DV), Carbohydrates 49g (16% DV), Dietary Fiber 11g (44% DV), Sugars 6g, **Added Sugars:** 0g, Protein 46g, Vitamin A 150%, Vitamin C 140%, Calcium 25%, Iron 45%.

15. Chicken or Salmon Caesar Salad

Ingredients
2 cups baby romaine and radicchio
1/2 cup Homemade Whole-Grain Croutons (p. 321)
2 tablespoons Caesar Dressing (p. 145)
4 ounces grilled chicken or salmon, cubed
1 tablespoon grated Parmesan cheese

Place greens on a plate. Top with croutons and drizzle with 1 tablespoon of Caesar Dressing. Add salmon or chicken. Drizzle the other tablespoon of dressing over all. Sprinkle with Parmesan cheese.

Per serving: Calories 560, Calories from Fat 310, Total Fat 35g (54% DV), Saturated Fat 6g (30% DV), Trans Fat 0g, Cholesterol 100mg (33% DV), So-

dium 490mg (20% DV), Carbohydrates 19g (6% DV), Dietary Fiber 4g (16% DV), Sugars 3g, **Added Sugars:** 0g, Protein 42g, Vitamin A 170%, Vitamin C 8%, Calcium 15%, Iron 20%.

16. Mediterranean Baby Spinach and Quinoa Salad

Ingredients
2 cups baby spinach
1/2 cup cooked quinoa
1/4 cup Marinated Olives (p. 176)
2 ounces feta cheese
1/2 cup Roma Tomato Basil Salsa (p. 172)

Place spinach on a plate. Top with quinoa, Marinated Olives, and feta and mix. Drizzle salsa over all.

Per serving: Calories 410, Calories from Fat 230, Total Fat 26g (40% DV), Saturated Fat 10g (50% DV), Trans Fat 0g, Cholesterol 50mg (17% DV), Sodium 1080mg (45% DV), Carbohydrates 29g (10% DV), Dietary Fiber 5g (20% DV), Sugars 5g, **Added Sugars:** 0g, Protein 15g, Vitamin A 130%, Vitamin C 40%, Calcium 40%, Iron 25%.

17. Chicken Fajita Taco Salad

Ingredients
1 romaine lettuce leaf
1/2 cup shredded cabbage
1/2 cup shredded carrots
1/2 cup shredded jicama
1/4 cup Almost Homemade Salsa (p. 234)
1 cup mixed sautéed bell pepper and onion
1/2 cup leftover fajita chicken

Place lettuce leaf on a plate. Toss cabbage, carrots, and jicama with Almost Homemade Salsa and place on lettuce. Top with bell pepper and onion mixture. Add fajita chicken. Optional: Put a whole-wheat tortilla on the bottom. This will add 110 calories.

Per serving: Calories 260, Calories from Fat 70, Total Fat 8g (12% DV), Saturated Fat 1.5g (8% DV), Trans Fat 0g, Cholesterol 60mg (20% DV), Sodium 600mg (25% DV), Carbohydrates 23g (8% DV), Dietary Fiber 8g (32% DV), Sugars 10g, **Added Sugars:** 0g, Protein 25g, Vitamin A 230%, Vitamin C 120%, Calcium 10%, Iron 15%.

18. Spinach Salad with Grilled Fish, Cherry Tomatoes, and Toasted Herb Nuts

Ingredients

2 cups baby spinach

2 tablespoons Balsamic Vinaigrette (p. 143)

1/4 cup Homemade Whole-Grain Croutons (p. 321)

4 ounces grilled salmon, swordfish, or tuna

1/2 cup halved or chopped cherry tomatoes or chopped ripe Roma tomatoes

1/4 cup nuts, toasted in a small pan over medium heat until brown, 3 to 4 minutes

Place baby spinach on a plate and drizzle with 1 tablespoon dressing. Top with croutons, then salmon and tomatoes. Drizzle with remaining 1 tablespoon of dressing. Sprinkle toasted nuts over all.

Per serving: Calories 740, Calories from Fat 490, Total Fat 57g (88% DV), Saturated Fat 8g (40% DV), Trans Fat 0g, Cholesterol 80mg (27% DV), Sodium 510mg (21% DV), Carbohydrates 24g (8% DV), Dietary Fiber 6g (24% DV), Sugars 5g, **Added Sugars:** 0g, Protein 39g, Vitamin A 130%, Vitamin C 45%, Calcium 15%, Iron 25%.

19. Braised Greens and Roasted Chicken over Pesto Barley Pilaf

Ingredients
1 romaine lettuce leaf
1 cup leftover braised greens
1/2 cup Whole-Grain Vegetable Pilaf
  (p. 371)
1/2 cup chopped leftover roasted chicken
1/2 cup Roma Tomato Basil Salsa (p. 172)

Add the lettuce leaf for aesthetics and top with braised greens. Spread pesto pilaf over greens, then add chicken. Top with salsa.

Per serving: Calories 460, Calories from Fat 210, Total Fat 23g (35% DV), Saturated Fat 4g (20% DV), Trans Fat 0g, Cholesterol 60mg (20% DV), Sodium 680mg (28% DV), Carbohydrates 34g (11% DV), Dietary Fiber 10g (40% DV), Sugars 3g, **Added Sugars:** 0g, Protein 31g, Vitamin A 240%, Vitamin C 70%, Calcium 25%, Iron 30%.

20. Chicken, Spanish Rice, and Black Bean Salad

Ingredients
2 cups mixed greens
1/2 cup leftover Spanish Brown Rice (p. 373)
1/2 cup cooked black beans, rinsed and drained
1/2 cup shredded leftover chicken
1/4 cup Almost Homemade Salsa (p. 234)

Place greens on a plate. Place Spanish Brown Rice in the middle of greens and top with cooked beans and chicken. Drizzle salsa over all.

Per serving: Calories 370, Calories from Fat 70, Total Fat 7g (11% DV), Saturated Fat 1.5g (8% DV), Trans Fat 0g, Cholesterol 60mg (20% DV), Sodium 570mg (24% DV), Carbohydrates 43g (14% DV), Dietary Fiber 12g (48% DV), Sugars 4g, **Added Sugars:** 0g, Protein 33g, Vitamin A 130%, Vitamin C 60%, Calcium 10%, Iron 25%

21. Cracked Wheat Salad with Roasted Veggies and Chickpeas

Ingredients
2 cups baby spinach
1 cup leftover Cracked Wheat Salad (p. 319)
1 cup leftover Roasted Mixed Vegetables (p. 454)
1/2 cup Roasted Chickpeas (p. 178)
1/4 cup Roma Tomato Basil Salsa (p. 172)

Place spinach on a plate. Place Cracked Wheat Salad in the center. Top with roasted veggies and chickpeas. Drizzle salsa over all.

22. Light Cobb Salad

Ingredients
2 cups shredded butter lettuce
2 tablespoons Ranch Dressing (p. 141)
1/2 cup chopped tomatoes
1/4 avocado, peeled and chopped
1/2 cup roasted zucchini
1/2 cup chopped chicken
2 slices turkey bacon, chopped
1 hard-boiled egg, peeled and chopped
1 slice Whole-Wheat Sponge Bread (p. 188)

Place shredded lettuce on a plate, then drizzle with 1 tablespoon of Ranch Dressing. Arrange the following ingredients in

little piles around the plate: chopped tomatoes, avocado, roasted zucchini, chicken,
turkey bacon, and hard-boiled egg. Drizzle
1 more tablespoon of dressing over all.
Serve sliced Whole-Wheat Sponge Bread on
the side.

Per serving: Calories 430, Calories
from Fat 250, Total Fat 28g (43% DV),
Saturated Fat 4g (20% DV), Trans Fat
0g, Cholesterol 0mg (0% DV), Sodium
920mg (38% DV), Carbohydrates 40g
(13% DV), Dietary Fiber 10g (40%
DV), Sugars 4g, **Added Sugars:** 0g,
Protein 9g, Vitamin A 140%, Vitamin C
80%, Calcium 10%, Iron 25%.

23. Tuna Niçoise

Ingredients
2 cups mixed greens
2 tablespoons Italian Vinaigrette Dressing
  (p. 139)
1/2 cup cubed roasted potatoes
1/2 cup steamed whole green beans (or
  frozen beans, thawed)
1 can (4 or 6 ounces) water-packed light
  tuna, drained, or fresh tuna
1/2 cup chopped Roma tomatoes

2 tablespoons Niçoise olives or Marinated
  Olives (p. 176)

Place greens on a plate and drizzle with 1
tablespoon of dressing. Arrange the following ingredients in little piles around the
plate: roasted potatoes, whole green beans,
tuna, chopped tomatoes, and olives. Drizzle
1 more tablespoon of dressing over all. This
is really good topped with cracked black
pepper.

Per serving: Calories 460, Calories
from Fat 230, Total Fat 26g (40% DV),
Saturated Fat 3g (15% DV), Trans Fat
0g, Cholesterol 35mg (12% DV), Sodium 630mg (26% DV), Carbohydrates
25g (8% DV), Dietary Fiber 6g (24%
DV), Sugars 5g, **Added Sugars:** 0g,
Protein 34g, Vitamin A 130%, Vitamin
C 50%, Calcium 10%, Iron 25%.

SESAME GINGER CABBAGE
WITH CARROTS AND CHICKEN

= Serves: 4   = Total time:
45 minutes (less
if you use leftover
cooked chicken

= Serving size: = Active time:
1/4 recipe   15 minutes

I'm a sucker for ginger. The ginger and apple cider really bring this dish out. Plus the cabbage delivers the requisite fiber. This crunchy salad, dressed lightly with cider vinegar and sesame oil, has Asian overtones. Served with brown rice, it makes a whole meal.

Ingredients

2 tablespoons canola oil

1/2 medium-size onion, yellow or white, peeled and finely diced

Salt

2 cloves garlic, peeled and minced

1/2 teaspoon peeled and finely grated fresh ginger

1 large carrot, scrubbed and cut into julienne strips

1/2 head green cabbage, thinly sliced

2 cups shredded chicken, about 1 pound

Fresh ground black pepper

1/2 teaspoon apple cider vinegar
1/4 teaspoon sesame oil
1 pinch (1/8 teaspoon) of crushed red
  pepper flakes

STEP 1: In a large sauté pan or skillet, heat the oil over medium-high heat. Add the onion and 1 pinch of salt and cook for 5 minutes until the onion softens and begins to brown. Reduce the heat to medium. Stir in the garlic, ginger, and carrot. Sauté for 1 minute.

STEP 2: Add the cabbage to the pan. Cook for 5 more minutes, until the cabbage is tender-crisp. Add the chicken, season with black pepper to taste, another pinch of salt, and the apple cider vinegar, sesame oil, and red pepper flakes.

STEP 3: Toss everything together until combined. Taste and add more seasonings. Serve immediately.

Recipe can be doubled.

VARIATIONS:
- Add chopped fresh scallions and cilantro.
- Add chopped kimchi (spicy Korean

fermented cabbage).
- Mix a couple of tablespoons of crunchy, no-sugar peanut butter with the vinegar and sesame oil before tossing.
- Toast 1/4 cup sesame seeds and toss them with the spices at the end.

GOES WELL WITH:
- Brown rice
- Sliced apples, mango, or watermelon

Per serving: Calories 180, Calories from Fat 50, Total Fat 6g (9% DV), Saturated Fat 1g (5% DV), Trans Fat 0g, Cholesterol 75mg (25% DV), Sodium 200mg (8% DV), Carbohydrates 7g (2% DV), Dietary Fiber 2g (8% DV), Sugars 3g, **Added Sugars:** 0g, Protein 25g, Vitamin A 160%, Vitamin C 80%, Calcium 15%, Iron 10%.

SAVORY WATERMELON AND FETA SALAD

= Makes: 8 cups
= Serving size: 1 cup plus lettuce leaf

= Total servings: 8
= Active time: 15 minutes
= Total time: 15 minutes

Ingredients

2 heads butter lettuce, leaves rinsed and patted dry

8 cups cubed seedless watermelon, chilled

1/2 cup Italian Vinaigrette Dressing (p. 139)

1/2 cup crumbled feta cheese

1/2 cup chopped fresh basil or mint

For 1 serving, place 2 large lettuce leaves on a salad plate. Top them with 1 cup of watermelon. Drizzle 1 tablespoon of Italian Vinaigrette Dressing over the watermelon. Sprinkle 1 tablespoon of feta cheese over the melon. Top with 1 tablespoon of the basil or mint.

On a large platter, arrange all of the lettuce leaves on the platter. Top them with all the 8 cups of watermelon. Drizzle the Italian dressing over the watermelon, sprinkle the feta cheese on top, and top with basil or mint.

VARIATIONS:

- Add a pinch cayenne pepper and a squeeze of lime juice instead of the Italian dressing.
- Use fresh mint in place of basil.

GOES WELL WITH:

- Vegetarian Bean Chili (p. 271)

- Quick Enchiladas (p. 400)
- Grilled or roasted meat

Per serving: Calories 160, Calories from Fat 110, Total Fat 12g (18% DV), Saturated Fat 2.5g (12% DV), Trans Fat 0g, Cholesterol 5mg (2% DV), Sodium 135mg (6% DV), Carbohydrates 12g (4% DV), Dietary Fiber 1g (4% DV), Sugars 9g, **Added Sugars:** 0g, Protein 3g, Vitamin A 45%, Vitamin C 20%, Calcium 6%, Iron 6%.

CHICKEN SALAD

= Makes: 5 cups   = Active time: 20 minutes

= Serves: 10   = Total time: 1 hour

= Serving size: 1/2 cup

It goes against decades of antifat conditioning, but the mayonnaise in this recipe won't kill you. This is a variation of the famous Waldorf salad, and it has ample protein and fiber. If you don't go nuts with the mayo, this dish has what your body really needs. Store-bought chicken salad always has way too much mayo. The goal is to use mayo that is high in monosaturated fats and low in omega-6s like rapeseed or flaxseed oil. Canola oil is OK, but higher in omega-6s than one would like. I personally like my chicken savory, not sweet. But this dish is a staple at Cindy's restaurant. It's great for school lunches and for picnics. If you're in a rush use "Just Chicken" from Trader Joe's.

Ingredients
1/2 cup raw cashews, toasted
3 cups diced cooked chicken
1 cup diced celery
1 cup diced crisp red apple, such as Fuji or Macintosh
About 1 cup of mayonnaise
1 teaspoon salt, or more to taste
1 teaspoon ground black pepper, or more to taste

STEP 1: Preheat the oven to 350°F.

STEP 2: Put the cashews in a small baking pan and toast them until lightly browned, about 8 minutes. Check every couple of minutes; nuts burn quickly. Remove and let cool to room temperature. Or toast in a small pan, for 3 to 5 minutes, until brown.

STEP 3: Place the chicken, celery, and

apple in a bowl and add the toasted cashews.

STEP 5: Add the mayonnaise, starting with
1/2 cup, and the salt and pepper. (Don't
use low-fat mayonnaise, it will taste thin
and won't be able to bind the salad.) Mix
well. Add more mayonnaise to your taste
and more salt and pepper as necessary. Chill
the salad for 30 minutes to bring out the
flavors and you are ready to go.

The recipe can be multiplied as desired.
Stored in a covered container in the
refrigerator, the chicken salad will keep
for three days.

VARIATIONS:
- Add 1/2 cup dried raisins or 3/4 cup
  fresh grapes, sliced in half.
- Add a tablespoon or so of lemon or
  lime juice to give it some kick.
- Double the amount of celery. Some
  people like this extra crunchy.

GOES WELL WITH:
- Whole-wheat bread and lettuce to
  make an awesome sandwich
- Whole-wheat tortillas or Middle
  Eastern lavash bread, as a wrap

- Mixed greens to make a salad

Per serving: Calories 270, Calories from Fat 200, Total Fat 22g (34% DV), Saturated Fat 3.5g (18% DV), Trans Fat 0g, Cholesterol 45mg (15% DV), Sodium 430mg (18% DV), Carbohydrates 4g (1% DV), Dietary Fiber < 1g (3% DV), Sugars 2g, **Added Sugars:** 0g, Protein 14g, Vitamin A 2%, Vitamin C 2%, Calcium 2%, Iron 6%.

NEWELL DUAL

= Makes: 1 cup

= Serves: 2

= Serving size: 1/2 cup

= Active time: 10 minutes

= Total time: 20 minutes

Cindy opened her first café on Newell Avenue in Walnut Creek. This tuna salad/ egg salad mash-up may sound a bit odd, but it became a best seller in her restaurant. Try it. It's a great way to make a little tuna go a long way. It's also the best way to get the highest quality protein with the least fat or sugar, even sneaking in a bit of fiber, and yet still delivering the most taste. This is a winner for school lunches. Put this on whole-grain bread with some lettuce and you can be sure this is one lunch your kids will look forward to at school.

Ingredients
1 can (6 ounces) water-packed light tuna, drained
2 hard-boiled eggs, grated
1/2 cup diced celery
2 tablespoons peeled and minced red onion
1 teaspoon lemon juice, or more to taste
1/4 cup mayonnaise

Put the tuna, eggs, celery, onion, lemon juice, and mayonnaise in a bowl and mix well. Chill at least 30 minutes before using.

The recipe can be multiplied. Stored in a plastic or glass sealed container in the refrigerator, the tuna salad will keep for up to three days.

VARIATIONS:
- If you prefer tuna packed in oil, use a little less mayonnaise.
- Use canned salmon in place of tuna.
- Use fresh fish in place of canned.
- Add 1 tablespoon chopped dill pickle.
- Substitute Italian dressing for mayonnaise.

GOES WELL WITH:
- Whole-wheat bread, in a sandwich
- Greens, to make a salad

Per serving: Calories 260, Calories from Fat 120, Total Fat 13g (20% DV), Saturated Fat 3g (15% DV), Trans Fat 0g, Cholesterol 230mg (77% DV), Sodium 160mg (7% DV), Carbohydrates 7g (2% DV), Dietary Fiber < 1g (2% DV), Sugars 3g, **Added Sugars:** 0g, Protein 27g, Vitamin A 8%, Vitamin C 6%, Calcium 6%, Iron 8%.

CRACKED WHEAT SALAD

= Makes: 6 cups

= Serving size: 1 cup for a main meal, 1/4 cup for a side

= Active time: 20 minutes

= Total time: 50 minutes

This dish is an excellent source of whole grains and vegetables. I love chewy grains and the wheat berries add a great texture. Add toasted chickpeas or tofu to this dish and make it a complete meal.

Ingredients
1 cup cracked bulgur wheat
2 cups boiling water

1 cup chopped fresh tomatoes
1 cup chopped cucumber
1 cup chopped fresh parsley
1/2 cup peeled and chopped red onion
1/4 cup toasted walnuts, chopped (optional)
1 avocado, chopped (optional)
1/2 cup pitted olives (optional)
1/2 cup feta cheese (optional)
1/2 cup olive oil
1 teaspoon dried dill or 1 tablespoon fresh dill
1 pinch (1/8 teaspoon) of cayenne pepper
1 teaspoon salt
1 teaspoon cracked black pepper
3 tablespoons fresh lemon juice

STEP 1: Pour water over grain and let stand for 30 minutes covered.

STEP 2: Cool grain to room temperature, then add tomatoes, cucumber, parsley, and red onion. You can also add other optional ingredients as well here.

STEP 3: Whisk olive oil, dill, cayenne pepper, salt, pepper, and lemon juice until dressing is combined. Toss grains and veggies with dressing. Serve at room temperature or chilled.

Stored in a covered container in the refrigerator, this keeps for up to two days. This does not freeze well.

VARIATIONS:
- Use Italian dressing instead of lemon juice and olive oil.
- Add 1 tablespoon fresh mint.

GOES WELL WITH:
- Lettuce

Per serving: Calories 260, Calories from Fat 160, Total Fat 19g (29% DV), Saturated Fat 2.5g (12% DV), Trans Fat 0g, Cholesterol 0mg (0% DV), Sodium 410mg (17% DV), Carbohydrates 22g (7% DV), Dietary Fiber 5g (20% DV), Sugars 2g, **Added Sugars:** 0g, Protein 4g, Vitamin A 25%, Vitamin C 40%, Calcium 4%, Iron 8%.

HOMEMADE WHOLE-GRAIN CROUTONS

= Makes: 2 cups

= Serving size: 1/4 cup

= Total servings: 8

= Active time: 10 minutes

= Total time: 20 minutes

These are great, very versatile. Use in soups and salads. Store in an airtight container for up to a month. They can be used as stuffing too.

Ingredients
2 tablespoons olive oil
2 cups 1-inch bread cubes, best with day-old or stale bread
1/2 teaspoon salt

STEP 1: Preheat the oven to 325°F.

STEP 2: Coat a bowl with the oil, then add the bread and toss with the salt.

STEP 3: Spread out on a baking sheet in a single layer. Toast in the oven for 10 minutes or until firm.

VARIATIONS:
- Use dried herbs such as Italian seasoning or oregano.
- Spice it up with cayenne.
- Try different oils like lemon oil or walnut oil.
- Toss in Parmesan cheese.
- Use Italian Vinaigrette Dressing

(p. 139), Caesar Dressing (p. 145) or Ranch Dressing (p. 141) in place of oil.

Per serving: Calories 80, Calories from Fat 40, Total Fat 5g (8% DV), Saturated Fat 0.5g (2% DV), Trans Fat 0g, Cholesterol 0mg (0% DV), Sodium 150mg (6% DV), Carbohydrates 9g (3% DV), Dietary Fiber 1g (4% DV), Sugars 1g, **Added Sugars:** 1g, Protein 2g, Vitamin A 0%, Vitamin C 0%, Calcium 0%, Iron 2%.

SANDWICHES THIRTEEN WAYS

Sandwiches are easier, but salads are healthier. But when you "gotta" have a sandwich, here are some healthy options. All recipes can be made with a whole-grain wrap, pita, or bread. You can also make an open-faced sandwich on our Whole-Wheat Sponge Bread (p. 188) or a lettuce wrap without any grains. Always add one cup of green salad or marinated raw vegetable salad to your meal and one tablespoon dressing of your choice. Add raw seeds such as sunflower, pumpkin, or chia seeds.

Each of the following recipes makes one sandwich. All recipes can be multiplied.

Since bread choices vary, nutritional info is for the sandwich fillings only.

1. Edamame (Vegan)

Ingredients
1/2 cup Edamame Spread (p. 183)
1 cup packed baby spinach
1/2 cup chopped tomatoes
3 slices each: paper-thin sliced cucumber and carrots
1 tablespoon Italian Vinaigrette Dressing (p. 139)

Per serving: Calories 440, Calories from Fat 340, Total Fat 38g (58% DV), Saturated Fat 5g (25% DV), Trans Fat 0g, Cholesterol 0mg (0% DV), Sodium 85mg (4% DV), Carbohydrates 16g (5% DV), Dietary Fiber 7g (28% DV), Sugars 5g, **Added Sugars:** 0g, Protein 12g, Vitamin A 90%, Vitamin C 50%, Calcium 10%, Iron 20%.

Stuff in a pita or have open-faced on whole-grain bread.

2. Pesto and Cheese

Ingredients
1/4 cup ricotta cheese
2 tablespoons Basil Pesto (p. 185)
1/2 cup sprouts
1 tablespoon sunflower seeds
1/4 cup grated carrots
1/4 cup chopped tomatoes
1/4 cup Spring mix

Spread ricotta cheese over bread or tortilla. Spread Basil Pesto over that. Top with sprouts, sunflower seeds, carrots, tomatoes, and Spring mix.

Per serving: Calories 380, Calories from Fat 290, Total Fat 33g (51% DV), Saturated Fat 9g (45% DV), Trans Fat 0g, Cholesterol 35mg (12% DV), Sodium 210mg (9% DV), Carbohydrates 10g (3% DV), Dietary Fiber 3g (12% DV), Sugars 3g, **Added Sugars:** 0g, Protein 12g, Vitamin A 160%, Vitamin C 20%, Calcium 25%, Iron 10%.

3. Hummus and Avocado

Ingredients

1/4 cup hummus

1/4 avocado, sliced or mashed

1/4 cup chopped or thinly sliced tomatoes

1/4 cup chopped or thinly sliced cucumber

1/2 cup packed baby spinach, sprouts, butter lettuce, or romaine

1 tablespoon dressing: Ranch (p. 141), Italian (p. 139), or Caesar (p. 145)

Spread hummus over bread, pita, or tortilla. Layer everything else over hummus and drizzle with dressing.

Per serving: Calories 260, Calories from Fat 160, Total Fat 18g (28% DV), Saturated Fat 2.5g (12% DV), Trans Fat 0g, Cholesterol < 5mg (1% DV), Sodium 280mg (12% DV), Carbohydrates 21g (7% DV), Dietary Fiber 7g (28% DV), Sugars 3g, **Added Sugars:** 0g, Protein 5g, Vitamin A 50%, Vitamin C 30%, Calcium 6%, Iron 10%.

4. Roasted Veggies and Hummus or Pesto

Ingredients

1/4 cup hummus, or a combination of 1 tablespoon Basil Pesto (p. 185) and hummus

1 cup chopped roasted veggies

1 tablespoon Roasted Tomatoes (p. 166)

Spring mix

Spread hummus over bread or tortilla wrap. Top with pesto, roasted veggies, tomatoes, and Spring mix.

Per serving: Calories 220, Calories from Fat 120, Total Fat 14g (22% DV), Saturated Fat 2g (10% DV), Trans Fat 0g, Cholesterol 0mg (0% DV), Sodium 510mg (21% DV), Carbohydrates 20g (7% DV), Dietary Fiber 4g (16% DV), Sugars 3g, **Added Sugars:** 0g, Protein 5g, Vitamin A 4%, Vitamin C 200%, Calcium 4%, Iron 10%.

5. Eggplant Parmesan or Stuffed Bell Peppers (p. 471)

Great in a wrap or on whole-grain bread (hot or cold).

Put lettuce on bread or wrap. Slice eggplant or peppers and layer over lettuce. (This will keep the bread from getting soggy.)

Per serving: Calories 340, Calories from Fat 160, Total Fat 18g (28% DV), Saturated Fat 11g (55% DV), Trans Fat 0g, Cholesterol 55mg (18% DV), Sodium 600mg (25% DV), Carbohydrates 26g (9% DV), Dietary Fiber 8g (32% DV), Sugars < 1g, **Added Sugars:** 0g, Protein 22g, Vitamin A 110%, Vitamin C 320%, Calcium 70%, Iron 40%.

6. Meatball Sandwich
Great on pita, a wrap, or whole-grain bread.

Ingredients
Two 2-ounce meatballs (see p. 415), sliced in half
1 cup chopped roasted veggies
1/2 cup romaine lettuce or field greens

Place meatball slices on bread, pita, or wrap. Top with roasted veggies and greens.

Per serving: Calories 310, Calories from Fat 170, Total Fat 19g (29% DV), Saturated Fat 6g (30% DV), Trans Fat 0g, Cholesterol 75mg (25% DV), Sodium 870mg (36% DV), Carbohydrates 15g (5% DV), Dietary Fiber 3g (12%

DV), Sugars 3g, **Added Sugars:** 0g, Protein 21g, Vitamin A 70%, Vitamin C 200%, Calcium 15%, Iron 20%.

7. Caesar Salad Wrap or Pita

Ingredients
2 cups baby romaine and radicchio
4 ounces leftover grilled chicken, cubed, or salmon, or simple turkey burger
1 tablespoon grated Parmesan cheese
2 tablespoons Caesar Dressing (p. 145)

Toss lettuce, leftover meat, cheese, and dressing in a bowl. Stuff into a wrap or pita.

Per serving: Calories 450, Calories from Fat 270, Total Fat 30g (46% DV), Saturated Fat 6g (30% DV), Trans Fat 0g, Cholesterol 100mg (33% DV), Sodium 260mg (11% DV), Carbohydrates 4g (1% DV), Dietary Fiber 2g (8% DV), Sugars 1g, **Added Sugars:** 0g, Protein 39g, Vitamin A 170%, Vitamin C 8%, Calcium 10%, Iron 15%.

8. Chicken Salad

Ingredients
1/2 cup Chicken Salad (p. 314)
1 large lettuce leaf
2 slices tomato
2 slices cucumber

Spread chicken salad on bread. Top with lettuce, tomato, and cucumber.

Per serving: Calories 280, Calories from Fat 200, Total Fat 22g (34% DV), Saturated Fat 3.5g (18% DV), Trans Fat 0g, Cholesterol 45mg (15% DV), Sodium 430mg (18% DV), Carbohydrates 7g (2% DV), Dietary Fiber 1g (4% DV), Sugars 4g, **Added Sugars:** 0g, Protein 15g, Vitamin A 10%, Vitamin C 15%, Calcium 2%, Iron 6%.

9. Grilled Chicken Sandwich

Ingredients
2 ounces leftover grilled chicken
1 cup chopped Roasted Mixed Vegetables (p. 454)
1 tablespoon Basil Pesto (p. 185)
1 tablespoon Roasted Tomatoes (p. 166)

1 ounce mozzarella, shredded
1/2 cup arugula

Toss leftover chicken, roasted vegetables, pesto, tomatoes, cheese, and arugula in a bowl. Spread on bread or a wrap.

> **Per serving:** Calories 380, Calories from Fat 220, Total Fat 25g (38% DV), Saturated Fat 5g (25% DV), Trans Fat 0g, Cholesterol 50mg (17% DV), Sodium 740mg (31% DV), Carbohydrates 15g (5% DV), Dietary Fiber 2g (8% DV), Sugars 10g, **Added Sugars:** 0g, Protein 25g, Vitamin A 25%, Vitamin C 200%, Calcium 25%, Iron 10%.

10. Joe's Delight

Ingredients
2 tablespoons whipped cream cheese
1/4 avocado, chopped
2 ounces sliced fresh turkey breast
1 tablespoon chopped toasted walnuts
1 large lettuce leaf, or 1/2 cup sprouts
2 large slices of tomato
2 slices cucumber

Spread cream cheese on one bread slice. Spread avocado on the other slice of bread. Add turkey and top with toasted walnuts, greens, tomato, and cucumber. Or, put everything in a wrap.

Per serving: Calories 300, Calories from Fat 200, Total Fat 23g (35% DV), Saturated Fat 8g (40% DV), Trans Fat 0g, Cholesterol 55mg (18% DV), Sodium 680mg (28% DV), Carbohydrates 12g (4% DV), Dietary Fiber 5g (20% DV), Sugars 5g, Protein 14g, **Added Sugars:** 0g, Vitamin A 30%, Vitamin C 25%, Calcium 6%, Iron 10%.

11. Steak Sandwich with Grilled Onions

Ingredients
3 ounces leftover steak
1 ounce blue cheese
1/2 cup leftover grilled onion and zucchini
1 tablespoon Barbecue Sauce (p. 152)

Layer ingredients over bread or wrap.

Per serving: Calories 360, Calories from Fat 210, Total Fat 24g (37% DV), Saturated Fat 9g (45% DV), Trans Fat 0g, Cholesterol 95mg (32% DV), Sodium 550mg (23% DV), Carbohydrates 6g (2% DV), Dietary Fiber 1g (4% DV), Sugars 2g, **Added Sugars:** 0g, Protein

29g, Vitamin A 8%, Vitamin C 90%, Calcium 20%, Iron 10%.

12. Newell Dual Salad

Ingredients
1/2 cup Newell Dual (p. 317)
1 large lettuce leaf

Top bread or wrap with Newell Dual salad and lettuce leaf.

Per serving: Calories 280, Calories from Fat 120, Total Fat 13g (20% DV), Saturated Fat 3.5g (18% DV), Trans Fat 0g, Cholesterol 230mg (77% DV), Sodium 160mg (7% DV), Carbohydrates 11g (4% DV), Dietary Fiber 2g (8% DV), Sugars 5g, **Added Sugars:** 0g, Protein 28g, Vitamin A 35%, Vitamin C 25%, Calcium 6%, Iron 10%.

13. Homemade Nut Butter and Jam or Banana Sandwich

Ingredients
2 tablespoons nut butter
1 small banana, sliced, or 2 tablespoons homemade jam

Top bread with nut butter and banana or jam.

Per serving: Calories 260, Calories from Fat 150, Total Fat 18g (28% DV), Saturated Fat 1.5g (8% DV), Trans Fat 0g, Cholesterol 0mg (0% DV), Sodium 0mg (0% DV), Carbohydrates 23g (8% DV), Dietary Fiber 5g (20% DV), Sugars 9g, **Added Sugars:** 0g, Protein 7g, Vitamin A 0%, Vitamin C 10%, Calcium 10%, Iron 8%.

Healthy Additions to Sandwiches:

Chopped raw nuts and seeds (sunflower, chia seeds, walnuts, slivered almonds, cashews)
Nut butters
Fresh avocado
Spinach
Mixed greens
Kale
Fresh grated carrots, jicama, beets
Sliced cucumbers
Bean sprouts, alfalfa sprouts, lentil sprouts, raddish sprouts (kind of peppery)
Roasted peppers, eggplant, zucchini, onions

Mustards: whole grain, spicy brown, Dijon
Greek yogurt
Ricotta cheese
Half dill pickles
Dressings: ranch dressing, Italian dressing, Caesar dressing, balsamic reduction
Cheeses: Swiss, mozzarella, goat, feta (anything you like)

■ ■ ■ ■

7

■ ■ ■ ■

CHAPTER 7
BEANS, GRAINS,
PIZZA, AND PASTA

The dishes in this chapter work well for lunch or dinner. Pasta and pizza are usually carb nightmares, but the versions in this book will keep your blood-sugar levels stable.

Recipes:

Spanish Brown Rice
Brown Rice with Lime and Cilantro
Green Pasta
Pasta with Crushed Tomatoes, Beef, and
 Spinach
Ricotta Gnocchi
Multi-Grain Flatbread Pizza

Beans and Legumes — a Tutorial

Split Peas and Lentils

Lentils are an inexpensive, healthy, and versatile food. They are probably the fastest cooking of all the legumes and are rich in antioxidants, selenium, and B vitamins, all of which boost the immune system. They are also packed with protein, rich in iron and folate, plus they are very high in fiber, which is good for digestive and heart health.

Lentils come in a variety of colors. Red lentils are the fastest cooking and are often used in Indian cuisine. The green and brown lentil varieties are more nutritious than the red variety.

Like beans, lentils and split peas are low in fat and high in protein and fiber; they have the added advantage of cooking quickly without the need for soaking.

Cooking Split Peas and Lentils

Spread beans out on a clean kitchen towel or rimmed baking sheet. Pick out and discard any shriveled or broken beans, stones or debris, and rinse in a fine sieve or colander under cold water.

Bring about 1 1/2 cups of water or broth to a boil for every cup of lentils or split peas. Add the lentils, allow water to return to boiling, reduce heat, partially cover pan, and let simmer for 30 to 45 minutes, depending on the variety.

Dry lentils and split peas can be added to soups and stews, just be sure that there is enough liquid (1 1/2 cups to every 1 cup of lentils) to compensate for absorption and expansion.

Dried Beans

Beans can be a wonderful part of a healthy meal; use them in chilis, soups, stews, salads, and dips. There are two ways to soak beans: overnight and by the quick-soak method. The soaking softens the beans and makes them cook more quickly. After soaking, beans cook in 1 1/2 to 2 hours. One cup of dried beans yields approximately 2 1/4 cups cooked beans.

To Soak Beans Overnight

Rinse the dried beans. Place the beans in a large bowl or saucepan and cover with three to four times as much water. Leave at least 4 hours or overnight. Drain water. Return to pot and cover with fresh, unsalted water: 3 cups water to 1 cup of beans.

The Quick-Soak Method

When you don't have time to let the beans soak overnight, put the beans in a large pot and add enough cold water to cover the beans by 3 inches. Do not cover the pot. Bring the water to a boil over medium-high heat. Reduce heat to medium, and continue simmering for 2 minutes. Remove from heat. Cover and let stand for 1 hour. Drain and rinse.

Cooking Beans

This method works for all dried beans: white beans, kidney beans, garbanzo beans or chickpeas, pinto beans, black beans.

Use 3 cups of water per 1 cup of soaked beans. Bring beans and water to a boil and cover.

Simmer beans gently for 2 hours with a lid to help keep their form.

Do not add salt during cooking! It will harden the outside of the beans, lengthening cooking time.

If more water is needed during the cooking process, add enough water to cover the beans by 2 to 3 inches.

Some people complain that beans cause gas. I often say, "Fat or fart" (see *Fat Chance* for the science). Drain and rinse the beans twice, as that will help minimize this side effect.

For optimal flavor store the beans in the refrigerator in their own cooking liquid; the flavor of cooked beans is always best on the second or third day.

Beans freeze well for up to three months, but drain the beans before freezing. The bean stock can be frozen separately for up to three months; both the beans and stock will keep in the refrigerator for up to one week.

LENTIL-BARLEY BURGERS WITH FRUIT SALSA

= Makes: 8 patties

= Serving size: 2 patties

= Active time: 30 minutes

= Total time: 30 minutes

I love the combination of the lentils and chewy barley. I like to use hulled barley, usually found in health food stores. This has everything in it: fruits, veggies, grain, and protein. It's a great lunch to pack. These can be cooked and frozen.

For Salsa:

Ingredients
1/4 cup finely chopped pineapple
1/4 cup finely chopped tomatillo
1 tablespoon fresh lime juice
1/4 mango, finely chopped
1/4 cup grape tomatoes, halved
1 serrano pepper, minced

For Burgers:

Ingredients
1/2 cup dried lentils
1 1/2 cups water
Non-aerosol cooking spray
1 cup peeled and chopped onion
1/4 cup grated carrot
2 teaspoons peeled and minced garlic
2 tablespoons tomato paste
1 teaspoon ground cumin
3/4 teaspoon dried oregano
1 1/2 teaspoons chili powder
3/4 teaspoon salt
3/4 cup cooked pearled barley (see p. 354)
2 large eggs, beaten

1/4 cup finely chopped fresh parsley
1/2 teaspoon ground black pepper
1/2 cup dry quinoa, cornmeal, or oatmeal
3 tablespoons canola or vegetable oil

STEP 1: Chop all the salsa ingredients and mix together in bowl. Cover and chill in the refrigerator.

STEP 2: In a medium-size pot, simmer the lentils in water for 15 to 20 minutes, or until tender. Drain the lentils, place half in a large bowl, and puree the other half in a blender or food processor. Add pureed lentils to the whole lentils in the bowl and mix.

STEP 3: Heat a large skillet over medium-high heat. Coat the pan with the cooking spray and add the onions and carrots. Sauté until tender, about 5 minutes.

STEP 4: Add the garlic to the pan and cook for 2 minutes, stirring. Next add the tomato paste, cumin, oregano, chili powder, and 1/4 teaspoon of the salt, cooking for 1 more minute, stirring.

STEP 5: Add the cooked onion-carrot mixture to the lentils in a large bowl. Add the remaining 1/2 teaspoon salt, the cooked barley, eggs, parsley, pepper, and quinoa or cornmeal. Mix well and put in the refrigerator for 1 hour or until firm. These can be made the night before.

STEP 6: To cook, heat a large skillet over medium-high heat with 1/2 tablespoon of the oil. Divide the lentil mixture into 8 portions and place flattened patties into the pan. Cook for 3 minutes on each side, or until just browned. Serve with the salsa.

This recipe can be multiplied. The patties will keep, wrapped individually, in the freezer for up to three months. Date and label! The salsa cannot be frozen.

VARIATIONS:
- Add some cayenne pepper.
- Use Almost Homemade Salsa (p. 234) in place of fruit salsa.
- Use brown rice in place of barley.

GOES WELL WITH:
- Roasted vegetables
- Sliced apples
- Spring mix and Italian Vinaigrette Dressing (p. 139)

Per serving: Calories 350, Calories

from Fat 130, Total Fat 14g (22% DV), Saturated Fat 2g (10% DV), Trans Fat 0g, Cholesterol 95mg (32% DV), Sodium 610mg (25% DV), Carbohydrates 44g (15% DV), Dietary Fiber 12g (48% DV), Sugars 8g, **Added Sugars:** 0g, Protein 13g, Vitamin A 45%, Vitamin C 40%, Calcium 8%, Iron 25%.

BLACK BEAN PATTIES

= Makes: 8 patties   = Active time: 30 minutes

= Serving size: 2 patties   = Total time: 30 minutes

If you like black beans, you are going to love these patties. They are great warm or cold.

Ingredients

3 tablespoons olive oil, divided

1 tablespoon peeled and chopped garlic

2 cups cooked black beans, rinsed and drained

1/4 cup bean water, saved before rinsing

1 cup dry cornmeal or quinoa

1 teaspoon chili powder

1 tablespoon chopped fresh oregano, or 1 teaspoon dried oregano

1/4 teaspoon salt

1 large egg, lightly beaten
1 egg white, lightly beaten

STEP 1: Combine 1 tablespoon oil, garlic, and beans in a blender or food processor. Pulse eight times or until the beans become a thick paste. Add the water. Scrape the bean mixture into a large bowl and add the cornmeal or quinoa.

STEP 2: Stir in the remaining ingredients. With moistened hands, divide the bean mixture into 4 equal portions (about 1/3 cup per portion), shaping into eight 3-inch patties.

STEP 3: Heat the remaining 2 tablespoons oil in a large skillet over medium-high heat. Add the patties to the pan and brown 4 minutes on the first side, reducing the heat if needed. Flip the patties and brown the second side for 2 to 3 minutes.

VARIATIONS:
- Bake in a loaf pan.
- Bake in a muffin pan.

GOES WELL WITH:
- Roma Tomato Basil Salsa (p. 172) on a bed of mixed greens

- Spanish Brown Rice (p. 373)
- Brown Rice with Lime and Cilantro (p. 375) with Savory Watermelon and Feta Salad (p. 312)

Per serving: Calories 340, Calories from Fat 120, Total Fat 13g (20% DV), Saturated Fat 2.5g (12% DV), Trans Fat 0g, Cholesterol 45mg (15% DV), Sodium 390mg (16% DV), Carbohydrates 41g (14% DV), Dietary Fiber 9g (36% DV), Sugars 2g, **Added Sugars:** 0g, Protein 14g, Vitamin A 6%, Vitamin C 2%, Calcium 10%, Iron 20%.

TOFU CRUSTED WITH OREGANO PESTO, CHEESE, AND BREAD CRUMBS

= Serves: 4

= Active time: 15 minutes

= Serving size: 1/4 recipe

= Total time: 30 minutes

Even if you're not a vegetarian, occasionally substituting tofu for meat is a healthy bet. Personally, I'm not a tofu fan. But you could do this with pork loin just as well. In any case, the nuts and cheese mean it won't last long in your house.

Ingredients

1 carton (12 ounces) firm tofu

1/2 cup dry cornmeal or quinoa

1/2 cup fresh oregano leaves, or 3 tablespoons dried oregano

2 garlic cloves, peeled and minced

2 tablespoons pine nuts or chopped almonds or sesame seeds

1/4 cup olive oil

Salt and pepper, to taste

1 cup grated Parmesan, Manchego, or
pecorino romano cheese

STEP 1: Drain the tofu on paper towels. Slice crosswise into 6 pieces. Cut each piece into triangles.

STEP 2: Put the quinoa or cornmeal into a small bowl.

STEP 3: In a blender, or food processor if you have one, add the oregano, garlic, and nuts. Process until all are finely chopped. Add 3 tablespoons olive oil. Process until a paste forms.

STEP 4: Season the dry tofu lightly with salt and pepper to taste. Rub the pesto mixture over the tofu triangles. Toss the cheese and the quinoa or cornmeal together in a small bowl. Press this into the tofu.

STEP 5: Heat a heavy skillet over medium heat. Add the tofu pieces and fry on both sides, about 3 minutes per side.

VARIATIONS:
- Use a different herb to make the pesto: basil, parsley, or tarragon would all work.
- For a quick version, coat tofu with Basil Pesto (p. 185) and proceed with recipe.
- Play around with different kinds of nuts: almonds, walnuts, or pecans.
- Use this preparation with meat, such as pork loin, boneless chicken thighs, or fish fillets.

GOES WELL WITH:
- Sliced tomato salad
- Green salad
- Steamed brown rice over polenta patties or quinoa
- Cracked wheat salad

Per serving: Calories 440, Calories from Fat 280, Total Fat 32g (49% DV), Saturated Fat 8g (40% DV), Trans Fat 0g, Cholesterol 20mg (7% DV), Sodium

640mg (27% DV), Carbohydrates 17g (6% DV), Dietary Fiber 4g (16% DV), Sugars 1g, **Added Sugars:** 0g, Protein 26g, Vitamin A 8%, Vitamin C 2%, Calcium 90%, Iron 25%.

WHOLE GRAINS — A TUTORIAL

Grains have become hugely popular lately not only because they are super nutritious and delicious, but also because they're not difficult to cook. If you can cook rice, you can cook grains. In general, 1/2 cup of cooked grains makes a reasonable serving.

Storing

Grains stored in airtight containers away from light, heat, and moisture should keep for a few months. Make sure to smell the grain before using it; if it smells strongly, it has probably gone bad.

Soaking

Soaking is not absolutely necessary, but it is recommended for hard grains like spelt and wheat berries — they will cook up more quickly if soaked and rinsed first.

Brown Rice

Brown rice is not milled and retains the bran and germ that surrounds the rice kernel, giving it a chewy texture and a flavor often described as nutty. It takes longer to cook, but it's more nutritious.

Short-Grain Brown Rice
Short and plump; about as long as it is wide. It sticks together when cooked and stays tender even at room temperature, like when it is used in sushi. When cooking, use 1 cup rice to 2 1/4 cups liquid and simmer for 45 minutes.

Long-Grain Brown Rice
Long and slender with a length that's four to five times its width. Its grains separate while being light and fluffy, making it a perfect side dish. When cooking, use 1 cup rice to 2 cups liquid and simmer for 45 minutes.

Cooking Rice
STEP 1: Bring water (and salt, if using) to a boil, add grains and return to a boil. Stir, reduce heat so the water just simmers, cover the pot tightly, and simmer. Do not lift the cover — releasing the steam will slow the cooking process.

STEP 2: Check grains for doneness by biting into one grain. Most whole grains will be slightly chewy after they are cooked.

STEP 3: When grains are done cooking, remove from heat and fluff them using a fork or chopstick. Cover again and allow to sit for 5 to 10 minutes before serving.

Barley

Barley is lightly milled to retain all of the germ and at least two thirds of the bran for a tender, slightly chewy texture and a mild flavor. Use in grain salads, soups, stews, and chilis. Try barley as a stuffing for peppers, tomatoes, or poultry. Barley comes in several varieties: "unhulled" barley is the most complete grain; "hulled" barley retains the bran; "pearled" barley has neither hull nor bran, but is still a pretty good source of fiber.

Cooking Barley

Use 3 cups liquid per 1 cup barley. Simmer for 40 minutes.

Quinoa

Pronounced "KEEN-wah," this grain is packed with nutrition and has a light, nutty flavor that works well in soups, salads, and pilafs.

Cooking Quinoa

When cooking, use 1 cup quinoa to 2 cups liquid. Bring to a boil and simmer covered for 15 minutes. Toss with a fork, cover again, and let sit for 5 more minutes.

Steel-Cut Oats

Chewier than rolled oats, steel-cut oats are groats (see p. 356) cut into smaller pieces.

Cooking Steel-Cut Oats

When cooking, use 1 cup oats to 4 cups liquid. Start in cold water and then simmer uncovered for 30 minutes.

Rolled Oats

Often called "old-fashioned oats," rolled oats are groats that have been steamed, rolled, and cut into flakes.

Cooking Rolled Oats

When cooking, use 1 cup oats to 2 cups liquid. Start in cold water, bring to a boil, then simmer for 10 to 15 minutes.

Cracked/Bulgur Wheat

Wheat berries cracked into small pieces. It's similar to oatmeal. Use in casseroles, salad, or as a stuffing.

Cooking Cracked/ Bulgur Wheat

Use 2 cups liquid for each 1 cup of wheat. Simmer covered for 20 minutes; let stand covered for 5 minutes.

Wheat Berries

Chewy texture, high in protein; wheat berries work well as a stuffing or added to a green salad. Wheat berries labeled "soft" cook more quickly.

Cooking Wheat Berries

When cooking, use 1 cup wheat berries to 4 cups liquid. Soak for 8 hours or overnight. Drain. Add water, bring to a boil, and simmer for 50 to 60 minutes.

Groats

Rich and hearty, a great alternative to oatmeal. Can be used in savory dishes like pilaf or stuffing.

Cooking Groats

When cooking, use 1 cup of groats for each 3 cups of liquid. Start in cold water, bring to a boil, and then simmer covered for 45 minutes. Turn off heat and let it sit for 15 minutes.

Cornmeal

Cornmeal is a coarse flour ground from dried maize or corn. You can buy it in fine, medium, or coarse consistencies.

Cooking Cornmeal

When cooking, use 1 cup of cornmeal for each 4 cups of liquid. Cook the same as you would cook polenta; the cornmeal will be done in 30 to 45 minutes.

Polenta

Polenta is coarse ground cornmeal boiled into a porridge and can be eaten directly, baked, fried, or grilled.

Cooking Polenta

When cooking, use 1 cup polenta for each 4 cups of liquid. I don't use instant polenta. It's more processed than the traditional grind. Add polenta to boiling water, gradually reducing the heat while stirring every 10 minutes. You can eat it after 45 minutes or so. The longer it cooks, the creamier it gets. If cooking longer, keep adding water as needed to keep it from getting too thick.

QUINOA AND BLACK BEAN BURRITO BOWL

= Serves: 4   = Active time: 15 minutes

= Serving size: 1 1/2 cups   = Total time: 20 minutes

This is an easy, packable lunch. It's good hot or cold. Here, quinoa takes the place of rice; it's got the most fiber of any food in the starch category. Teamed up with black beans it's full of protein. This is vegetarian, but if you need your meat fix, add 1 pound of browned ground turkey and serve it as the main dish of a Mexican fiesta!

Ingredients

1 cup quinoa, rinsed

2 1/2 cups water

1 tablespoon olive oil

1/4 cup peeled and minced onion

1 clove garlic, peeled and minced

2 cans (15 ounces each) black beans, or 2 cups black beans, cooked, rinsed, and drained

1/2 cup chopped fresh cilantro

1 tablespoon mild chili powder

1 pinch (1/8 teaspoon) of cayenne pepper

1/4 cup fresh lime juice

1 teaspoon salt
2 cups shredded lettuce

Optional Topping Ingredients:
Grated cheddar or Jack cheese
Sour cream or Greek yogurt
Pico de gallo or salsa
Diced seeded tomatoes
Hot sauce or Sriracha sauce
Sliced avocado
Guacamole
Corn kernels

STEP 1: Pour the quinoa into a saucepan along with 2 cups of water. Bring the quinoa to a boil, then reduce heat to a low simmer. Cover the pot. Let the quinoa simmer for about 20 minutes, until it becomes tender and all the liquid has been absorbed. Keep a close eye on the pot to make sure the quinoa doesn't burn.

STEP 2: While quinoa is cooking, heat the oil in another saucepan over medium heat. Add the minced onion to the saucepan and sauté for 3 to 5 minutes, until it softens and begins to turn brown. Add the minced garlic to the pot and sauté for 1 to 2 minutes longer.

STEP 3: Add the black beans to the saucepan along with the remaining 1/2 cup water, 2 tablespoons of cilantro, the chili powder, and cayenne pepper. Bring the beans to a boil, then reduce the heat to medium-low. Let the beans simmer until the liquid is mostly evaporated, 15 minutes. Stir in 2 tablespoons of fresh lime juice. Season with salt to taste.

STEP 5: When the quinoa is fully cooked, remove it from the heat and fluff it with a fork. Use the fork to mix in 2 tablespoons cilantro and 2 tablespoons fresh lime juice. Season with salt to taste.

STEP 6: Assemble your burrito bowls. Divide the cilantro-lime quinoa among 4 bowls. Top each portion with 1/2 cup of lettuce and 1 tablespoon of cilantro. Top each portion of lettuce with simmered black beans. Top the black beans with your choice of toppings. Serve warm or cold.

This recipe can be doubled.

VARIATIONS:
- Use cooked barley, cracked wheat, or brown rice in place of quinoa.
- Add roasted vegetables.

GOES WELL WITH:
- Fresh fruit salad

Per serving: Calories 320, Calories from Fat 60, Total Fat 7g (11% DV), Saturated Fat 1g (5% DV), Trans Fat 0g, Cholesterol 0mg (0% DV), Sodium 630mg (26% DV), Carbohydrates 52g (17% DV), Dietary Fiber 12g (48% DV), Sugars < 1g, **Added Sugars:** 0g, Protein 14g, Vitamin A 40%, Vitamin C 10%, Calcium 6%, Iron 25%.

QUINOA AND VEGETABLE CHILI

= Makes: 1 gallon   = Active time: 25 minutes

= Serving size: 1 1/2 cups   = Total time: 45 minutes

Quinoa can serve the same role as potatoes or rice, but it is absorbed into our systems much more slowly. This avoids the blood sugar spikes often caused by eating other starches. Quinoa also provides a good source of omega-3 fats, and is one of the best plant sources of protein. Here's a Latin approach to this lesser-known whole grain.

Ingredients

1/4 cup olive oil

1 cup onion, peeled and chopped

1 cup carrots, chopped into 1/2-inch pieces

1 cup celery, chopped into 1/2-inch pieces

4 garlic cloves, peeled and minced

2 cups red bell peppers, chopped into 1/2-inch pieces

2 cups zucchini, chopped into 1/2-inch pieces

1/4 cup chili powder

1 tablespoon ground cumin

1 tablespoon Spanish smoked paprika

2 teaspoons salt

1 1/2 cups water

2 cups vegetable stock

1/2 cup quinoa, rinsed

1 can (28 ounces) crushed tomatoes, or 3 cups chopped fresh tomatoes

4 cups cooked beans, rinsed and drained, or 2 cans (15 ounces each) pinto, black, or kidney beans

STEP 1: Heat a large stockpot over medium-high heat. Add oil to pan; swirl to coat. Add the onion, carrots, and celery; sauté 5 minutes. Add the garlic. Sauté for 2 more minutes. Add the bell peppers and zucchini and sauté for 5 minutes or until tender.

362

STEP 2: Stir in the chili powder, cumin, and paprika. Stir constantly for 30 seconds. Add the salt, water, stock, quinoa, tomatoes, and beans; bring to a boil. Reduce heat to medium-low; cover the pot and let simmer until the quinoa is tender, 20 minutes.

VARIATIONS:
- Replace the quinoa with 1 cup of cooked barley or 1 cup of cooked brown rice.
- Add 1 pound of ground cooked turkey or beef.
- Add cheese and sour cream.

GOES WELL WITH:
- Green salad
- Fresh fruit

Per serving: Calories 230, Calories from Fat 70, Total Fat 8g (12% DV), Saturated Fat 1g (5% DV), Trans Fat 0g, Cholesterol 0mg (0% DV), Sodium 960mg (40% DV), Carbohydrates 34g (11% DV), Dietary Fiber 11g (44% DV), Sugars 5g, **Added Sugars:** 0g, Protein 10g, Vitamin A 80%, Vitamin C 70%, Calcium 10%, Iron 20%.

GREENS AND BARLEY GRATIN

= Serves 6

= Serving size:
One 2-by-2-inch square

= Active time:
20 minutes

= Total time:
1 hour

This is a great brunch or potluck dish. It keeps well and tastes good at room temperature.

Ingredients

2 tablespoons olive oil

1 cup peeled and chopped yellow onion

4 large cloves garlic, peeled and sliced

3 cups Swiss chard, beet greens, spinach, or kale, washed and dried, ribs removed, chopped and set aside

1 teaspoon salt

1 teaspoon fresh thyme leaves, or 1/2 teaspoon dried thyme

1 teaspoon cracked black pepper

3 eggs, beaten

1/2 cup half-and-half or whole milk

1 teaspoon Dijon mustard

1 cup cooked barley or brown rice

1/2 cup (about 2 ounces) grated Gruyère cheese

2 tablespoons freshly grated Parmesan cheese

STEP 1: Preheat the oven to 375°F.

STEP 2: Heat the oil in a large skillet over medium heat. Add the onion and sauté until tender, about 5 minutes. Add the garlic, chopped chard ribs, and a pinch of salt. Sauté just until the garlic becomes fragrant, 1 to 2 minutes. Do not overcook the garlic, it will become bitter.

STEP 3: Stir in the chopped greens and thyme and toss together. Season with salt and pepper to taste. Remove from heat.

STEP 4: In a large bowl, whisk the eggs, milk, and Dijon mustard. Add salt and cracked pepper. Stir in the cooked greens mixture, the barley, and cheese. Mix well.

STEP 5: Grease a 2-quart gratin dish, or shallow baking dish, with oil or cooking spray. Scrape the mixture from the bowl into the dish and bake in the oven for 35 to 40 minutes, or until sizzling and lightly browned on the top and sides. Remove from the oven. Allow to sit for at least 10 minutes before serving.

This recipe can be multiplied.

VARIATIONS:
- Use kale and brown rice.

GOES WELL WITH:
- Roasted chicken or turkey
- Pickled beets
- Salad
- Roasted leg of lamb
- Berry Compote (p. 225) with yogurt

Per serving: Calories 200, Calories from Fat 100, Total Fat 12g (18% DV), Saturated Fat 4g (20% DV), Trans Fat 0g, Cholesterol 105mg (35% DV), Sodium 700mg (29% DV), Carbohydrates 16g (5% DV), Dietary Fiber 4g (16% DV), Sugars 3g, **Added Sugars:** 0g, Protein 10g, Vitamin A 120%, Vitamin C 35%, Calcium 25%, Iron 15%.

CREAMY POLENTA WITH FRESH CORN

= Makes: 4 cups   = Active time: 15 minutes

= Serving size: 3/4 cup   = Total time: 1 hour

Fresh corn adds texture to creamy polenta. You can use fresh corn or frozen corn in this recipe. This is a sweet and wonderful dish. Sometimes, I boil the stripped corn-cobs in the water for 15 minutes to get all the sweetness out of the cob. Then I remove the cobs and proceed with the instructions below. You don't need to add refined sugar to make things sweet!

Ingredients
4 cups water or vegetable stock
Salt
1 cup coarse cornmeal (polenta)
2 cups fresh corn, off the cob

STEP 1: Bring water or stock and salt to a boil in a large pot over high heat.

STEP 2: Once the liquid is boiling, slowly add the cornmeal, stirring constantly with a whisk to keep lumps from forming.

STEP 3: When the grain is mixed smoothly into the liquid, bring to a full boil, then reduce the heat to low and simmer gently for 30 minutes. Stir occasionally to keep the polenta from sticking.

STEP 4: Add the corn kernels to the polenta and cook for an additional 30 minutes, covered. You may need to add up to 1 cup of water to keep it from becoming stiff.

VARIATIONS:

- Add a small bit of cheese to the mixture once it's cooked.
- Add garlic or chopped herbs such as basil or parsley.

GOES WELL WITH:

- Grilled, roasted, or sautéed meats and vegetables of all kinds
- Stews of all kinds

Per serving: Calories 280, Calories from Fat 30, Total Fat 3.5g (5% DV), Saturated Fat 0g (0% DV), Trans Fat 0g, Cholesterol 0mg (0% DV), Sodium 125mg (5% DV), Carbohydrates 57g (19% DV), Dietary Fiber 1g (4% DV), Sugars 0g, **Added Sugars:** 0g, Protein 7g, Vitamin A 0%, Vitamin C 0%, Calcium 0%, Iron 10%.

"ALMOST RISOTTO" BROWN RICE PILAF WITH VEGGIES

= Serves: 6   = Active time: 20 minutes

= Serving size: 1 cup   = Total time: 30 minutes

This recipe tastes a lot like traditional risotto and it's a lot better for you. And you don't have to stir it constantly as it cooks, a must in traditional risotto recipes.

Ingredients

1 cup peeled and chopped onion
1 tablespoon butter
2 tablespoons olive oil
1 tablespoon peeled chopped garlic
1 cup diced zucchini
1 cup diced mushrooms
1 tablespoon fresh rosemary, or 1 teaspoon
 dried rosemary
2 cups cooked brown rice or barley
1 cup water or vegetable stock
1/2 cup grated Parmesan cheese

STEP 1: Sauté the onion in the butter and 1 tablespoon of the olive oil in a medium-size saucepan over medium-high heat until it begins to soften and brown, 3 to 5 minutes. Add the garlic and sauté for 2 minutes. Then add the zucchini, mushroom, and rosemary and continue to sauté 5 more minutes. Add the brown rice or barley to the pot. Cook until the grain begins to brown a little.

STEP 2: Stir in the water or vegetable stock and Parmesan cheese to the pot. Cover and cook on low for 15 minutes, melting the cheese and allowing the flavors to meld. Turn off the heat, and let it sit until ready to serve.

VARIATIONS:
- Use chopped leftover roasted vegetables in place of the onions, zucchini, and mushrooms.
- Change up the kind of herbs: basil, parsley, thyme, tarragon, cilantro, and dill all work well here.
- Soft veggies work best in this recipe: sweet peppers, kale, and spinach are good.

GOES WELL WITH:
- Any roasted or grilled meat or tofu
- Stews and chilis
- Stuffed bell peppers
- Roasted vegetables

Per serving: Calories 270, Calories from Fat 130, Total Fat 14g (22% DV), Saturated Fat 5g (25% DV), Trans Fat 0g, Cholesterol 20mg (7% DV), Sodium 220mg (9% DV), Carbohydrates 29g (10% DV), Dietary Fiber 3g (12% DV), Sugars 3g, **Added Sugars:** 0g, Protein 8g, Vitamin A 6%, Vitamin C 15%, Calcium 15%, Iron 6%.

WHOLE-GRAIN VEGETABLE PILAF

= Serves 6
= Serving size: 3/4 cup

= Active time: 10 minutes
= Total time: 30 minutes

Barley, wheat berries, and veggies team up to make a lovely side dish.

Ingredients
1/4 cup olive oil
1/2 cup carrots, scrubbed and chopped
1/2 cup chopped celery
1/2 cup onion, peeled and chopped
1/2 cup chopped zucchini
1/2 bell pepper, ribs and seeds removed, chopped
1 cup cooked barley
1/2 cup cooked wheat berries
1 cup cooked cracked wheat
1 cup Vegetable Stock (p. 160)
1 teaspoon salt, or to taste

STEP 1: Heat the oil in a saucepan over medium heat. Add the carrots, celery, and onions and sauté until tender, about 5 minutes.

STEP 2: Add the zucchini and bell peppers and cook an additional 3 minutes, until tender and brown. Add the barley, wheat berries, cracked wheat, and Vegetable Stock and lower the heat to medium. Cook covered for 5 minutes, add salt to taste, then turn off heat and let sit until ready to serve.

VARIATIONS:
- Add a few cloves of peeled and chopped garlic.
- Sprinkle with chopped parsley just before serving.

GOES WELL WITH:
- Makes a great stuffing for turkey or chicken
- Meat or fish as a side dish

Per serving: Calories 160, Calories from Fat 80, Total Fat 9g (14% DV), Saturated Fat 1.5g (8% DV), Trans Fat 0g, Cholesterol 0mg (0% DV), Sodium 20mg (1% DV), Carbohydrates 18g (6% DV), Dietary Fiber 5g (20% DV), Sugars 2g, **Added Sugars:** 0g, Protein 3g, Vitamin A 40%, Vitamin C 25%, Calcium 2%, Iron 6%.

SPANISH BROWN RICE

= Makes: 4 cups
= Active time: 20 minutes

= Serving size: 1/2 cup
= Total time: 1 hour

An "exotic" staple in the 1950s, Spanish rice with less processed grain updates an old standard, and adds loads of fiber. The thing that makes this dish work is the brown rice, which ups the fiber and downs the insulin response. If you add ground beef, this is an easy dish to turn into a full meal.

Ingredients

2 tablespoons olive oil

1 cup peeled and chopped onion

1 tablespoon peeled and chopped garlic

1 cup cored, seeded, and chopped red bell pepper

2 cups uncooked brown rice

3 1/2 cups water

1 cup crushed tomatoes

1 tablespoon chili powder

1 tablespoon cumin

1 1/2 teaspoons kosher salt, or 3/4 teaspoon table salt

STEP 1: Heat oil in a skillet over medium heat. Add the onion, garlic, and bell pepper and sauté until veggies are tender. Add the rice and cook until rice begins to toast, about 2 minutes. Add the water, crushed tomatoes, chili powder, cumin, and salt. Bring to a boil.

STEP 2: Once the rice is boiling, turn heat down to low and simmer until all the liquid is absorbed and the rice is tender, about 45 minutes.

VARIATIONS:
- Add cilantro to rice at end of cooking.
- Add 1 pound of ground meat, browned, to make a whole meal.

GOES WELL WITH:
- Roasted chicken
- Roasted pork loin
- Chili

Per serving: Calories 230, Calories from Fat 45, Total Fat 5g (8% DV), Saturated Fat 1g (5% DV), Trans Fat 0g, Cholesterol 0mg (0% DV), Sodium 280mg (12% DV), Carbohydrates 42g (14% DV), Dietary Fiber 3g (12% DV), Sugars 2g, **Added Sugars:** 0g, Protein

5g, Vitamin A 20%, Vitamin C 40%, Calcium 4%, Iron 10%.

Brown Rice with Lime and Cilantro

= Serves 4   = Active time: 10 minutes

= Serving size: 1/2 cup   = Total time: 45 minutes

Brown rice means fiber. Lime and cilantro means flavor. This makes a flavorful bed for chili, filling for a burrito, or a great side dish for grilled meat or fish. It takes time, so start this first before preparing the other parts of the meal.

Ingredients
1 tablespoon butter
1 cup brown rice
1 lime, juiced
1 1/2 cups water
3 tablespoons chopped cilantro, or more if desired

STEP 1: Melt the butter in a medium saucepan over medium heat.

STEP 2: Add the rice and the juice from half the lime. Stir briskly until the juice has evaporated and the rice begins to smell a little nutty, about 1 to 2 minutes.

STEP 3: Add the water and bring to a boil.

STEP 4: Reduce the heat to low. Cook, covered until air tunnels form in the rice and the liquid is completely absorbed, about 1 hour.

STEP 5: Add juice from the other half of the lime and more water if needed. Stir and fluff the rice.

STEP 6: Add cilantro as desired and serve.

This recipe can be multiplied.

VARIATIONS:
- Change the citrus and the herb: substitute lemon juice for lime; and basil for cilantro.
- Substitute parsley for cilantro for a milder dish.

GOES WELL WITH:
- Chilis, stews, curries
- In burritos, or alongside Latin dishes
- Grilled meats and fish

Per serving: Calories 200, Calories from Fat 35, Total Fat 4g (6% DV), Saturated Fat 2g (10% DV), Trans Fat 0g, Cholesterol 10mg (3% DV), Sodium 30mg (1% DV), Carbohydrates 37g (12% DV), Dietary Fiber 2g (8% DV), Sugars 0g, **Added Sugars:** 0g, Protein 4g, Vitamin A 4%, Vitamin C 4%, Calcium 2%, Iron 4%.

GREEN PASTA

= Makes: 4 cups = Active time: 20 minutes
= Serving size: 1 cup = Total time: 45 minutes

The spinach makes this more mild than traditional Basil Pesto sauce (p. 185). Kids really enjoy this, and so do adults. Use the sauce for cheese tortellini or ravioli. Make the sauce and pasta ahead of time; it will last up to three days. Then just heat and toss on a busy weeknight.

Ingredients
1/2 pound whole-grain angel hair pasta or spaghetti
1 cup packed fresh spinach, chopped
1 cup basil leaves, packed
3 cloves garlic, minced

1 tablespoon olive oil
1/2 cup low-fat milk
Salt and pepper, to taste
1/2 cup mozzarella cheese, shredded

STEP 1: Cook the pasta according to package directions. In a blender, or food processor if you have one, blend the spinach and basil until mixed.

STEP 2: In a large saucepan, sauté the garlic in olive oil. Add the milk and spinach mixture to the saucepan. Bring to a boil and reduce heat to simmer. Stir occasionally until the sauce thickens slightly. Remove from heat. Add the pasta; season with salt and pepper. Sprinkle with the cheese. Serve immediately.

VARIATIONS:
- Replace pasta with any grain.
- Add grilled chicken or shrimp.
- Make it a great cold pasta salad. Use penne or fusilli, and just add olives and chopped tomatoes.

GOES WELL WITH:
- Roasted chicken
- Flat iron steak or tri-tip

- Roasted vegetables
- Sliced melons

Per serving: Calories 200, Calories from Fat 80, Total Fat 9g (14% DV), Saturated Fat 3.5g (18% DV), Trans Fat 0g, Cholesterol 20mg (7% DV), Sodium 370mg (15% DV), Carbohydrates 20g (7% DV), Dietary Fiber 4g (16% DV), Sugars 3g, **Added Sugars:** 0g, Protein 13g, Vitamin A 90%, Vitamin C 25%, Calcium 35%, Iron 10%.

PASTA WITH CRUSHED TOMATOES, BEEF, AND SPINACH

= Makes: 2 quarts sauce (use 1 quart sauce per 1 pound pasta)
= Serves: 8

= Serving size: 1 cup sauce, 2 ounces pasta

= Active time: 20 minutes
= Total time: 30 minutes

Pasta is the hook for kids. That can be a problem if that's all they eat. But this sauce extends the pasta. You're getting the fiber into the sauce. And the meat makes it worthwhile. If you put the vegetables on the

379

side, the kids would eat the pasta and leave the vegetables. But by mixing the veggies into the sauce, kids won't turn this down.

This recipe makes a large batch, enough for a family gathering. If you're not serving a crowd, freeze half the sauce to use later, and use only 1 pound pasta, 1 pound spinach, and 1/2 cup Parmesan cheese.

Ingredients
3 teaspoons salt
1/4 cup canola oil
1 cup peeled and chopped yellow onion
1/4 cup peeled and chopped garlic
2 pounds ground meat
1/4 cup Italian seasoning
1/2 teaspoon crushed red pepper flakes
8 cups Marinara Sauce (p. 149) or two 28-ounce cans crushed tomatoes
2 pounds pasta, any kind
2 pounds fresh or frozen spinach, Swiss chard, or kale
1 cup grated Parmesan cheese

STEP 1: Fill the stockpot two-thirds full with water. Add 1 teaspoon salt to the water, cover, and place over high heat until it boils.

STEP 2: Pour the oil into a second stockpot. Add the onions and cook gently over medium heat for 5 minutes. Add the garlic and cook for 2 more minutes.

STEP 3: Add the meat to the onions and garlic. Cook until the meat loses its pink color, about 5 minutes. Add the Italian seasoning and crushed red pepper flakes and stir together with the meat. Add the Marinara Sauce. Simmer uncovered on medium heat for 20 minutes.

STEP 4: Add the pasta to the boiling water in the first stockpot. Cook until tender, 8 to 10 minutes. Add the spinach to the pasta water 30 seconds before the noodles are done. Drain the pasta and spinach. Spray a large serving dish with cooking spray. Pour the pasta and spinach back into the pot. Pour the sauce over the pasta and mix. Transfer to a serving dish and top with the cheese. Serve.

This sauce can be frozen. Divide among four separate containers, add 1/2 pound cooked pasta, and a small bag of spinach and you've got a quick meal.

VARIATIONS:
- Use fresh or frozen kale or chard.
- Add 2 cups white or red beans to sauce.
- Add 2 pounds of cooked ground beef, turkey, or Homemade "Sausage" (p. 231).
- Add roasted zucchini and bell pepper.
- Add fresh basil just before serving.

GOES WELL WITH:
- Green salad
- Sliced fresh fruit

Per serving: Calories 420, Calories from Fat 110, Total Fat 12g (18% DV), Saturated Fat 4g (20% DV), Trans Fat 0g, Cholesterol 40mg (13% DV), Sodium 810mg (34% DV), Carbohydrates 57g (19% DV), Dietary Fiber 5g (20% DV), Sugars < 1g, **Added Sugars:** 0g, Protein 26g, Vitamin A 130%, Vitamin C 50%, Calcium 20%, Iron 40%.

RICOTTA GNOCCHI

= Serves: 4   = Active time:
                       20 minutes
= Serving size: = Total time:
  1/2 cup   30 minutes

Gnocchi are often made with potatoes, and that can be difficult. It takes a long time to make the potato mixture. And while they are little pillows of heaven, they do have a high glycemic index and generate a mega-insulin response. These gnocchi, because they are made with whole-grain flour and cheese, might be an imitation of the more traditional version, but no one will know, or care. They're way healthier.

Be quick and gentle with these. They're amazing.

Ingredients
1 cup ricotta cheese
1 large egg
1/4 cup finely grated Parmesan cheese
1/2 cup semolina flour, plus extra for rolling
  dough
1/2 cup unbleached all-purpose flour
1 teaspoon salt

STEP 1: Combine the ricotta cheese and

egg in a large bowl and mix thoroughly. Add the Parmesan cheese. Mix.

STEP 2: Add the flours to the cheese mixture. Continue to mix with a fork until the dough comes together. It will be soft and moist. Don't overmix.

STEP 3: Turn the dough out onto a lightly floured, flat surface. Work with your hands to form a smooth ball.

STEP 4: Divide the dough into 4 pieces, as if you were slicing a loaf of bread. Roll each slice into a long rope, about 1 inch in diameter. Spreading your fingers, roll from the center out to the edge of the rope.

STEP 5: Position 2 of the ropes parallel to each other. Cut 2 ropes at a time, at 1-inch intervals. Roll each piece off the back of a fork to make imprints that will help hold the sauce.

STEP 6: Transfer gnocchi pieces to a lightly floured, or nonstick, baking sheet so they don't stick together. Place in the freezer while you make the rest of the batch. If you plan to save any gnocchi for future use, allow them to freeze entirely on the baking sheet before storing in a plastic bag. This will keep the frozen gnocchi from sticking together.

STEP 7: Fill a large stockpot with water and add salt.

STEP 8: Add the gnocchi to the boiling water. Gently stir with a wooden spoon, to prevent gnocchi from sticking to each other, or to the bottom of the pot. When gnocchi begin to rise to the top, this signals that they are done. Scoop them out with a fine mesh strainer or a bamboo wire skimmer. Don't drain in a colander, because they'll stick together. Transfer to a serving dish. Add sauce of your choice to each layer of gnocchi, so that you don't have to stir them and risk damaging the delicate pasta. Top with extra Parmesan and serve.

This recipe can be multiplied. It will keep in the refrigerator and freezes well, uncooked, for up to three months.

VARIATIONS:
- Add 2 tablespoons minced sun-dried tomatoes or minced fresh parsley into dough.
- The next day, use fresh spinach in

the bottom of a baking pan. Top with leftover gnocchi, and cover with crushed tomatoes, beef, and spinach (see p. 379).

GOES WELL WITH:
- Marinara Sauce (p. 149)
- Basil Pesto (p. 185) and a little bit of cream
- Cauliflower Béchamel Sauce (p. 158)
- Green salad with Balsamic Vinaigrette Dressing (p. 143)
- Sliced melons

Per serving: Calories 280, Calories from Fat 100, Total Fat 11g (17% DV), Saturated Fat 7g (35% DV), Trans Fat 0g, Cholesterol 85mg (28% DV), Sodium 170mg (7% DV), Carbohydrates 29g (10% DV), Dietary Fiber < 1g (4% DV), Sugars 0g, **Added Sugars:** 0g, Protein 15g, Vitamin A 8%, Vitamin C 0%, Calcium 20%, Iron 10%.

MULTI-GRAIN FLATBREAD PIZZA

= Makes:
two small pizzas
= Serves: 6

= Active time:
15 minutes
= Total time:
1 hour
45 minutes

= Serving size:
1/3 of pizza

The fiber in this crust (cornmeal, rolled oats) makes this pizza much more filling. That means you'll eat fewer slices. It's a crunchier and more substantial alternative to traditional crust, which has little fiber and lots of sugar. The whole grains in this recipe add the fiber that conventional pizza crust lacks, making a healthy version of what's so often labeled "junk food."

There's no sugar in the pizza sauce, which is definitely not true of frozen pizza or pizza from a chain like Domino's. Add lots of whole milk mozzarella cheese.

Make the Crust:
1 teaspoon yeast
1/2 cup warm water
1 cup coarse-ground cornmeal (polenta)
3/4 cup boiling water
2 cups mixed grains (2/3 cup semolina, 2/3

cup wheat flour, 2/3 cup rolled oats)
1 pinch (1/8 teaspoon) of salt
Semolina flour for rolling the dough
2 tablespoons olive oil

STEP 1: Sprinkle the yeast over the warm water in a small bowl. Let it sit for 5 minutes until the yeast dissolves, and begins to bubble.

STEP 2: In another small bowl, combine the cornmeal with the boiling water.

STEP 3: In a large mixing bowl, add half of the mixed grains and a good pinch of salt. Make a well in the center of the mixed grains, then add the dissolved yeast and water mixture. Gradually stir the mixed grains into the liquid using a wooden spoon. Then gradually add the cornmeal mixture, and all but 1/2 cup of the mixed grains until the dough comes together. Continue to mix until the dough is "raggedy."

STEP 4: Place 1/2 cup flour on a large cutting board and transfer the dough onto the flour. Oil your hands and knead the dough for about 4 minutes. The dough should be a little wet.

STEP 5: Rinse the mixing bowl and dry with a towel. Rub lightly with 1 tablespoon olive oil. Place the kneaded dough in the bowl and cover with a damp towel. Set aside until the dough has doubled in size, about 1 hour.

STEP 6: The dough makes enough for two small pizzas or two long flatbreads on cookie sheets. Using an oiled rolling pin or your hands, roll the dough onto an oiled cookie sheet or pan. This will be a slightly wet dough.

Make the Pizza Sauce:
2 pounds (about 10 to 12) Roma tomatoes
1 tablespoon olive oil
1 pinch (1/8 teaspoon) of salt

STEP 1: Wash tomatoes, core and cut in half. Cut in half again and then into thirds. Toss the tomatoes with the oil and pinch of salt.

STEP 2: Either roast in the oven at 425°F for 20 minutes or sauté in a pan on high heat for 10 minutes. The tomatoes should be browned and soft.

STEP 3: Cool and spread the tomatoes over the pizza crust.

The sauce can be made a day or two ahead of time and stored in an airtight container in the refrigerator.

Make the Topping:
2 medium bell peppers
2 medium zucchinis
2 tablespoons olive oil
1 recipe pizza sauce (see above) or Basil Pesto (p. 185)
1 pound grated mozzarella or 8 ounces grated mozzarella and 8 ounces ricotta

STEP 1: Preheat the oven to 425°F.

STEP 2: Cut the ends from the bell peppers and remove the seeds. Cut the peppers in half and julienne (thinly slice).

STEP 3: Cut the zucchini in half lengthwise and then into thin half circles.

STEP 4: Sauté the red bell peppers in 1 tablespoon olive oil over high heat until lightly browned. Remove from the pan into a small bowl.

STEP 5: Add 1 tablespoon olive oil to the pan, then add the zucchini and sauté over high heat until lightly browned.

STEP 6: Divide the sauce evenly between two pizza crusts.

STEP 7: Divide the vegetables (combo or separate) between both pizzas.

STEP 8: Sprinkle the cheese on top of the vegetables. Bake for 25 to 30 minutes, on the bottom rack. Check the crust by lifting up with a spatula. It should be brown, not soggy, on the bottom.

This recipe can be multiplied.

VARIATIONS:
- Vary the toppings: mushrooms, fresh spinach, eggplant, Homemade "Sausage" (p. 231), grilled chicken, fresh corn.
- Add fresh basil leaves and/or chopped garlic to the topping.
- For "white pizza" use Cauliflower Béchamel Sauce (p. 158) and mozzarella.
- Vary the sauces: fresh pesto or salsa (goes great with the chicken, corn,

and spinach).
- Use the sauce on pasta, fish, or chicken.

GOES WELL WITH:
- Green salad

Per serving: Calories 590, Calories from Fat 240, Total Fat 27g (42% DV), Saturated Fat 10g (50% DV), Trans Fat 0g, Cholesterol 40mg (13% DV), Sodium 80mg (3% DV), Carbohydrates 58g (19% DV), Dietary Fiber 8g (32% DV), Sugars 7g, **Added Sugars:** 0g, Protein 31g, Vitamin A 35%, Vitamin C 100%, Calcium 60%, Iron 15%.

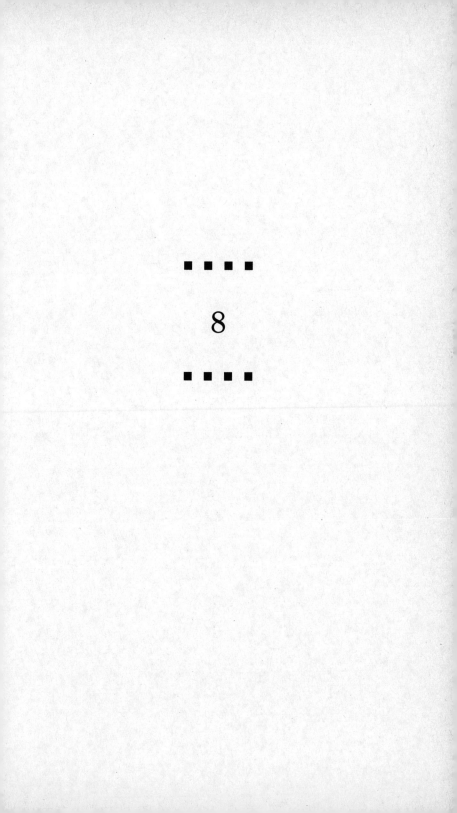

8

CHAPTER 8
MEAT, POULTRY, AND FISH

In this chapter, you'll find lovely main courses. Most are quick enough to serve on a busy weeknight. Many are good enough to be the centerpiece for a holiday meal, a brunch, or a dinner party.

Remember: Meat and fat are not bad for you. Just consume them in reasonable portions. The serving sizes here are a good guideline.

Make sure to cook meat, poultry, and fish until it reaches the minimum safe temperature. Generally cook poultry to 165°F, fish to 145°F, beef to 145°F for medium-rare or 170°F for well done, and pork to 165 °F. Check http://www.foodsafety.gov/keep/charts/mintemp.html for a complete list.

Also remember to let meat, poultry, and fish "rest" for 5 to 15 minutes before serving (less time for fish). This allows the temperature and the juices to equalize throughout.

Recipes:

Pork Loin with Apples and Onions
Quick Enchiladas
Slow Oven-Smoked Brisket
Seared and Roasted Leg of Lamb
Caprese-Style Polenta and Steak
Chili Colorado
Italian-Style Meatballs, Patties, or Meat Loaf
Chicken Braised with Onions and Tomatoes Five Ways
Roasted Chicken: Whole or Pieces
Quinoa Turkey Casserole
Roast Turkey
Simple Turkey Meatballs
Quick Chicken Tikka Masala
Salmon Milanese
No-Guilt Fish Tenders
Old-Fashioned Beef Stew and Vegetables

PORK LOIN WITH APPLES AND ONIONS

= Serves: 6 = Active time: 15 minutes

= Serving size: 4 ounces = Total time: 1 hour

Pork and fruit just go together. This dish is amazingly simple but good enough to serve to company. Pork is "the other white meat" low in fat, high in protein. Pork does have a fairly hefty dose of omega-6s, as does chicken, so make sure you also get some omega-3s in your diet somewhere (either from salmon or sardines or flaxseed or walnuts); so make a salad with the leftovers! The sweetness of this dish comes from the apples, not from added, refined sugar.

Ingredients

1 boneless pork loin, 1 1/2 pounds
1/4 cup olive oil or safflower oil
1 tablespoon chopped fresh sage, or 1 teaspoon dried sage
1 tablespoon fresh rosemary, or 1 teaspoon dried rosemary
1 tablespoon salt
2 tablespoons cracked black pepper
1 pound yellow onions, peeled and sliced
1 pound Granny Smith apples or other tart apples, cored and sliced

STEP 1: Preheat the oven to 375°F.

STEP 2: Toss the pork loin with 2 tablespoons of the olive oil. Mix the sage, rosemary, salt, and pepper in a shallow dish, then roll the pork in the herb mix.

STEP 3: Heat a sauté pan over medium-high heat. Sear the meat on all sides until browned, about 2 minutes per side. Transfer the pork loin to a plate.

STEP 4: Add the remaining 2 tablespoons of olive oil to the sauté pan. Add the onions and apples and cook until lightly browned, 5 minutes.

STEP 5: Line a large rectangular roasting pan with parchment paper. Spread the sautéed onions and apples over the bottom of the pan. Top with the pork and put the pan in the oven. Roast the pork until the internal temperature measured on an instant-read meat thermometer is 165°F, about 40 minutes. When the onions and apples begin to caramelize and everything's all brown and toasty, remove the pan from the oven.

STEP 6: Transfer the pork to a cutting board and cover it with aluminum foil to keep warm. Let the meat rest for 10 minutes. This allows the temperature and the juices to equalize throughout the roast, so that it's juicier, easier to slice, and easier to chew. Slice the pork into 1/4-inch thick pieces.

STEP 7: When you're ready to serve, spread the caramelized onions and apples over the bottom of a platter. Take sliced pork pieces and fan them out on top. Pour any accumulated juices from the pan over everything.

VARIATIONS:
- Add a couple of cups of sliced or chopped fennel to the onions and apples.
- Add 1 cup diced or shredded celery root.
- Add 1 cup sliced beets.
- Use another fruit: 1 pound of peaches or plums would work nicely.
- Add a bit of balsamic vinegar to give the dish more complex flavoring.

GOES WELL WITH:
- Quinoa
- Brown rice
- Potatoes or sweet potatoes, mashed, broiled, or baked
- Roasted cauliflower

Per serving: Calories 350, Calories from Fat 150, Total Fat 17g (26% DV), Saturated Fat 4g (20% DV), Trans Fat 0g, Cholesterol 90mg (30% DV), So-

dium 1240mg (52% DV), Carbohydrates 19g (6% DV), Dietary Fiber 4g (16% DV), Sugars 11g, **Added Sugars:** 0g, Protein 32g, Vitamin A 2%, Vitamin C 15%, Calcium 6%, Iron 10%.

QUICK ENCHILADAS

= Serves: 4   = Active time: 20 minutes

= Serving size: 2 enchiladas   = Total time: 40 minutes

Enchiladas are a quick, easy dinner and really tasty when you make your own sauce. You don't have to give up the taste of Mexican food to eat healthy. People think that eating Mexican food means chips and salsa, rice, beans, and the tortilla. But there is so much more than that! This is a balanced Mexican meal.

Ingredients
1/2 cup peeled and finely chopped yellow onion
1 tablespoon oil, olive or safflower
1 pound ground meat or chopped chicken
1/2 teaspoon salt
1 pound chopped zucchini
8 corn tortillas (6 inches each)
2 cups Enchilada Sauce (p. 147)

1 cup grated cheddar cheese, Monterey
  Jack, or a mixture
Non-aerosol cooking spray

STEP 1: Preheat the oven to 400°F.

STEP 2: Sauté the onion in a large skillet
with the olive oil over medium-high heat.
Once the onion has started to soften, add
the ground meat and salt. Continue to cook,
breaking up the meat, until the meat loses
its pink color. Add the zucchini and cook
until tender, about 5 minutes.

STEP 3: To soften the corn tortillas and
make them easier to roll, heat them in a
microwave for 30 seconds, or warm them
individually in a nonstick skillet for about
30 seconds per side. Spray or grease an
8-by-10-inch baking dish. Spread 1 cup of
Enchilada Sauce on the bottom of the baking dish. One by one, dip each tortilla into
the Enchilada Sauce, moistening both sides.
Fill each with 1/2 cup of the meat-and-
vegetable mixture, roll the tortilla up, and
place it seamside down in the baking dish.

STEP 4: Pour the remaining Enchilada
Sauce over the rolled tortillas. Sprinkle with
the grated cheese.

STEP 5: Bake the enchiladas for 15 to 20 minutes. Remove them when the cheese has melted and the sauce is bubbling.

VARIATIONS:

- Add more spices to the meat mixture. One teaspoon each of any of the following would work well: minced garlic, oregano, cumin, coriander, or chili powder.
- Add vegetables to the meat mixture. Add 1/2 cup of any of the following: chopped olives, chopped sweet peppers, spinach, mushrooms, or chopped scallions. Or add all of them.
- Punch up the spiciness: Take a few peppers from a can of chipotle peppers in adobo, about 1 tablespoon, chop them, and add them to the meat mixture. Or remove the seeds and ribs from a few small jalapeño peppers and add about 1 tablespoon chopped jalapeños to the meat mixture.
- Top each serving with some or all of the following: 1 tablespoon of whole milk yogurt, sour cream and some chopped cilantro, a little crumbly queso fresco (ricotta salata cheese

would also work if the Mexican cheese is not available), sliced avocado, or chopped fresh tomatoes.
- In place of corn tortillas, layer everything with polenta squares.

GOES WELL WITH:
- Green salad
- Fresh fruit

Per serving: Calories 570, Calories from Fat 280, Total Fat 31g (48% DV), Saturated Fat 9g (45% DV), Trans Fat 0g, Cholesterol 105mg (35% DV), Sodium 790mg (33% DV), Carbohydrates 38g (13% DV), Dietary Fiber 6g (24% DV), Sugars 6g, **Added Sugars:** 0g, Protein 37g, Vitamin A 40%, Vitamin C 35%, Calcium 35%, Iron 25%.

SLOW OVEN-SMOKED BRISKET

= Serves: 8

= Active time: 15 minutes

= Serving size: 4 ounces

= Total time: 7 to 8 hours

Tough cuts of meat slow cooked with a great rub are fantastic; this meat can go with so many dishes. Brisket comes from the lower chest of beef or veal. It used to be marketed as a thrifty cut of meat. Because cattle do not have collar bones, these muscles must support 60 percent of the animal's weight. That means brisket has a lot of connective tissue to it. It must be cooked slowly for a long time to become tender. But prepared properly, brisket can be sublime. When I was growing up in Brooklyn, brisket was a holiday treat. This recipe is a best seller at Cindy's restaurant. Use the leftovers in soups, burritos, and casseroles.

Ingredients
1/2 cup Barbecue Rub (p. 171)
3-pound brisket (make sure it still has both the fat cap and the lean meat)

STEP 1: Place a rack in the middle of the oven and preheat the oven to 250°F.

STEP 2: Line a large baking sheet with parchment paper or foil to catch the fat drippings. Place a roasting rack in the center of the sheet. Massage the rub all over the brisket. For double protection against hard-to-clean drips, line another rimmed baking sheet with aluminum foil and place it on the bottom rack of the oven to catch drippings. Place the brisket on the rack on the baking sheet and bake it on the middle rack of the oven for 7 to 8 hours. When a fork can poke the roast as easily as a potato, the brisket is done. If it's not soft all the way through, it's not done. It should look very dark on the outside but it will be yummy and tender on the inside.

STEP 3: Remove the brisket from the oven and let it cool for 15 minutes, to let the temperature and juices equalize. Cut off and discard the fat. Slice and serve.

Brisket freezes well. Slice the meat and wrap it in airtight packages. Make sure to label and date them. Frozen brisket keeps for one month. Thaw by transferring to the refrigerator overnight. Or you can defrost it in the microwave.

VARIATIONS:
- Pork shoulder can be cooked the same way; bake it for 5 hours. Cooking time will vary depending on size of cut. Use the fork test.
- A whole chicken prepared this way will be done in 2 1/2 hours. Cooking time will vary depending on the size of the chicken. The internal temperature should be 155° to 165°F.

- Whole salmon covered with Barbecue Sauce (p. 152) bakes for 2 hours. Cooking time will vary depending on the size of the fish. The internal temperature should be 145°F, and the flesh should flake easily.

GOES WELL WITH:
- Nana's Italian Vegetable Stew (p. 465)
- Whole-Grain Vegetable Pilaf (p. 371)
- Roasted beets and kale
- Applesauce (p. 226)
- Coleslaw
- Sliced melon

Per serving: Calories 310, Calories from Fat 210, Total Fat 23g (35% DV), Saturated Fat 9g (45% DV), Trans Fat 0g, Cholesterol 95mg (32% DV), Sodium 970mg (40% DV), Carbohydrates 5g (2% DV), Dietary Fiber 2g (8% DV), Sugars 1g, **Added Sugars:** 0g, Protein 19g, Vitamin A 20%, Vitamin C 4%, Calcium 4%, Iron 15%.

SEARED AND ROASTED LEG OF LAMB

= Serves: 8   = Active time:
                  20 minutes
= Serving size: = Total time:
  4 ounces   1 hour

This is such an easy and tasty way to do leg of lamb. Cindy's students went wild over it. Ask the butcher at your meat counter to butterfly the lamb for you. Butchers will also cut chickens and grind meats at no extra charge if asked.

Ingredients

1 cup finely chopped fresh flat-leaf parsley
1/4 cup packed fresh mint leaves, chopped,
   or 1 1/3 tablespoons dried mint
1/4 cup packed fresh basil leaves, chopped,
   or 1 1/3 tablespoons dried
1 tablespoon chopped fresh rosemary
3 tablespoons peeled and minced garlic
1 teaspoon crushed red pepper flakes
1/4 cup olive oil
1 tablespoon balsamic vinegar
1 teaspoon sea salt or kosher salt
1 butterflied leg of lamb, about 5 pounds
Non-aerosol cooking spray

STEP 1: Preheat the oven to 350°F.

STEP 2: Place the parsley, mint, basil, rosemary, garlic, and red pepper flakes in a blender or food processor and blend them until they make a paste. Scrape the herb paste into a bowl. Stir in the olive oil, balsamic vinegar, and salt. Set aside 2 tablespoons of the marinade to serve with the lamb.

STEP 3: Place the lamb in a large plastic bag with the marinade and shake to coat. Let the lamb marinate in the refrigerator for 2 hours, or overnight.

STEP 4: Remove the lamb from the bag. Discard the bag and marinade. Spray a large skillet with non-aerosol cooking spray. Heat the pan to medium-high. Sear the lamb on all sides until brown, 6 to 8 minutes per side. Line a roasting pan with parchment paper or foil; this eases clean-up. Place the lamb on a roasting rack in the pan. Roast the lamb in a preheated oven until the internal heat registers 140°F on an instant-read meat thermometer, 25 to 35 minutes.

STEP 5: Take the lamb from the oven and allow it to rest for 10 to 15 minutes before slicing. Top with any accumulated juices. Serve with the reserved marinade.

VARIATION:
- Use a cracked pepper rub or the Barbecue Rub (p. 171) in place of the marinade.

GOES WELL WITH:
- Roasted Root Vegetables (p. 456)
- Applesauce (p. 226)
- Tossed salad with Italian Vinaigrette Dressing (p. 139)

Per serving: Calories 240, Calories from Fat 160, Total Fat 18g (28% DV), Saturated Fat 7g (35% DV), Trans Fat 0g, Cholesterol 70mg (23% DV), Sodium 330mg (14% DV), Carbohydrates < 1g (0% DV), Dietary Fiber 0g (0% DV), Sugars 0g, **Added Sugars:** 0g, Protein 19g, Vitamin A 6%, Vitamin C 8%, Calcium 2%, Iron 10%.

CAPRESE-STYLE POLENTA AND STEAK

= Serves: 4   = Active time: 20 minutes

= Serving size: 1/4 recipe   = Total time: 1 hour

When you make polenta, always double the recipe because it freezes well. Just pour the extra polenta onto a sheet pan with a rim, making sure the polenta is at least 1 inch thick. Cool the polenta in the refrigerator until firm, then cut it into 3-inch squares. Make sure they are tightly wrapped individually. Don't forget to label and date. Polenta squares can be kept frozen for up to one month.

Ingredients

Four 3-inch polenta squares (see p. 245)
1 tablespoon olive oil
1/2 cup Basil Pesto (p. 185)
1 pound flat iron, New York, or tri-tip steak, cut into 4 portions
4 Roma tomatoes, sliced
4 ounces fresh mozzarella cheese, sliced
Fresh basil leaves (optional)

STEP 1: Grill or heat the polenta squares. Meanwhile, brush 2 tablespoons of the pesto on the steaks.

STEP 2: Heat the oil in a large heavy skillet over medium heat. Add the steaks and cook on each side to desired doneness, 7 to 10 minutes: 145°F for rare, 170°F for well done, turning once. Let rest for 5 minutes to let temperature and juices equalize.

STEP 3: Place a square of polenta on each of 4 plates. Top with the tomatoes, cheese, and then the sliced beef. Drizzle the remaining 6 tablespoons of pesto over the meat and tomatoes. Sprinkle chopped fresh basil leaves on top, if using.

VARIATIONS:
- In place of polenta, use 8 ounces cooked rigatoni.
- In place of polenta, use any leftover whole grain, like barley, brown rice, or quinoa.
- Make an open-faced sandwich on Whole-Wheat Sponge Bread (p. 188), sliced and toasted.
- Use Roma Tomato Basil Salsa (p. 172) in place of the tomatoes and pesto.

GOES WELL WITH:
- Sliced fresh melon
- A mixed field greens salad with Italian dressing

Per serving: Calories 460, Calories from Fat 250, Total Fat 28g (43% DV), Saturated Fat 6g (30% DV), Trans Fat 0g, Cholesterol 40mg (13% DV), Sodium 340mg (14% DV), Carbohydrates 32g (11% DV), Dietary Fiber 3g (12%

DV), Sugars 9g, **Added Sugars:** 0g,
Protein 20g, Vitamin A 30%, Vitamin C
15%, Calcium 25%, Iron 15%.

CHILI COLORADO

= Serves: 6

= Serving size:
2 cups for a main dish,
1 cup for a starter

= Active time:
20 minutes

= Total time:
3 hours

Ingredients

For the Sauce:
8 ounces dried Guajillo chilies, or any other
Mexican chili such as chipotle or ancho
pasilla (They come in 1-pound bags; use
half a bag.)
3 cups water

For the Stew:
1/2 cup of olive oil or safflower oil
2 cups peeled and chopped yellow onion
4 cloves of garlic, peeled and chopped
1 1/2 pounds beef stew meat, cut into 1/2-
inch pieces
1 cup unbleached all-purpose flour
3 cups liquid, water or stock
1 tablespoon cracked black pepper

1 tablespoon salt
2 cups 1-inch pieces scrubbed potatoes
2 cups 1-inch pieces scrubbed carrots

STEP 1: Prepare the chilies. Place the chilies in a medium-size pot, add the water, and boil until very soft, 30 minutes. Place the chilies in a blender with 1 cup of their cooking liquid and puree until smooth. Add liquid as necessary to form 3 cups smooth sauce. Pass the sauce through a fine mesh strainer to remove any seeds and tough skin. Set aside.

STEP 2: Heat 1/4 cup oil in a cast-iron or stainless steel pot. (Make sure it has a tight fitting lid.) Sauté the onions until brown and tender, about 5 minutes. Add the garlic and sauté for 2 more minutes. Remove the onions and garlic from the pot with a slotted spoon and reserve in a small bowl.

STEP 3: In a large bowl, dredge the meat in the flour. Shake off excess flour. Add the remaining oil to the pot and cook the meat in two batches over medium-high heat, quickly browning. Remove the meat, and reserve on a plate.

STEP 4: Deglaze the pot. Add the water

and chili sauce to the pot. Bring to a boil while scraping up the brown bits from the bottom of the pot.

STEP 5: Reduce the heat to low. Return the meat and the aromatics to the liquid in the pot. Slowly cook the stew over low heat, covered, so that the liquid barely simmers. Simmer for 2 hours.

STEP 6: After the meat has had a chance to cook for a while, add the potatoes and carrots. Cook until the meat is fork tender, about 1 hour. Add salt and pepper to taste.

VARIATIONS:
- Use chicken thighs.
- Use pork shoulder.
- Add kale or chard, shredded, at the very end.

GOES WELL WITH:
- Steamed brown rice or barley
- Sautéed mushrooms
- Green salad and sliced apples with lemon juice

Per serving: Calories 590, Calories from Fat 370, Total Fat 41g (63% DV), Saturated Fat 12g (60% DV), Trans Fat

0g, Cholesterol 80mg (27% DV), Sodium 1270mg (53% DV), Carbohydrates 31g (10% DV), Dietary Fiber 3g (12% DV), Sugars 4g, **Added Sugars:** 0g, Protein 23g, Vitamin A 70%, Vitamin C 15%, Calcium 4%, Iron 20%.

ITALIAN-STYLE MEATBALLS, PATTIES, OR MEAT LOAF

= Serves: 5   = Active time: 10 minutes

= Serving size: 1/5 of recipe   = Total time: 30 minutes

Most meatball recipes call for bread crumbs, or bread pieces soaked in milk, or crushed crackers. They're just as good if you use a whole grain like uncooked rolled oats, cooked brown rice, or cooked quinoa, and the whole grains make the resulting dish more healthy.

Ingredients
1 pound ground beef or ground turkey
1/2 cup ricotta cheese
1/4 cup Parmesan cheese
1/4 cup Marinara Sauce (p. 149)
1 egg
2 ounces uncooked rolled oats or uncooked bulgar wheat, or cooked brown rice or

cooked quinoa

1 cup chopped spinach, frozen or fresh

1/2 cup shredded zucchini

1 teaspoon salt

1 teaspoon ground black pepper

1 teaspoon garlic powder

1 pinch (1/8 teaspoon) of cayenne or crushed red pepper flakes (optional)

STEP 1: Measure all the ingredients into a large bowl. Mix well. I find that clean hands work best.

STEP 2: Form the meat mixture into your desired shape: meatballs, patties, or a loaf.

STEP 3: If making patties or meatballs, brown in a frying pan with 1 to 2 tablespoons oil and add to your Marinara Sauce. If making a loaf, place in an oiled 9-by-5 inch loaf pan, or form into a loaf shape and place on a foil-lined baking sheet, and bake at 350°F for 45 minutes to 1 hour.

VARIATIONS:

- Add 2 tablespoons toasted pine nuts, chopped.
- Use 1 teaspoon roasted or sautéed garlic instead of powder.
- Add 2 tablespoons of chopped fresh

parsley, or chopped fresh basil.
- If making meat loaf, top with several thin strips of bacon.

GOES WELL WITH:
- Spaghetti
- Polenta
- Whole grains
- Tossed green salad

Per serving: Calories 340, Calories from Fat 180, Total Fat 21g (32% DV), Saturated Fat 8g (40% DV), Trans Fat 0.5g, Cholesterol 115mg (38% DV), Sodium 670mg (28% DV), Carbohydrates 12g (4% DV), Dietary Fiber 2g (8% DV), Sugars < 1g, **Added Sugars:** 0g, Protein 26g, Vitamin A 40%, Vitamin C 6%, Calcium 15%, Iron 20%.

CHICKEN BRAISED WITH ONIONS AND TOMATOES FIVE WAYS

= Serves: 6	= Active time: 15 minutes
= Serving size: 1 1/2 cups	= Total time: 35 minutes

This is five dishes in one. Let your imagination run wild.

Ingredients

1 pound chicken breast

1 teaspoon salt

4 tablespoons of the rub of your choice (see recipes below)

2 tablespoons olive oil

1 cup peeled and chopped yellow onion

1 can (15 ounces) crushed tomatoes

1/2 cup water

STEP 1: Cut chicken breast meat into 1-inch pieces. Toss with the salt and rub and set aside.

STEP 2: Heat the olive oil in a large pot or pan over medium-high heat. Add the onion and sauté until translucent. Add the chicken pieces and sear.

STEP 3: Add the crushed tomatoes and water. Bring to a boil. Reduce heat to low and simmer, uncovered, for 20 minutes.

STEP 4: Taste and adjust seasonings.

Can be frozen for up to three months. Label and date!

Per serving: Calories 230, Calories from Fat 90, Total Fat 10g (15% DV),

Saturated Fat 1.5g (8% DV), Trans Fat 0g, Cholesterol 75mg (25% DV), Sodium 860mg (36% DV), Carbohydrates 10g (3% DV), Dietary Fiber 2g (8% DV), Sugars 1g, **Added Sugars:** 0g, Protein 26g, Vitamin A 15%, Vitamin C 20%, Calcium 4%, Iron 10%.

There are endless variations on the basic recipe above. As Cindy likes to say, you can travel around the world just by changing the seasonings. Here are four variations to get your imagination going.

Italian-Style Chicken Cacciatore

Add:
1 1/2 cups chopped bell peppers
1 cup chopped zucchini
1 cup chopped mushrooms
2 to 4 tablespoons Italian seasoning

Toss chicken in Italian seasoning before cooking.

Add the additional vegetables after the onions are browned.

VARIATIONS:
- Add greens such as spinach or kale when you add the mushrooms.

419

- Add a handful of olives.
- Add a tablespoon of balsamic vinegar.
- Use more spices. Add garlic if you like. Add a tablespoon or two of other fresh European herbs such as rosemary and oregano. Use 1 teaspoon if herbs are dried.

Per serving: Calories 250, Calories from Fat 90, Total Fat 10g (15% DV), Saturated Fat 1.5g (8% DV), Trans Fat 0g, Cholesterol 75mg (25% DV), Sodium 870mg (36% DV), Carbohydrates 15g (5% DV), Dietary Fiber 4g (16% DV), Sugars 3g, **Added Sugars:** 0g, Protein 27g, Vitamin A 20%, Vitamin C 80%, Calcium 8%, Iron 15%.

Mexican Chicken with Peppers and Onions

Add:

2 cups sweet peppers, ribs and seeds removed, diced into 1/2-inch pieces

Rub:

1 tablespoon of chili powder
1 teaspoon ground cumin
1 teaspoon dried oregano, or 1 tablespoon

fresh oregano
1/4 teaspoon cayenne pepper

Toss chicken with rub. Add the peppers to the onions once browned.

VARIATIONS:
- Top with chopped fresh cilantro.
- Top with sliced fresh avocado.

Per serving: Calories 260, Calories from Fat 90, Total Fat 11g (17% DV), Saturated Fat 1.5g (8% DV), Trans Fat 0g, Cholesterol 75mg (25% DV), Sodium 900mg (38% DV), Carbohydrates 15g (5% DV), Dietary Fiber 5g (20% DV), Sugars 3g, **Added Sugars:** 0g, Protein 27g, Vitamin A 35%, Vitamin C 120%, Calcium 8%, Iron 15%.

Asian-Style Chicken with Peppers and Onions

Add:
1 cup diced celery
1 cup diced carrots
2 cups diced sweet peppers, any color

Rub:

2 tablespoons five-spice powder
Use 2 tablespoons peanut oil instead of
  olive oil

Add celery and carrots to onions and cook
until tender. Add peppers halfway through
cooking process.

VARIATIONS:
- Add a drizzle of sesame oil just
  before serving.
- Sprinkle with chopped cilantro just
  before serving.
- Add a bit of hot sauce, such as Sriracha or chili garlic.

Per serving: Calories 340, Calories
from Fat 110, Total Fat 12g (18% DV),
Saturated Fat 2.5g (12% DV), Trans Fat
0g, Cholesterol 95mg (32% DV), Sodium 1560mg (65% DV), Carbohydrates 21g (7% DV), Dietary Fiber 7g
(28% DV), Sugars 5g, **Added Sugars:**
0g, Protein 39g, Vitamin A 130%, Vitamin C 130%, Calcium 15%, Iron 25%.

Indian-Style Chicken Curry

Add:
1 cup diced carrots
1 cup 1-inch chopped potatoes
1 cup frozen peas

Rub:
1 tablespoon curry powder
1 teaspoon cumin
1 teaspoon garlic powder
Clarified butter or olive oil
1/4 cup Greek yogurt
1 tablespoon fresh or 1 teaspoon dried dill

Add carrots to onion and sauté until soft. Add potatoes. Proceed with recipe. Toss chicken with spice mixture. About 5 minutes before recipe is done, add peas. Top with Greek yogurt, and garnish with dill.

VARIATION:
- Add 1 teaspoon of garam masala (an Indian spice blend) to the sauce.

GOES WELL WITH:
- Brown rice
- Polenta
- Barley
- Quinoa

- Salad
- Fresh fruit

VARIATIONS:

- Add spinach or kale to any of the above recipes. Sheer brilliance! No one will notice the extra nutrients and fiber.
- Use boneless chicken thighs, often cheaper, in place of chicken breasts.

Per serving: Calories 370, Calories from Fat 110, Total Fat 13g (20% DV), Saturated Fat 2g (10% DV), Trans Fat 0g, Cholesterol 80mg (27% DV), Sodium 1000mg (42% DV), Carbohydrates 31g (10% DV), Dietary Fiber 7g (28% DV), Sugars 7g, **Added Sugars:** 0g, Protein 34g, Vitamin A 140%, Vitamin C 45%, Calcium 15%, Iron 25%.

ROASTED CHICKEN: WHOLE OR PIECES

= Serves: 5

= Serving size:
2 pieces (each breast
cut in half again

= Active time:
10 minutes

= Total time:
Whole: 1 hour
30 minutes

= Total time:
Pieces:
45 minutes

When I have a lot of time, I like to roast a whole chicken, carve off the meat, take the bones and the drippings, put it in a pot, cover it with water, and make chicken stock. But sometimes I'm in a hurry and I just want roasted chicken and roasting pieces is faster. This recipe works either way.

Ingredients
1 whole chicken or cut up into 10 pieces
2 tablespoons olive oil or rice bran oil
1 tablespoon salt
1 tablespoon cracked black pepper
1 tablespoon fresh sage, or 1 teaspoon dried sage
Non-aerosol cooking spray

STEP 1: Preheat the oven to 400°F.

STEP 2: Put the chicken into a big bowl. Rub oil all over the chicken.

STEP 3: Rub the chicken on both sides with salt, pepper, and sage. Spray cooking oil onto a pan or line a pan with parchment paper or foil.

Whole:

Bake whole chicken in a roasting pan for 1 hour 25 minutes or until juices run clear, and the internal temperature registers 165°F.

Pieces:

Bake chicken pieces on a sheet pan lined with foil or parchment paper for 35 to 40 minutes, or until juices run clear and temperature registers 165°F.

VARIATIONS:
- For spices, use Barbecue Rub (p. 171) or fresh rosemary, salt, and lemon zest.
- Rub chicken with Basil Pesto (p. 185).

GOES WELL WITH:
- Roasted potato wedges
- Brown rice pilaf
- Barley pesto
- Sweet potato oven fries

Per serving: Calories 370, Calories from Fat 250, Total Fat 28g (43% DV), Saturated Fat 7g (35% DV), Trans Fat 0g, Cholesterol 115mg (38% DV), Sodium 1290mg (54% DV), Carbohydrates < 1g (0% DV), Dietary Fiber 0g (0% DV), Sugars 0g, **Added Sugars:** 0g, Protein 29g, Vitamin A 4%, Vitamin C 4%, Calcium 2%, Iron 8%.

QUINOA TURKEY CASSEROLE

= Serves: 8	= Active time: 30 minutes
= Serving size: 1 cup	= Total time: 30 minutes

Cindy's grandmother loved the combination of curry powder and sage that's used in this casserole. This is not a common spice mixture, but keep an open mind: It's delicious.

Ingredients

3 cups water or broth
1 1/2 cups quinoa
3 tablespoons canola oil
1 onion, coarsely chopped
2 carrots, coarsely chopped
2 ribs celery, coarsely chopped
1 pound ground turkey
1 tablespoon curry powder
1 teaspoon dried sage
1 teaspoon salt
1 teaspoon pepper
1 pound Brussels sprouts, shaved very thin
2 tablespoons butter

STEP 1: Bring the water or broth to boil in a 4-quart pot. Add the quinoa. Reduce heat to low and simmer for 15 minutes. Remove from heat and let cool for 5 minutes. Fluff the quinoa with a fork.

STEP 2: Heat 2 tablespoons of oil in a large pan over medium-high heat. Add the onion, carrots, and celery. Sauté until golden brown, about 5 minutes. Add the ground turkey, curry powder, sage, salt, and pepper, breaking up the meat and cooking it until no longer pink, another 5 minutes. Add the meat-and-vegetable mixture to the pot of quinoa. Mix, and cover to keep warm.

STEP 3: Meanwhile, in the pan you used to brown the turkey, sauté the Brussels sprouts in the butter and 1 tablespoon of oil until they begin to brown slightly. Then lower the heat, cover and steam for 6 to 8 minutes, until tender. Add the Brussels sprouts to the quinoa mixture and stir. Season to taste and serve.

VARIATIONS:
- Use a different kind of meat: Ground beef and ground lamb both work well in this casserole.
- Use a different kind of vegetable. Strong flavored veggies work best in this dish. Try broccoli, cabbage, cauliflower, or kale.
- For a richer dish, top the casserole with 1/4 cup grated Parmesan cheese.

GOES WELL WITH:
- Tossed green salad
- Plain Greek yogurt and berries for dessert

Per serving: Calories 420, Calories from Fat 170, Total Fat 19g (29% DV), Saturated Fat 5g (25% DV), Trans Fat 0g, Cholesterol 60mg (20% DV), So-

dium 220mg (9% DV), Carbohydrates 39g (13% DV), Dietary Fiber 7g (28% DV), Sugars 4g, Protein 24g, Vitamin A 80%, Vitamin C 110%, Calcium 10%, Iron 25%.

ROAST TURKEY

= Serves: 10 to 12   = Total time: Varies depending on the size of the turkey

= Serving size: 4 ounces

= Active time: 15 minutes

Roast turkey shouldn't just be for holidays. Ask your butcher to cut it up for you, if you want to save time and hassle.

Ingredients
1 turkey (10 to 12 pounds), whole or cut into 8 pieces
1/4 cup olive oil or soft butter
2 tablespoons salt
2 tablespoons cracked black pepper
1 tablespoon curry powder
1 tablespoon fresh sage, or 1 teaspoon dried sage

STEP 1: Preheat the oven to 375°F.

STEP 2: Line a baking or roasting pan with parchment paper or foil.

STEP 3: Rub the turkey with the oil or butter, as if you were putting lotion on. Mix the salt, pepper, curry powder, and sage together and rub onto the turkey. Place the turkey onto pan and place in the oven. If you have a roasting rack, then place the turkey on that, and place the rack and bird in the pan.

Whole Turkey:

For whole turkey, place in a roasting pan and cover with foil. Bake for 2 1/2 to 3 hours, or until internal temperature registers 160°F. Take foil off for last 45 minutes so turkey can brown.

Turkey Pieces:

You can ask your butcher to cut up the whole turkey. For turkey pieces, place on a sheet pan. Bake for 1 1/2 to 2 hours, or until internal temperature registers 165°F.

VARIATIONS:
- Use Barbecue Rub (p. 171).

- Use salt, cracked pepper, and rosemary.

GOES WELL WITH:
- Roasted potatoes
- Nana's Italian Vegetable Stew (p. 465)
- Caesar salad
- Warm Applesauce (p. 226)

Per serving: Calories 260, Calories from Fat 100, Total Fat 11g (17% DV), Saturated Fat 2.5g (12% DV), Trans Fat 0g, Cholesterol 130mg (43% DV), Sodium 1140mg (48% DV), Carbohydrates < 1g (0% DV), Dietary Fiber 0g (0% DV), Sugars 0g, **Added Sugars:** 0g, Protein 36g, Vitamin A 0%, Vitamin C 0%, Calcium 4%, Iron 15%.

SIMPLE TURKEY MEATBALLS

= Serves: 4	= Active time: 25 minutes
= Serving size: 4 ounces	= Total time: 25 minutes

This is one of my favorite combinations. The peppers keep the turkey from drying out. I make the meatballs ahead of time, cook them, and freeze them. They're good for a quick lunch or dinner, and are simple and healthy.

Ingredients
1 pound ground turkey
2 tablespoons extra-virgin olive oil
1/2 teaspoon salt
1/2 teaspoon ground black pepper
1/2 cup finely chopped red bell pepper
1/2 cup finely chopped green onion

STEP 1: Put the ground turkey in a bowl. Add 1 tablespoon of the olive oil and a dash of salt and black pepper. Add the bell pepper and green onion.

STEP 2: Roll the turkey mixture into small balls, about 1 1/2 inches in diameter.

STEP 3: Heat the remaining 1 tablespoon of olive oil (or use non-aerosol cooking spray) in a medium-size saucepan on high heat. Add the turkey meatballs and cook until browned and the internal temperature reaches 165°F, about 5 minutes per side.

VARIATION:
- Add 1 teaspoon peeled and minced fresh ginger to the ground turkey.

GOES WELL WITH:

- Pasta or in a chili
- Ratatouille (p. 468)
- Barley, brown rice, or quinoa
- Green salad
- Sliced melon

Per serving: Calories 170, Calories from Fat 100, Total Fat 11g (17% DV), Saturated Fat 2.5g (12% DV), Trans Fat 0g, Cholesterol 55mg (18% DV), Sodium 50mg (2% DV), Carbohydrates 2g (1% DV), Dietary Fiber < 1g (2% DV), Sugars 1g, **Added Sugars:** 0g, Protein 16g, Vitamin A 20%, Vitamin C 45%, Calcium 2%, Iron 6%.

QUICK CHICKEN TIKKA MASALA

= Serves: 4   = Active time: 20 minutes
= Serving size: 1/4 recipe   = Total Time: 40 minutes

Takeout food is convenient, but alas, often filled with fat, sugar, and salt. This version of an Indian takeout staple is ethnic food without the guilt.

Ingredients

4 teaspoons garam masala*

1/2 teaspoon salt

1/4 teaspoon ground turmeric

1/2 cup unbleached all-purpose flour

1 pound chicken tenders

4 teaspoons canola oil, divided

6 cloves garlic, peeled and minced

1 large sweet onion, peeled and diced

4 teaspoons minced peeled fresh ginger, or
   1 tablespoon ground ginger

1 can (28 ounces) plum tomatoes with their
   juices

1/3 cup heavy (whipping) cream

1/2 cup chopped fresh cilantro, for garnish

STEP 1: Stir together the garam masala, salt, and turmeric in a small dish. Place the flour in a shallow dish. Sprinkle the chicken with 1/2 teaspoon of the spice mixture and dredge in the flour. Reserve the remaining spice mix and 1 tablespoon of the remaining flour.

STEP 2: Heat 2 teaspoons oil in a large skillet over medium-high heat. Cook the chicken until browned, 1 to 2 minutes per side. Transfer to a plate.

* Garam masala is a blend of spices used in Indian cooking. Usually includes cardamom, black pepper, nutmeg, fennel, cumin, and coriander.

STEP 3: Heat the remaining 2 teaspoons oil in the pan over medium-low heat. Add the garlic, onion, and ginger and cook, stirring often until starting to brown, 5 to 7 minutes. Add the reserved spice mix and cook, stirring until fragrant, 30 seconds to 1 minute. Sprinkle the reserved 1 tablespoon flour and stir until coated.

STEP 4: Add the tomatoes and their juices. Bring to a simmer, stirring and breaking up the tomatoes with a wooden spoon. Cook, stirring often, until thickened and the onion is tender, 3 to 5 minutes.

STEP 5: Stir in the cream. Add the chicken and any accumulated juices to the pan. Bring to a simmer and cook over medium-low heat until the chicken is cooked through, 3 to 4 minutes. Garnish with the cilantro.

GOES WELL WITH:
- Steamed brown rice
- Barley
- Salad and fresh fruit

Per serving: Calories 330, Calories from Fat 110, Total Fat 12g (18% DV), Saturated Fat 4g (20% DV), Trans Fat 0g, Cholesterol 85mg (28% DV), So-

dium 460mg (19% DV), Carbohydrates 28g (9% DV), Dietary Fiber 5g (20% DV), Sugars 6g, **Added Sugars:** 0g, Protein 29g, Vitamin A 15%, Vitamin C 100%, Calcium 15%, Iron 30%.

SALMON MILANESE

= Serves: 4 to 6 people with leftovers

= Total time: 35 to 45 minutes, depending on the thickness of the salmon

= Active time: 10 minutes

I love this simple, yet tasty, salmon. You can prep this dish the day before and then just pop it in a hot oven for 20 to 30 minutes. When the onions and tomatoes are brown, it's done. I like to toss zucchini with a little bit of olive oil and roast them with the salmon. Serve on top of raw spinach and let the warm salmon wilt the spinach.

Ingredients
2 pounds salmon, pin bones removed with tweezers
1 pound Roma tomatoes, diced into 1/4-inch pieces

1 cup yellow onion, peeled and diced into 1/4-inch pieces
2 teaspoons salt
1 teaspoon fresh cracked pepper
1/4 cup olive oil
2 fresh lemons, sliced
1/4 cup chopped fresh basil

STEP 1: Preheat the oven to 400°F.

STEP 2: Place the salmon in a lightly oiled 8-by-12-inch baking dish, skin-side down.

STEP 3: In a bowl, toss the tomatoes and onion with the salt, cracked pepper, and olive oil and place on top of the salmon.

STEP 4: Top with the lemon slices, place in the oven, and bake for 20 to 30 minutes (depending on the thickness of the salmon). The onion and tomatoes should be browned. The salmon should be firm to the touch.

STEP 5: Remove from the oven. Sprinkle with the basil.

VARIATIONS:
• Gently using two spatulas when salmon is done, move fish to a bed

of fresh spinach or kale.

- Surround salmon with 1-inch pieces of zucchini and bell peppers and roast with salmon, onions, and tomatoes.
- Spread 1/2 cup of fresh pesto over the salmon before adding the tomato and onion mixture.

GOES WELL WITH:
- Quinoa
- Brown rice
- Barley pilaf
- Summer slaw salad: raw broccoli, or shaved Brussels sprouts tossed in a lemon and yogurt dill dressing
- Sliced melons for a refreshing dessert
- Savory Watermelon and Feta Salad (p. 312)

Per serving: Calories 230, Calories from Fat 110, Total Fat 12g (18% DV), Saturated Fat 2g (10% DV), Trans Fat 0g, Cholesterol 50mg (17% DV), Sodium 680mg (28% DV), Carbohydrates 5g (2% DV), Dietary Fiber 1g (4% DV), Sugars 3g, **Added Sugars:** 0g, Protein 24g, Vitamin A 20%, Vitamin C 20%, Calcium 4%, Iron 6%.

No-Guilt Fish Tenders

= Serves: 4 = Active time: 10 minutes

= Serving size: 4 ounces = Total time: 35 minutes

Here's an alternative to a Filet-O-Fish sandwich, which has crazy amounts of bad fat (one-third of the recommended daily amount) and as much sugar as half a can of soda. The Japanese bread crumbs, panko, are key here. They make the tenders crunchy and satisfying.

Flat white fish means lots of protein, and wild flat white fish means omega-3s. Remember, farmed fish eat corn, which means omega-6s. The quinoa or cornmeal provide some carbohydrates, but you're holding it together with egg (protein), not fat (mayonnaise).

Ingredients
1 pound of meaty white fish fillets: cod, haddock, or pollock
2 eggs
2 cups dry panko, quinoa, or cornmeal
1/2 teaspoon salt
1/2 teaspoon pepper

1 pinch (1/8 teaspoon) of cayenne pepper
Non-aerosol cooking spray

STEP 1: Preheat the oven to 425°F.

STEP 2: Slice the fish into 1/2-inch strips.

STEP 3: Line a cookie sheet or large baking pan with parchment paper or foil.

STEP 4: Beat the eggs in a medium-size bowl until frothy. Pour the panko, quinoa, or cornmeal into a large dish or baking pan with the salt, pepper, and cayenne. Dip the fish strips in the beaten eggs, then into the quinoa or cornmeal. Spray both sides with non-aerosol cooking spray. Place on the prepared cookie sheet or baking pan.

STEP 5: Bake for 20 minutes, until coating is browned and crunchy.

VARIATIONS:
- Use chicken tenders or turkey tenders in place of fish.
- Top it with Marinara Sauce (p. 149) and grated Parmesan cheese.
- It's fine to play around with the spices in the bread crumb mix: Add dried seasoned salt, garlic powder,

oregano, thyme, or parsley.
- Add a couple squirts of hot sauce to the eggs.
- Serve over a salad.
- Use as a sandwich filling.

GOES WELL WITH:
- A little bit of tartar sauce (Just mix mayo with minced parsley, pickles, and green onions: avoid the bottled stuff!)
- Roma Tomato Basil Salsa (p. 172) or Fresh Fruit Salsa (p. 174)
- Green salad
- Rice dishes
- Whole-Wheat Sponge Bread (p. 188)
- Sliced tomatoes

Per serving: Calories 330, Calories from Fat 50, Total Fat 6g (9% DV), Saturated Fat 1.5g (8% DV), Trans Fat 0g, Cholesterol 145mg (48% DV), Sodium 850mg (35% DV), Carbohydrates 39g (13% DV), Dietary Fiber 2g (8% DV), Sugars 3g, **Added Sugars:** 0g, Protein 28g, Vitamin A 4%, Vitamin C 0%, Calcium 10%, Iron 20%.

OLD-FASHIONED BEEF STEW
AND VEGETABLES

= Serves: 6   = Active time:
                  20 minutes
= Serving size: = Total time:
  2 cups   3 hours

Stew is the quintessential comfort food. There is something about the rich sauce, tender meat, and flavor-infused vegetables that warms the body. Best of all, stews are easy to make if you follow a few simple steps.

Stews taste great as soon as the meat becomes tender, but if you have leftovers, let cool and then keep them in the refrigerator overnight. They will taste even better the next day, after the flavors have had more time to marry. You can freeze leftovers for up to three months. Don't forget to label and date.

Ingredients
1/2 cup oil: olive, safflower, or rice bran
1 cup chopped celery
1 cup chopped and peeled onions
1 cup chopped carrots
1 teaspoon dried thyme, or 1 tablespoon
  fresh thyme

4 cloves garlic, peeled and chopped

1 cup unbleached all-purpose flour

1 1/2 pounds beef stew meat

8 cups liquid (water, wine, stock, or a mixture)

1 teaspoon salt

1 tablespoon cracked black pepper

2 cups 1-inch pieces scrubbed carrots or parsnips

2 cups scrubbed diced potatoes

STEP 1: Heat 1/4 cup of oil in a cast-iron or stainless steel pot. (Make sure it has a tight-fitting lid.) Sauté the celery, onions, carrots, thyme, and garlic in the pot until brown and tender. When aromatic vegetables are brown, remove them from the pot with a slotted spoon and reserve in a small bowl.

STEP 2: Place the flour in a bowl. Dredge the meat, shaking off the excess flour. Add the remainder of oil to the pot and cook the meat over medium-high heat, quickly browning but not cooking. Do this in small batches. Take the meat out and reserve on plate.

STEP 3: Add the liquid to the pot and bring to a boil while scraping up the brown bits from the bottom of the pot. While it dissolves it will add flavor to the gravy.

STEP 4: Reduce the heat to low and return the meat and the aromatics to the liquid. It's very important that the stew must simmer and not boil. Slowly cook the stew over low heat so the liquid barely simmers. Cover and cook for 2 hours.

STEP 5: After the meat has had a chance to cook for a while, add the 1-inch pieces of carrot and the potatoes. Cook until the meat is fork tender, about an hour. Adjust the salt and pepper and serve.

VARIATIONS:

Lamb Stew
1 1/2 pounds boned leg of lamb
Herbs: thyme, parsley
Veggies: pearl onions, carrots

Pork Stew
1 1/2 pounds pork shoulder, or pork tenderloin
Herbs: chili powder, cumin, coriander
Veggies: peppers, onions, potatoes

Chicken Stew

1 1/2 pounds boneless chicken thighs
Herbs: thyme
Veggies: pearl onions, carrots, parsnips

All these stews may be doubled or tripled. They freeze well.

- About 10 minutes before serving, add any leftover grains you need to use up.
- Sprinkle with fresh herbs before serving.
- Add 1 to 2 teaspoons hot sauce.
- Add several cloves of garlic, minced.
- Add a few tablespoons of lemon juice or vinegar just before serving.
- Use broth or bean water instead of plain water.

GOES WELL WITH:
- Steamed brown rice or barley
- Add kale or chard at the very end
- Sautéed mushrooms
- Green salad and sliced apples with lemon juice
- Polenta
- Any whole grain
- Whole-Wheat Sponge Bread (p. 188)

Per serving: Calories 660, Calories

from Fat 360, Total Fat 40g (62% DV), Saturated Fat 8g (40% DV), Trans Fat 0g, Cholesterol 100mg (33% DV), Sodium 150mg (6% DV), Carbohydrates 37g (12% DV), Dietary Fiber 3g (12% DV), Sugars 2g, **Added Sugars:** 0g, Protein 37g, Vitamin A 110%, Vitamin C 10%, Calcium 6%, Iron 35%.

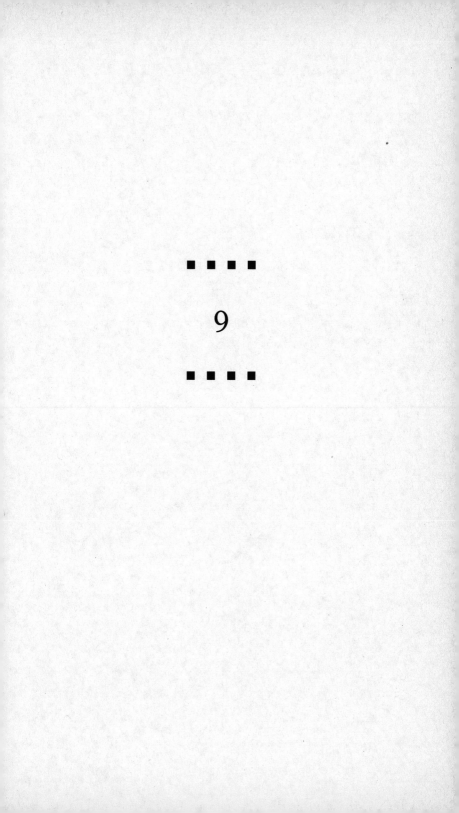

9

CHAPTER 9
VEGETABLES

Obviously, I'm a big fan of vegetables. You don't need complicated recipes to roast, steam, or grill vegetables. By all means, chop vegetables raw. Put them in everything! But sometimes, vegetables deserve special treatment. Here are some favorite, and special, veggie dishes.

Recipes:

Oven-Grilled Vegetables Four Ways
Pickled Beets
Braised Greens
Roasted Cauliflower with Yogurt Cream
  Sauce
Nana's Italian Vegetable Stew
Ratatouille
Stuffed Bell Peppers
Sky's the Limit Stuffed Potatoes
Stewed Fresh Tomatoes and Okra
Spaghetti Squash with Marinara Sauce

OVEN-GRILLED VEGETABLES FOUR WAYS

= Makes: 4 cups = Active time: 15 minutes

= Serving size: 3/4 cup = Total time: 45 minutes

Almost every vegetable tastes better when it's grilled or roasted. The high temperature caramelizes the outside. At the same time, the heat punches up the natural sweetness within each morsel. Remember to season them with some garlic powder or seasoned salt as well. My kids won't eat steamed asparagus, but they will eat grilled asparagus. This recipe grills the vegetables in the oven, but they are even better on the outdoor grill! If you use a grill, make sure to use a veggie grilling pan so that the pieces don't drop into the fire.

Below are four of our favorite roasted veggies, but you can use any mixture of what's in your fridge or in the market.

Roasted Cauliflower

Ingredients
1 head cauliflower
2 tablespoons olive oil or vegetable oil

1 teaspoon salt
1 teaspoon dried dill

STEP 1: Preheat the oven to 425°F.

STEP 2: Rinse the cauliflower. Chop the whole head, including the core and the stem, into 1-inch pieces. Place the cauliflower in a large bowl and toss with the oil, salt, and dill.

STEP 3: Line a large baking sheet with a piece of parchment paper. Pour the cauliflower on top. Bake in the oven until brown, 30 minutes. Cool for 5 minutes and serve.

Per serving: Calories 60, Calories from Fat 40, Total Fat 5g (8% DV), Saturated Fat 0.5g (2% DV), Trans Fat 0g, Cholesterol 0mg (0% DV), Sodium 420mg (18% DV), Carbohydrates 5g (2% DV), Dietary Fiber 2g (8% DV), Sugars 2g, **Added Sugars:** 0g, Protein 2g, Vitamin A 0%, Vitamin C 80%, Calcium 2%, Iron 2%.

Roasted Mixed Vegetables

Ingredients

2 bell peppers, each cored, seeded, and cut into 6 pieces

1 small yellow onion, peeled and cut into 4 four pieces

2 medium-size zucchini, cut in half, length-wise, and then cut crosswise into 3 pieces

1/2 pound white button or cremini mushrooms, cut in half

2 tablespoons olive oil

1 teaspoon salt

STEP 1: Preheat the oven to 425°F.

STEP 2: Place the bell peppers, onion, zucchini, and mushrooms in a large bowl and toss with the oil and salt.

STEP 3: Line a large baking sheet with a piece of parchment paper. Pour the vegetable mixture on top. Bake the vegetables in the oven until brown, 30 minutes. Cool for 5 minutes and serve.

Per serving: Calories 110, Calories from Fat 80, Total Fat 9g (14% DV), Saturated Fat 1g (5% DV), Trans Fat 0g, Cholesterol 0mg (0% DV), Sodium

370mg (15% DV), Carbohydrates 8g (3% DV), Dietary Fiber 2g (8% DV), Sugars 3g, **Added Sugars:** 0g, Protein 2g, Vitamin A 4%, Vitamin C 190%, Calcium 2%, Iron 4%.

Roasted Shaved Brussels Sprouts

Ingredients
2 pounds Brussels sprouts
2 tablespoons olive oil
1 teaspoon salt

STEP 1: Preheat the oven to 425°F.

STEP 2: Slice the Brussels sprouts thinly. Place them in a bowl and toss them with the oil and salt.

STEP 3: Line a large baking sheet with a piece of parchment paper. Pour the Brussels sprouts on top. Bake the Brussels sprouts in the oven until brown, about 20 minutes. Cool for 5 minutes and serve.

Per serving: Calories 70, Calories from Fat 40, Total Fat 4.5g (7% DV), Saturated Fat 0.5g (2% DV), Trans Fat 0g, Cholesterol 0mg (0% DV), Sodium 410mg (17% DV), Carbohydrates 7g

(2% DV), Dietary Fiber 3g (12% DV), Sugars 2g, **Added Sugars:** 0g, Protein 3g, Vitamin A 10%, Vitamin C 110%, Calcium 4%, Iron 6%.

Roasted Root Vegetables

Ingredients
1/2 pound parsnips or acorn squash
1/2 pound carrots or butternut squash
1/2 pound rutabaga or sweet potatoes
1/2 pound beets (red or golden)
1/2 cup olive or vegetable oil (set aside 1 tablespoon for the beets)
1 teaspoon of salt

STEP 1: Preheat the oven to 425°F.

STEP 2: Scrub all of the vegetables and cut into 1-inch cubes. If you like, peel the acorn squash and butternut squash, if using. It's also good with the peel on, and the peel adds extra fiber.

STEP 3: Place all of the vegetables except the beets in a bowl and toss them with 7 tablespoons of the oil and the salt. Toss the whole unpeeled beets separately with the remaining tablespoon oil.

STEP 4: Place parchment paper in the bottom of a roasting pan. Put the cubed root vegetables in the pan, then place the unpeeled beets on top. Cover the pan with aluminum foil. Bake the vegetables covered for 20 minutes. Remove the foil and bake the vegetables, until tender and brown, 15 minutes longer.

Per serving: Calories 180, Calories from Fat 100, Total Fat 11g (17% DV), Saturated Fat 1.5g (8% DV), Trans Fat 0g, Cholesterol 0mg (0% DV), Sodium 320mg (13% DV), Carbohydrates 21g (7% DV), Dietary Fiber 6g (24% DV), Sugars 10g, **Added Sugars:** 0g, Protein 2g, Vitamin A 150%, Vitamin C 40%, Calcium 6%, Iron 6%.

VARIATIONS FOR ALL RECIPES:
- Play around with seasonings: Add whole peeled garlic cloves, 1 cup peeled pearl onions, onion powder, rosemary, or chili powder to the oil when you toss the vegetables.
- Sprinkle chopped fresh herbs on the veggies just before serving. Basil, cilantro, and parsley always work well.
- Sprinkle veggies with lemon juice

and a couple tablespoons of Parmesan cheese before serving.

GOES WELL WITH:

- Roasted or grilled meats or fish
- Polenta
- Quinoa, farro, or barley and browned ground meat; mix them together
- Salad
- Added to a frittata, or an egg scramble
- Pasta and Basil Pesto (p. 185) or Marinara Sauce (p. 149)

PICKLED BEETS

= Makes: 6 servings   = Active time: 10 minutes

= Serving size: 4 ounces   = Total time: 1 hour

Canned beats do a great disservice to nutrition, yuck. Everybody hates beets until they've had these pickled beets. They can last for up to two months in the fridge, but they don't even last a week in my house.

Ingredients
1 1/2 pounds beets, rinsed and chopped into 1-inch pieces
1 cup apple cider vinegar

2 cups water
1 teaspoon salt
1 bay leaf
4 cloves garlic, peeled
6 sprigs fresh thyme
5 whole peppercorns

Place the beets, cider vinegar, water, salt, bay leaf, garlic, thyme, and peppercorns in a 2-quart stainless steel pot and bring to a boil over medium-high heat. Reduce the heat to medium-low and let the beets simmer until fork tender but not mushy, about 35 to 40 minutes. Chill in the cooking liquid. Serve the beets room temperature or cold.

Stored in an airtight container, the beets will keep for up to one month in the refrigerator. Pickled beets do not freeze well.

VARIATION:
• Use red or golden beets.

GOES WELL WITH:
• Brisket
• Salad
• Just for a snack
• Sliced cheese, as a starter

Per serving: Calories 35, Calories from Fat 0, Total Fat 0g (0% DV), Saturated Fat 0g (0% DV), Trans Fat 0g, Cholesterol 0mg (0% DV), Sodium 400mg (17% DV), Carbohydrates 7g (2% DV), Dietary Fiber 2g (8% DV), Sugars 4g, Protein 1g, **Added Sugars:** 0g, Vitamin A 0%, Vitamin C 8%, Calcium 2%, Iron 4%.

BRAISED GREENS

= Serves: 4 = Total time: 10 minutes

= Active time: 5 minutes

Try to eat greens every day. Broccoli rabe, mustard greens, beet tops, escarole, spinach, it's all green. Any greens can be cooked this way. (It's actually a great way to use them up if they are starting to wilt or you just have too much.)

Ingredients
2 large bunches greens, about 1 pound
About 2 tablespoons extra-virgin olive oil
3 cloves garlic, peeled and minced, chopped, or sliced
Salt

STEP 1: Clean the greens by filling a clean sink or a large bowl with water and soaking the leaves to loosen any sand or dirt. Drain. Put the greens in a salad spinner to remove any excess moisture or blot them with a clean dish towel or paper towels.

STEP 2: Heat 2 tablespoons olive oil in a large skillet over medium-high heat. Add the garlic and sauté until it is just beginning to brown, about 1 minute.

STEP 3: Add the greens to the skillet, packing them down with your hand a bit if you need to. Use a couple spatulas to lift the greens and turn them over in the skillet so that you coat more of them with the olive oil and garlic. Do this a couple of times. Cover the skillet and cook for 1 minute. Uncover the skillet and turn the greens over again. Cover the skillet and cook for an additional minute. (I often find it helpful to cook greens in batches so that the leaves don't go overboard.)

STEP 4: After 2 minutes of cooking covered, the greens should be completely wilted. Remove them from the heat. Drain any excess moisture from the skillet. Add a little more olive oil and sprinkle with salt to taste. Serve immediately.

VARIATIONS:
- Use chard, mustard greens, spinach, escarole, beet tops.
- Chop the stems of the greens, sauté these first, then remove them. Proceed with recipe and add the stems at the end. (Don't do this with kale, though.)
- For kale, remove the stems, use the leaves only; the stems are bitter.
- Use a different oil, flavored, or a nut oil.
- Throw cooked Italian sausage or barley or farro on top, or red chili peppers, to make a whole meal.

GOES WELL WITH:
- Anything

Per serving: Calories 80, Calories from Fat 50, Total Fat 5g (8% DV), Saturated Fat 1g (5% DV), Trans Fat 0g, Cholesterol 0mg (0% DV), Sodium 130mg (5% DV), Carbohydrates 7g (2% DV), Dietary Fiber 4g (16% DV), Sugars < 1g, **Added Sugars:** 0g, Protein 5g,

Vitamin A 300%, Vitamin C 80%, Calcium 15%, Iron 25%.

ROASTED CAULIFLOWER WITH YOGURT CREAM SAUCE

= Serves: 6 = Active time: 15 minutes

= Serving size: 1 cup = Total time: 40 minutes

Cauliflower is terrific in just about any preparation. Take cauliflower, yogurt, pomegranate seeds, and you've got a simple creative, flavorful, wonderful dish. The contrast of colors and textures here is lovely.

Ingredients
1 large head cauliflower, cut into 1-inch, bite-size florets
2 tablespoons extra-virgin olive oil
1 tablespoon whole cumin seeds
Kosher salt
1/2 tablespoon freshly ground black pepper
1 cup plain yogurt, for serving
1/4 cup packed fresh mint, chopped, for garnish
1/4 cup pomegranate seeds, for garnish

STEP 1: Preheat the oven to 425°F.

STEP 2: Toss the cauliflower florets with the oil, cumin seeds, 1/2 tablespoon of salt, and the pepper.

STEP 3: Line a baking sheet with waxed paper or parchment paper and spread the cauliflower on it in an even layer. Roast the cauliflower, stirring it occasionally, until just tender and browned on the edges, 20 to 30 minutes.

STEP 4: In a bowl mix the yogurt and a pinch of salt. Top the cauliflower with the yogurt and sprinkle the chopped mint and pomegranate seeds on top.

GOES WELL WITH:
- Roasted chicken
- Lamb
- Barley or brown rice

Per serving: Calories 90, Calories from Fat 45, Total Fat 5g (8% DV), Saturated Fat 1g (5% DV), Trans Fat 0g, Cholesterol < 5mg (1% DV), Sodium 250mg (10% DV), Carbohydrates 9g (3% DV), Dietary Fiber 3g (12% DV), Sugars 5g, **Added Sugars:** 0g, Protein 4g, Vitamin A 0%, Vitamin C 100%, Calcium 10%, Iron 4%.

NANA'S ITALIAN VEGETABLE STEW

= Serves: 6   = Active time:
                                    15 minutes
= Serving size: = Total time:
   1 cup   40 minutes

Where better to hide vegetables than in a vegetable stew? Again, seasoning is everything. And Parmesan cheese works wonders — it has enough salt to make this savory without being biting.

Cindy's grandmother, Nana, always kept a thriving vegetable garden. This endlessly variable stew was a staple of her summer kitchen. Now that Cindy's a Nana herself and has her own cooking class and this great garden at school, she makes this Italian vegetable stew regularly. You can vary the green vegetables, but don't let this get too heavy by adding extra potatoes. It should be bright and refreshing.

Ingredients

8 ounces potatoes, unpeeled and diced into 1-inch pieces

1 pound cauliflower, chopped into 2-inch pieces

8 ounces broccoli, cleaned and chopped into 2-inch pieces

8 ounces fresh green beans, or frozen if out of season

8 ounces zucchini or yellow squash, cleaned and chopped into 2-inch pieces

1 bunch (8 ounces) chard, cleaned and chopped

1 bunch (8 ounces) kale, cleaned, stemmed, and chopped

1 tablespoon garlic or shallots, peeled and chopped

1/4 cup extra-virgin olive oil

4 ounces Parmesan cheese, shaved or grated

STEP 1: Add about 3 inches of water to a large stockpot. Layer the cubed potatoes in the water. The liquid should just reach to the top of the potatoes. Add the cauliflower (in layers), then the broccoli, then the green beans, and then the zucchini to the pot. Then add the chard and kale.

STEP 2: Bring everything to a boil over medium heat, then reduce heat to low and simmer for 10 minutes.

STEP 3: Use a long knife or a skewer to test the potatoes. When the metal glides softly into the potatoes, they're done. Pour the water and veggies into a strainer, and then return the vegetables to the pot.

STEP 4: In a medium-size pan, sauté the garlic in the olive oil for about 1 minute. Add to the vegetable mixture with the Parmesan cheese and stir gently.

VARIATIONS:
- Add fresh herbs, 1/4 cup basil or parsley, if you have them.
- Add extra garlic, or use both garlic and shallots.
- Add 1/2 cup chopped prosciutto to the oil when you sauté the garlic.
- Add 2 cups of cannellini beans to make a kind of minestrone.
- If fresh produce is scarce, this recipe also works well with frozen veggies. Substitute 1 pound frozen chopped spinach for the leaf veggies.

GOES WELL WITH:
- Crusty whole-wheat French bread
- Farro
- Brown Rice
- Green Salad

Per serving: Calories 130, Calories from Fat 70, Total Fat 8g (12% DV), Saturated Fat 2.5g (12% DV), Trans Fat 0g, Cholesterol 10mg (3% DV), Sodium 220mg (9% DV), Carbohydrates 11g

(4% DV), Dietary Fiber 3g (12% DV), Sugars 3g, **Added Sugars:** 0g, Protein 7g, Vitamin A 90%, Vitamin C 120%, Calcium 15%, Iron 8%.

RATATOUILLE

= Serves: 10   = Active time: 20 minutes

= Serving size: 1 cup   = Total time: 1 hour 30 minutes

Ratatouille is not just a cute animated film about a rat who wants to be a Parisian chef. Ratatouille is delicious, filling, low-calorie, and a staple of French cuisine. *Touiller* means "to toss," or "to mix up." Accordingly this dish is a stewed mix of eggplant, zucchini, tomatoes, and European herbs such as marjoram, basil, thyme, or a green herb mix such as "herbes de Provence." This version calls for Italian seasoning because it's readily available almost everywhere. What makes the dish is the seasonings: lots of thyme, lots of marjoram, lots of oregano, and lots of olive oil.

French chefs argue endlessly about the best way to make ratatouille: Should the vegetables be sautéed separately to preserve the flavor of each and then combined? Should they be layered and baked? Here, we opt for simple: Just combine everything and cook. You can also do this in a crockpot.

Ingredients
2 large eggplants, unpeeled, cut into 1-inch dice
1/4 cup olive oil
1 yellow onion, peeled and finely chopped
2 cloves garlic, peeled and finely chopped
2 tablespoons Italian seasoning
1 teaspoon salt
1/4 teaspoon cayenne pepper (if you want more kick, add 1 teaspoon)
2 bell peppers, any color, seeds and ribs removed, cut into 1-inch dice
2 large zucchini, unpeeled, cut into 1-inch dice
1 can (15 ounces) diced tomatoes
1 can (15 ounces) crushed tomatoes

STEP 1: Soak the diced eggplant in salted water for 5 minutes to draw out the bitterness. Rinse the eggplant, place it in a saucepan, cover it with water, and boil for 3 minutes. Drain well.

STEP 2: Heat the olive oil in a large skillet over medium heat. Add the onion and sauté for 5 minutes until the onion softens. Add the garlic and sauté for an additional 2 minutes. Add the Italian seasoning, salt, and cayenne. Then, add the bell peppers, zucchini, diced and crushed tomatoes, and the eggplant. Sauté over medium heat for 6 to 8 minutes.

STEP 3: Reduce the heat to low. Simmer the stew until it is thick and the flavors have blended, about 30 minutes.

VARIATIONS:
- Simmer the ratatouille a bit more to get rid of extra moisture, then use it as a filling for an omelet or savory crepes.
- Toss with pasta and sprinkle with Parmesan cheese for a one-dish meal.
- Experiment with herbs. Add fresh herbs if available.

GOES WELL WITH:
- Grilled meats and fish
- Pasta
- Brown rice
- Barley or farro
- Scrambled eggs or an omelet, mixed in
- Frittatas, baked in

Per serving: Calories 110, Calories from Fat 50, Total Fat 6g (9% DV), Saturated Fat 1g (5% DV), Trans Fat 0g, Cholesterol 0mg (0% DV), Sodium 350mg (15% DV), Carbohydrates 15g (5% DV), Dietary Fiber 5g (20% DV), Sugars 2g, **Added Sugars:** 0g, Protein 3g, Vitamin A 15%, Vitamin C 130%, Calcium 6%, Iron 10%.

STUFFED BELL PEPPERS

= Serves: 6	= Active time: 15 minutes
= Serving size: 1/2 pepper	= Total time: 1 hour 5 minutes

Here's another way to disguise vegetables and fiber for kids. Give them ricotta cheese, and they'll eat peppers and spinach willingly. Kids don't like bitter vegetables the first time they're offered. The rule is: Whenever you're serving a bitter vegetable, add cheese to remove the bitterness.

Ingredients
5 cups fresh spinach, or 10 ounces frozen
   chopped spinach, thawed
3 medium-size bell peppers
1 cup ricotta cheese

1 cup grated Monterey Jack cheese, or other cheese

1/4 cup grated Parmesan cheese

1/2 teaspoon garlic powder, or to taste

1/2 teaspoon cracked black pepper, or to taste

1/4 cup Italian seasoning

1 can (28 ounces) crushed tomatoes

STEP 1: Preheat the oven to 400°F.

STEP 2: Drain the thawed spinach if using frozen and squeeze as much water as you can from it. (You can do this by squeezing handful by handful, or you can put all the spinach in a kitchen towel, twist the ends, and squeeze until most of the excess water has been removed.) Stem the bell peppers and cut them in half. Remove the peppers' ribs and seeds.

STEP 3: Combine the ricotta, Jack cheese, and 2 tablespoons of the Parmesan in a large bowl. Mix with your hands, or with a spoon. Add the spinach, garlic powder, and cracked black pepper. Mix until combined.

STEP 4: Mix the Italian seasoning with the crushed tomatoes and pour into a greased 9-by-9-inch or 8-by-10-inch baking pan.

Divide the spinach-cheese mixture in 6 equal portions and stuff the peppers. Place the stuffed peppers side by side in the baking pan. Sprinkle with the remaining 2 tablespoons of grated Parmesan.

STEP 5: Cover the peppers with aluminum foil and bake in the oven for 30 minutes. Uncover the peppers, then bake them until brown, an additional 20 minutes. Remove the peppers when they have softened and the tomato sauce is bubbling. Let the peppers sit for 15 minutes before serving.

This recipe can be doubled.

VARIATIONS:
- Double the number of peppers. Add 1 pound of browned ground meat to the spinach-cheese mixture.
- Double the number of peppers. Add 2 cups of cooked brown rice, cooked cracked wheat, or cooked quinoa.
- Add a couple cloves of minced garlic and a couple tablespoons of dried or fresh oregano to the cheese mixture.
- Add 1/4 cup chopped fresh basil or 2 tablespoons dried basil to the cheese mixture.
- Add 1/4 cup chopped sun-dried

tomatoes to the cheese mixture.
- Add 1 pound of fresh spinach in a layer between the crushed tomatoes and the peppers; it will wilt and form a delicious base to the dish.
- Add 8 ounces corn niblets, fresh or frozen, to the spinach-cheese mixture.

Stuffed Zucchini
4 medium-size zucchini

Cut the zucchini in half lengthwise. Using a spoon, hollow out the zucchini. Stuff them with the cheese filling. Bake the zucchini following the recipe for stuffed peppers.

Stuffed Portobello Mushrooms
6 large portobello mushrooms

Remove the stems from the mushrooms, stuff them with the cheese filling. Do not add the tomato sauce. Bake the stuffed mushrooms on a sheet pan until cheese is browned, 25 minutes. Serve with Whole-Grain Vegetable Pilaf (p. 371).

GOES WELL WITH:
- Brown rice
- Polenta

- Farro
- Green salad

Per serving (stuffed bell pepper): Calories 340, Calories from Fat 160, Total Fat 18g (28% DV), Saturated Fat 11g (55% DV), Trans Fat 0g, Cholesterol 55mg (18% DV), Sodium 600mg (25% DV), Carbohydrates 26g (9% DV), Dietary Fiber 8g (32% DV), Sugars < 1g, **Added Sugars:** 0g, Protein 22g, Vitamin A 110%, Vitamin C 320%, Calcium 70%, Iron 40%.

SKY'S THE LIMIT STUFFED POTATOES

= Serves: 6   = Active time: 20 minutes

= Serving size: 1/2 potato   = Total time: 1 hour 30 minutes

Stuffed potatoes get no respect. If you add just a little milk, some cheese, and vegetables, you'll feel so decadent, and so satisfied. This dish is balanced. It has just enough cheese to satisfy, a dash of milk, and vegetables. Here's a way to hide greens: in potatoes. Cheese and meat are the great equalizers. It's Healthy Potato Skins! No kid has ever turned down a potato skin, even if it's stuffed with something healthy. An extra bonus: You won't fall asleep from sugar shock after eating this dish. Add a green salad and a sliced apple, and you've got a whole meal.

The only limit to this dish is your imagination: Add more spices, scallions, meat, even tomato sauce. The key is the ratios here. It's heavy on veggies, 2 to 3 pounds total, light on milk: no butter, only 1/2 cup of milk and 3/4 pound cheese.

Ingredients

3 large russet baking potatoes (8 to 10 ounces each)

1/4 cup olive oil or vegetable oil

1/2 cup milk

12 ounces mozzarella and Monterey Jack cheeses, shredded and mixed

3 pounds cooked vegetables (see the variations below)

Salt and pepper

3 tablespoons grated Parmesan cheese

STEP 1: Preheat the oven to 400°F.

STEP 2: Scrub the potatoes. Poke each potato with a fork several times to let the steam escape as it cooks. Rub the potatoes with the oil, then place them on a baking sheet. Bake the potatoes until a tester goes into the potato flesh smoothly, 1 hour. Remove them from the oven. Let sit for 10 minutes until cool enough to handle.

STEP 3: Cut the warm potatoes in half lengthwise. Holding each potato with a pot holder, scoop out the pulp into a large bowl. Return the potato skins to baking sheet. Add the milk and mozzarella and Jack cheeses to the potato pulp and mash coarsely. Fold in the vegetables. Season with salt and pepper to taste.

STEP 4: Divide the potato-vegetable mixture among the potato skins. Top with the Parmesan cheese.

STEP 5: Bake in the oven until the filling is hot and the cheese has melted, 30 minutes.

Per serving (stuffed bell pepper): Calories 340, Calories from Fat 160, Total Fat 18g (28% DV), Saturated Fat 11g (55% DV), Trans Fat 0g, Cholesterol 55mg (18% DV), Sodium 600mg (25% DV), Carbohydrates 26g (9% DV), Dietary Fiber 8g (32% DV), Sugars < 1g, **Added Sugars:** 0g, Protein 22g, Vitamin A 110%, Vitamin C 320%, Calcium 70%, Iron 40%.

VARIATIONS:

Broccoli–Cheddar Cheese Potatoes

2 bunches broccoli, 2 to 3 pounds total, cut in florets, steamed or boiled until just tender

1/2 cup milk

1 teaspoon salt

1 teaspoon ground black pepper

12 ounces cheddar cheese, grated, in place of the mozzarella

Toss broccoli, milk, salt, pepper, and 10 ounces cheese with potato flesh. Stuff skins and sprinkle remaining cheese over all. Roast in the oven at 400°F for 25 minutes, or until heated through and brown.

Cauliflower Stuffed Potatoes

One head of cauliflower, cut in florets, tossed with 1 to 2 tablespoons olive oil, roasted in a 400°F oven until tender, 25 minutes. You can also steam the cauliflower until tender.

1/2 cup milk

1 teaspoon salt

1 teaspoon black pepper
12 ounces cheddar cheese, grated, in place
  of the mozzarella

Toss cauliflower, milk, salt, pepper, and 10 ounces cheese with potato flesh. Sprinkle remaining 2 ounces of cheese over all. Roast in a 400°F oven for 25 minutes, or until heated through and brown.

Italian Veggie Stuffed Potatoes

1 1/2 pounds diced zucchini, steamed, sautéed, or roasted
1 1/2 pounds chopped mushrooms, raw, sautéed, or roasted
12 ounces mozzarella cheese, grated
1/4 cup milk
1 tablespoon Italian seasoning
1 teaspoon salt
1 teaspoon ground black pepper
1 cup Marinara Sauce (p. 149)

Toss zucchini, mushrooms, 10 ounces mozzarella, milk, Italian seasoning, salt, and pepper with the potato flesh. Stuff potato skins. Top all with the Marinara Sauce, spreading a little on the top of each potato. Top with remaining 2 ounces of mozzarella. Roast them in a 400°F oven until heated through and browned, 25 minutes.

Greek Stuffed Potatoes

1 1/2 pounds diced zucchini, steamed, sautéed, or roasted

1 1/2 pounds cherry tomatoes or 1-inch tomato pieces

1/2 cup chopped olives, any kind

1/2 cup chopped parsley

12 ounces feta cheese

1 teaspoon dried dill

Toss zucchini, tomatoes, olives, half the parsley, and the cheese with potato flesh. Stuff potato skins. Roast in 400°F oven until tender and browned, 25 minutes. Top with remaining chopped parsley and dill.

Beef and Greens Stuffed Potatoes

1/2 cup rinsed and sliced leeks, sautéed until tender

1/2 cup peeled and chopped onion, sautéed until tender

1/2 pound ground beef, cooked

1 teaspoon salt

1 pound greens (kale, broccoli rabe, spinach, or a mixture), wilted

1/4 pound mushrooms, raw or sautéed

2 chopped fresh tomatoes (It's OK to use a 14-ounce can of diced tomatoes, if fresh are not available.)

12 ounces Monterey Jack cheese, grated

Toss leeks, onion, ground beef, salt, greens, mushrooms, tomatoes, and 10 ounces cheese with potato flesh. Taste filling and adjust seasoning. Stuff skins with mixture. Top with remaining 2 ounces cheese. Bake in a 400°F oven for 25 minutes, or until brown.

VARIATIONS:
Play around with more exotic cheeses: Use blue cheese, feta, smoked gouda, Gruyère.
Add more spices and/or herbs: dill, basil, cayenne, snipped chives, chopped scallions.
Add a different meat: 1/2 pound ground beef, turkey, or pork; 1/4 pound cooked bacon, or 1/4 pound prosciutto, diced.

GOES WELL WITH:
- Green salad
- Sliced fruit

STEWED FRESH TOMATOES AND OKRA

= Serves: 4   = Active time:
                        15 minutes
= Serving size: = Total time:
  1/2 cup   35 minutes

Okra is not well-known outside the southern United States. It's wonderful though, especially when it is stewed slowly with ripe fresh tomatoes.

Ingredients

3/4 cup peeled and chopped sweet onion (1 small, or 1/2 medium-size onion)

2 tablespoons olive oil

2 cups fresh okra, rinsed, trimmed, and sliced, or frozen okra

3 medium-size ripe tomatoes, chopped, or 1 can (14 ounces) whole peeled tomatoes with their juice

1/2 teaspoon salt

Freshly ground black pepper

STEP 1: In a saucepan or sauté pan with a close-fitting lid, sauté the onion in the olive oil over medium heat until softened, but not browned, about 5 minutes.

STEP 2: Reduce the heat to low and stir in

the okra and tomatoes. Add the salt, cover and simmer for 15 minutes. Remove from heat and season with pepper to taste.

VARIATIONS:
- Add 1 teaspoon cayenne pepper.
- Add 1 cup cooked barley or cooked brown rice.
- Add 1/2 cup chopped fresh basil or 1/2 cup chopped fresh cilantro.
- Add 1 cup chickpeas.

GOES WELL WITH:
- Roasted meats
- Grilled fish
- Green salad and/or fresh fruit

Per serving: Calories 100, Calories from Fat 60, Total Fat 7g (11% DV), Saturated Fat 1g (5% DV), Trans Fat 0g, Cholesterol 0mg (0% DV), Sodium 300mg (12% DV), Carbohydrates 10g (3% DV), Dietary Fiber 3g (12% DV), Sugars 4g, **Added Sugars:** 0g, Protein 2g, Vitamin A 20%, Vitamin C 40%, Calcium 6%, Iron 4%.

SPAGHETTI SQUASH
WITH MARINARA SAUCE

= Makes: 6 cups, may vary depending on the size of the squash

= Serving size: 1 cup

= Active time: 15 minutes

= Total time: 1 hour 15 minutes

We all love pasta, but a steady diet of pasta is an insulin nightmare. Spaghetti squash makes a healthy pasta substitute. Because the long strips of spaghetti squash look like pasta, kids will eat it. And grown-ups don't have to feel guilty about seconds!

Ingredients
1 large spaghetti squash, about 2 1/2 pounds
3 cups of Marinara Sauce (p. 149)
1/4 cup grated Parmesan cheese (optional)
1/4 cup chopped fresh basil (optional)

STEP 1: Position an oven rack in the center of the oven. Preheat the oven to 350°F.

STEP 2: Place the squash in a baking pan on the rack in the center of the oven and bake the squash until a fork can easily pierce the squash, 1 hour.

STEP 3: Cool the squash until it is easy to handle. Split the squash in half lengthwise. Using a large spoon, remove the seeds from the center of the squash and discard them.

STEP 4: Using a fork, hold a squash half over a large bowl and scrape the flesh from the skin, working lengthwise.

STEP 5: Toss with the Marinara Sauce. Sprinkle the Parmesan cheese and basil on top, if using. Serve.

VARIATIONS:
- Grate zucchini lengthwise, and steam it. Top with Marinara Sauce (p. 149).
- Use Basil Pesto (p. 185) instead of Marinara Sauce.
- Use Roma Tomato Basil Salsa (p. 172) instead of Marinara Sauce.
- Add leftovers to vegetable soup.

GOES WELL WITH:
- Simple Turkey Meatballs (p. 432)
- Grilled meats
- Tofu

Per serving: Calories 90, Calories from Fat 20, Total Fat 2g (3% DV), Saturated Fat 0g (0% DV), Trans Fat 0g, Cholesterol 0mg (0% DV), Sodium 230mg (10% DV), Carbohydrates 17g (6% DV), Dietary Fiber 2g (8% DV), Sugars 0g, **Added Sugars:** 0g, Protein 3g, Vitamin A 15%, Vitamin C 20%, Calcium 6%, Iron 10%.

■ ■ ■ ■

10

■ ■ ■ ■

CHAPTER 10
SCRATCH BAKING

I'm not against treats. I love treats. But don't mistake treats for everyday fare. When you do splurge, make it worth it. The recipes in this chapter are worth it. Enjoy!

Recipes:

Whole-Wheat Crust
Corn Cakes
Whole-Wheat Banana-Veggie Bread
Chocolate Chip Banana Bread
New York Cheesecake
Cindy's Super Awesome Chocolate Chip Cookies
Whole-Wheat Biscotti
Apple Pie
Four-Berry Pie with Oatmeal Crumb Topping
Oatmeal Cookies
Peach or Stone Fruit Crumble with Oatmeal Topping

Carrot Cake
Di Noci Italian Cookies
Chocolate Ganache Without the Cake
Zucchini Bread

WHOLE-WHEAT CRUST

= Makes: 1 crust = Active time:
10 minutes
= Serving size: = Total time:
1/8 recipe 40 minutes

Whole-wheat flour is still flour, and will be rapidly absorbed, causing an insulin spike, so this is not perfect. But hey, for a crust, it's as good as it's going to get. Compared to standard crust recipes, this one does have some fiber to slow absorption and induce satiety.

This is an all-purpose, whole-grain crust. You can use it for quiche, pies, savory turnovers, little pastries. The whole grain gives this crust heft and flavor, so you don't need added sugar or salt.

Ingredients
4 tablespoons (1/2 stick) chilled butter
3 tablespoons coconut oil
1 1/3 cups whole-wheat flour
2/3 cup unbleached all-purpose flour

1 egg, beaten lightly with a fork
2 to 3 tablespoons ice water
Non-aerosol cooking spray

STEP 1: Put the butter, coconut oil, and whole-wheat and all-purpose flours in a medium-size bowl. Mix with your hands, rubbing the flour and fats together between your fingers until it resembles wet sand.

STEP 2: Add the beaten egg to the ice water, then add to the dough 1 tablespoon at a time, until you can bring the dough together with your hands to form a ball.

STEP 3: Chill the dough for at least 30 minutes before rolling it out. Roll the dough between two sheets of plastic wrap or waxed paper. Place a pie pan on top to measure; it should be a half an inch wider than the pie pan.

STEP 4: Spray the pie pan with non-aerosol cooking spray. Remove one sheet of plastic wrap (or waxed paper) from the dough and place the uncovered side into the pie pan and gently push down. Peel off the second sheet.

This recipe can be multiplied. It can be

rolled into flat round sheets and frozen for up to three months. Wrap well in plastic wrap to prevent freezer burn. Be sure to label and date.

Per serving: Calories 180, Calories from Fat 80, Total Fat 9g (14% DV), Saturated Fat 4.5g (22% DV), Trans Fat 0g, Cholesterol 40mg (13% DV), Sodium 90mg (4% DV), Carbohydrates 22g (7% DV), Dietary Fiber 2g (8% DV), Sugars 0g, **Added Sugars:** 0g, Protein 5g, Vitamin A 10%, Vitamin C 0%, Calcium 2%, Iron 8%.

CORN CAKES

= Makes: 16 corncakes or muffins

= Active time: 20 minutes

= Total time: 40 minutes

= Serving size: 16

Cindy serves these corn cakes at her restaurant with vegetarian chili on top. Sprinkle with cheddar cheese and you've got a great meal.

Ingredients
3 large eggs
2 cups buttermilk (If you don't have but-

termilk, add 1/4 cup lemon juice to 1 3/4 cups milk and let it sit for 20 minutes.)

2 tablespoons honey (optional)

1/2 cup fresh or canned peppers (if fresh, diced, sautéed, and cooled)

6 scallions, both white and green parts, finely chopped

3 cups fresh or frozen corn, lightly sautéed in 1 tablespoon oil and cooled

12 ounces cornmeal

12 ounces semolina flour

2 teaspoons baking powder

1 teaspoon baking soda

1 teaspoon garlic powder

1 teaspoon salt

Non-aerosol cooling spray

STEP 1: Mix the eggs and buttermilk in a large bowl with a whisk. Add the honey, if using. Then add the peppers, scallions, and corn kernels.

STEP 2: In separate bowl, mix the cornmeal, semolina flour, baking powder, baking soda, garlic powder, and salt. Mix until blended. Add to wet ingredients in large bowl. Mix until just blended.

STEP 3: Using a scoop or tablespoon, place spoonfuls of batter on a skillet that has been sprayed with non-aerosol cooking spray.

STEP 4: Cook the cakes like pancakes, 5 to 7 minutes per side, until browned.

Use immediately, or keep in the refrigerator for two days. Or the cakes can be frozen for up to a month. Wrap them individually in plastic wrap. Date and label! Reheat the cakes in a microwave or oven.

VARIATIONS:
- Cook in a muffin tin.

GOES WELL WITH
- Chili
- Salsa, cheese, and avocado
- Barbecued meats
- Salad

Per serving (without honey): Calories 290, Calories from Fat 30, Total Fat 3.5g (5% DV), Saturated Fat 1g (5% DV), Trans Fat 0g, Cholesterol 35mg (12% DV), Sodium 280mg (12% DV), Carbohydrates 57g (19% DV), Dietary Fiber 5g (20% DV), Sugars 2g, **Added Sugars:** 0g, Protein 10g, Vitamin A 4%,

Vitamin C 2%, Calcium 8%, Iron 15%.

WHOLE-WHEAT BANANA-VEGGIE BREAD

= Makes: 1 loaf   = Active time:
                    15 minutes
= Serving size: = Total time:
  4-ounce piece   35 to 40 minutes

There's enough sugar in the raisins and bananas to make this bread sweet. You don't need more. The rolled oats have lots of fiber. Carrots and zucchini lend that great density and texture. The yogurt adds tang. The result? A moist, satisfying loaf.

Ingredients
1 3/4 cups whole-wheat flour
1 cup old-fashioned rolled oats
1 teaspoon baking soda
1/4 teaspoon salt
1 pound or 3 ripe bananas, mashed
1/2 cup plain yogurt, nonfat Greek yogurt
  works best
1/2 cup shredded carrots
1/2 cup shredded zucchini
1/2 cup raisins (optional)
2 tablespoons honey
2 eggs

1/3 cup safflower oil

1 teaspoon vanilla extract

STEP 1: Preheat the oven to 350°F. Grease a 9-by-5-inch loaf pan or 8-by-8-inch baking pan.

STEP 2: Whisk together the flour, oats, baking soda, and salt in a large bowl.

STEP 3: In a medium bowl, mash the bananas. Stir in the remaining ingredients.

STEP 4: Fold the banana mixture into the flour mixture. Do not overmix; it will make the loaf tough.

STEP 5: Pour the batter into the prepared pan.

STEP 6: Bake the loaf for 25 to 30 minutes, or until a toothpick or skewer inserted into the middle comes out clean.

VARIATIONS:
- Use a muffin pan. This recipe will make about 12 muffins. You can freeze them, then defrost as needed on busy mornings.
- Add a few more spices: 1/2 teaspoon

cinnamon, 1/4 teaspoon nutmeg, and 1/8 teaspoon allspice would all make good additions.

- Toss in a 1/2 cup of chopped toasted walnuts or pecans when you fold the bananas and flour together.

GOES WELL WITH:
- Breakfast egg dishes
- Sliced fruit and yogurt
- A dollop of Greek yogurt or sour cream
- Butter

Per serving: Calories 300, Calories from Fat 100, Total Fat 11g (17% DV), Saturated Fat 1.5g (8% DV), Trans Fat 0g, Cholesterol 40mg (13% DV), Sodium 240mg (10% DV), Carbohydrates 43g (14% DV), Dietary Fiber 6g (24% DV), Sugars 10g, **Added Sugars:** 4g, Protein 9g, Vitamin A 20%, Vitamin C 8%, Calcium 6%, Iron 10%.

Chocolate Chip Banana Bread

= Makes: 3 loaves, or one 9-by-13-inch baking pan

= Active time: 15 minutes

= Total time: 1 hour 10 minutes

= Serving size: 4-ounce piece

When you've got bananas that have gone too ripe for your taste, peel them, pop them in a freezer bag, and save for recipes like this.

Many banana recipes go over the top with sugar. This recipe uses whole-grain flours and cuts the sugar in half. This bread is so rich, many people mistake it for brownies. For everyday meals, leave out the chocolate chips. Save the chips for special occasions.

Ingredients
2 cups whole-wheat flour
3 cups rolled oats
2 cups unbleached all-purpose flour
1/2 cup brown sugar
1 tablespoon baking soda
1 tablespoon baking powder
2 tablespoon ground cinnamon

2 cups semisweet chocolate chips (optional)
4 bananas, mashed (about 4 cups)
2 cups vegetable oil, canola, safflower, or
  coconut
6 eggs
2 tablespoons vanilla extract
1/2 cup honey or unsweetened applesauce

STEP 1: Preheat the oven to 350°F.

STEP 2: Whisk together whole-wheat flour, oats, unbleached all-purpose flour, brown sugar, baking soda, baking powder, cinnamon, and 1 cup chocolate chips, if using, in a large bowl. Reserve 1 cup chocolate chips.

STEP 3: Whisk together the bananas, oil, eggs, vanilla, and honey (or applesauce) in a medium bowl.

STEP 4: Fold the wet mixture into the dry mixture. Do not overmix; it will make the loaf tough.

STEP 5: Grease a 9-by-13-inch baking pan, or three loaf pans, and pour in the batter. Sprinkle reserved chocolate chips on top, if using.

STEP 6: Bake sheet pan for 1 hour; if making loaves, for 40 minutes. The bread is done when it's firm or when a toothpick or skewer inserted into the middle comes out clean. Let cool and slice.

This recipe can be multiplied.

VARIATIONS:
- Leave out the chocolate chips. Pour into muffin pan. Freeze and defrost in microwave as needed.
- Top with 1/2 cup of chopped toasted walnuts, pecans, or extra chocolate chips before baking.
- Use a mixture of applesauce and bananas.

GOES WELL WITH:
- Breakfast egg dishes
- Sliced fruit and yogurt
- Greek yogurt or sour cream
- Butter

Per serving: Calories 380, Calories from Fat 190, Total Fat 21g (32% DV), Saturated Fat 4.5g (22% DV), Trans Fat 0g, Cholesterol 0mg (0% DV), Sodium 220mg (9% DV), Carbohydrates 47g (16% DV), Dietary Fiber 4g (16% DV), Sugars 21g, **Added Sugars:** 25g, Protein 5g, Vitamin A 0%, Vitamin C 6%, Calcium 6%, Iron 10%.

NEW YORK CHEESECAKE

= Serves: 12   = Total time:
                     1 hour 15 minutes
= Active time:
   15 minutes

I'm from New York City; how could this book not have a New York Cheesecake recipe?

Ingredients
Whole-Wheat Crust (p. 490)
2 1/2 pounds cream cheese, softened
1 cup sugar
3 tablespoons unbleached all-purpose flour
1 tablespoon vanilla extract
1 cup sour cream
4 large eggs
2 cups plain Greek yogurt
2 cups fresh or frozen berries

STEP 1: Preheat the oven to 325°F.

STEP 2: Press the Whole-Wheat Crust firmly onto bottom of a 9-inch spring form pan or an 8-by-10-inch baking pan. Bake for 10 minutes at 325°F.

STEP 3: Beat the cream cheese, 1 cup of sugar, flour, and vanilla until well blended. Add the sour cream and mix well. Then add the eggs, one at a time, and mix until just blended. Pour the mixture over the crust. Lower oven temperature to 300°F.

STEP 4: Bake in the oven for 1 hour 10 minutes or until the center is just about set. Run a knife or metal spatula around the rim of the pan to loosen the cake. Let cool before removing. Refrigerate at least 4 hours or overnight.

STEP 5: Top with 2 cups of thick Greek yogurt. Sprinkle with berries and serve.

Per serving: Calories 570, Calories from Fat 360, Total Fat 41g (63% DV), Saturated Fat 23g (115% DV), Trans Fat 0g, Cholesterol 190mg (63% DV), Sodium 410mg (17% DV), Carbohydrates 38g (13% DV), Dietary Fiber 2g (8% DV), Sugars 25g, **Added Sugars:** 17g, Protein 13g, Vitamin A 35%, Vitamin C 30%, Calcium 20%, Iron 8%.

CINDY'S SUPER AWESOME CHOCOLATE CHIP COOKIES

= Makes: Thirty 1-ounce cookies

= Serving size: 1 cookie

= Active time: 10 minutes

= Total time: 30 minutes

Real oats mean fiber, and chocolate chip cookies are a great way to hide it. The chips make all the difference. Try low-sugar dark chocolate chips, ones that use cacao and cocoa butter, not synthetic oils. There's nothing worse than a synthetic chocolate chip cookie. What a waste of a dessert . . .

The secret here is creaming the butter and sugar by hand, and then forming the cookies together with your hands. Because you're handling the flour less, fewer strands of gluten form. The more gluten strands, the tougher pastries usually come out. These emerge from the oven crunchy on the outside, soft and rich on the inside.

Ingredients

1 cup packed brown sugar

4 ounces (1 stick) butter, unsalted, at room temperature

2 tablespoons coconut oil

1 large egg

1 teaspoon vanilla extract
1 teaspoon baking soda
2 cups of the best chocolate chips
1 cup rolled oats (not quick-cooking or instant)
1 1/4 cups unbleached all-purpose flour

STEP 1: Preheat the oven to 350°F.

STEP 2: Mash together the brown sugar, butter, and oil in a large bowl with a fork. Don't use a mixer! You want the butter and sugar to be combined well. The ideal is not chunky, but not whipped super smooth either.

STEP 3: Beat the egg in a small bowl and add it to the creamed butter mixture. Mix with a wooden spoon. Add the vanilla and baking soda and mix.

STEP 4: Add the chocolate chips, oats, and flour.

STEP 5: Mix with your hands, pulling and pushing the ingredients until they come together. The mixture will be very dry. Don't overmix.

STEP 6: Line two cookie sheets with

parchment or waxed paper. Pull off little balls of dough and place 2 inches apart on the cookie sheets.

STEP 7: Bake for 10 minutes with racks on the upper third and lower third of the oven. Rotate and switch cookie sheets halfway through baking to allow for oven hot spots. Remove when just starting to brown, let cool and serve.

This recipe can be doubled.

Per serving: Calories 180, Calories from Fat 80, Total Fat 9g (14% DV), Saturated Fat 5g (25% DV), Trans Fat 0g, Cholesterol 90mg (30% DV), Sodium 85mg (4% DV), Carbohydrates 20g (7% DV), Dietary Fiber < 1g (3% DV), Sugars 13g, **Added Sugars:** 13g, Protein 5g, Vitamin A 4%, Vitamin C 0%, Calcium 4%, Iron 4%.

WHOLE-WHEAT BISCOTTI

- = Makes 50 to 75 mini bis- = Total time:
  cotti   40 minutes
- = Active time:
  10 minutes

Cindy has served this Italian cookie in her restaurant for more than thirty years.

Ingredients
4 eggs, beaten, plus 1 egg for egg wash
2 cups sugar
1 tablespoon vanilla extract
2 cups whole-wheat flour
4 teaspoons baking powder
1 tablespoon anise seed
5 ounces whole almonds, toasted
1/4 cup unbleached all-purpose flour
1 teaspoon water

STEP 1: Preheat the oven to 325°F.

STEP 2: Using an electric mixer, beat the eggs, sugar, and vanilla in a large bowl until well blended.

STEP 3: Whisk together the whole-wheat flour, baking powder, and anise seed in a separate bowl, then add slowly to the egg mixture. Stir in the almonds.

506

STEP 3: Place the dough on a floured table and cut into 6 equal portions. Roll each portion like a log, 1-inch wide and 8 to 10 inches long (like a snake).

STEP 4: Place onto a parchment- or waxed-paper-lined sheet pan. Beat together the remaining egg and 1 teaspoon water. Brush the egg wash on the tops of the logs.

STEP 5: Bake for 30 minutes. Remove from the oven. While still hot, cut each log into about finger-width sizes.

STEP 6: For a softer cookie, let sit on counter until cool and then store in an airtight container.

For a drier Italian-style cookie, turn oven off, place sliced cookies back on cookie sheet, and let cookies stay in the oven for an additional hour. Make sure you turn off the oven!

This recipe can be multiplied. It can be stored in an airtight container for up to two months.

Per serving: Calories 100, Calories from Fat 15, Total Fat 2g (3% DV),

Saturated Fat 0g (0% DV), Trans Fat 0g, Cholesterol 15mg (5% DV), Sodium 45mg (2% DV), Carbohydrates 18g (6% DV), Dietary Fiber 1g (4% DV), Sugars 9g, **Added Sugars:** 9g, Protein 3g, Vitamin A 0%, Vitamin C 0%, Calcium 4%, Iron 4%.

APPLE PIE

= Makes: 1 pie   = Active time:
                            15 minutes
= Serves: 8   = Total time:
                            1 hour 15 minutes

Look, it's a pie. It's going to be sweet. And there's going to be sugar. Just make it special, and this pie is. Most of the sugar comes from the apples. It's got one-third less added sugar than a standard apple pie, and it's extended by the cornstarch. The crust uses coconut oil instead of trans-fat-loaded shortening, and it's held together with whole-wheat flour and rolled oats. This pie is as "safe" as you can make a pie.

For the Pie Blend:
1/4 cup white sugar
1/4 cup brown sugar
1/4 cup cornstarch

For the Filling:

4 to 5 Granny Smith apples, peeled and
 sliced
1 tablespoon lemon juice
1 tablespoon ground cinnamon

STEP 1: Preheat the oven to 350°F.

STEP 2: Make the Whole-Wheat Crust (p.
490). You will need to double the crust
recipe.

STEP 3: Make the pie blend: Mix together
the white sugar, brown sugar, and cornstarch in a small bowl.

STEP 4: Toss the apples with the lemon
juice, cinnamon, and pie blend.

STEP 5: Roll out the first crust into an 11-
inch diameter circle. Transfer to a 9-inch
pie plate. Roll out the second crust. Fill the
pie bottom with the fruit. Top with the
second crust, fold the extra pie crust under
and crimp. Cut a few holes in the top crust
to let the steam escape.

STEP 6: Bake for 50 to 60 minutes, depending on your oven. Let rest for 30
minutes before serving. Lasts for two days,

but this pie never stays around that long!

Store at room temperature. Do not refrigerate as the crust will get wet.

VARIATIONS:
- Use any kind of fruit, fresh or frozen: fresh over-ripe peaches, plums, apricots, nectarines, fresh or frozen berries, cherries, strawberry rhubarb . . . yum! The pie blend works well with all of these.
- Add a pinch of nutmeg to pie filling.
- Add a teaspoon of lemon zest to pie filling with the lemon juice.
- If using cherries, add 1/2 teaspoon of almond extract to the pie filling.

GOES WELL WITH:
- Cheddar cheese slices
- A dollop of whipped cream or Greek yogurt

Per serving: Calories 510, Calories from Fat 160, Total Fat 18g (28% DV), Saturated Fat 9g (45% DV), Trans Fat 0g, Cholesterol 75mg (25% DV), Sodium 190mg (8% DV), Carbohydrates 83g (28% DV), Dietary Fiber 9g (36% DV), Sugars 30g, **Added Sugars:** 13g,

Protein 10g, Vitamin A 20%, Vitamin C 2%, Calcium 4%, Iron 15%.

FOUR-BERRY PIE WITH OATMEAL CRUMB TOPPING

= Makes: 1 pie

= Serves: 8 to 10

= Active time: 20 minutes

= Total time: 1 hour 50 minutes

Cindy's girlfriend Denise was a terrible cook, but she always asked what she could bring to gatherings. One day, Cindy asked her to bring berries. Denise showed up with two 6-packs of berries that she had bought several days earlier at the farmers' market. The berries were barely good enough to use, but Cindy mixed them all together and made a pie/cobbler. Everyone lost their minds, it was so good. Cindy later developed this into her restaurant's Four-Berry Pie.

Ingredients
Whole-Wheat Crust (p. 490)
1 1/2 cups frozen strawberries
1 1/2 cups frozen raspberries
1 1/2 cups frozen blueberries
1 1/2 cups frozen blackberries

For the Filling:
1/4 cup sugar
1/4 cup brown sugar
1/4 cup cornstarch

For the Oatmeal Crumb Topping:
2 cups rolled oats
1/4 cup unbleached all-purpose flour
1/2 cup minced almonds
3 tablespoons brown sugar
5 tablespoons butter, softened

STEP 1: Preheat the oven to 300°F.

STEP 2: Line a 9-inch pie plate with Whole-Wheat Crust. Trim and crimp the edges.

STEP 3: Mix the berries in a bowl.

STEP 4: In a separate bowl, combine the pie filling ingredients.

STEP 5: Mix the oatmeal crumb topping in a separate bowl.

STEP 6: In the prepared pie crust, add 1 1/2 cups of berries and sprinkle with the pie filling. Repeat with the remaining berries, drizzling pie filling after each layer.

STEP 7: Top with the oatmeal crumb topping. Bake for 1 hour and 15 minutes or until firm. Let sit for at least 1 hour to cool.

VARIATION:
- Top with pie crust in place of oatmeal crumb topping.

Per serving: Calories 340, Calories from Fat 100, Total Fat 11g (17% DV), Saturated Fat 5g (25% DV), Trans Fat 0g, Cholesterol 20mg (7% DV), Sodium 5mg (0% DV), Carbohydrates 59g (20% DV), Dietary Fiber 8g (32% DV), Sugars 31g, **Added Sugars:** 18g, Protein 5g, Vitamin A 6%, Vitamin C 35%, Calcium 6%, Iron 10%.

OATMEAL COOKIES

= Makes:
  20 large cookies
  or 36 small cookies

= Active time:
  15 minutes

= Total time:
  35 to 40 minutes

These cookies are crunchy, chewy, satisfying, what dessert should be.

Ingredients

6 ounces (1 1/2 sticks) butter or margarine (coconut oil, Promise, or Heart Smart)
2 tablespoons milk
1 teaspoon vanilla extract
1 large egg
1 1/4 cups old-fashioned rolled oats
1 cup raisins or mixed dried fruit, chopped
3/4 cup unbleached all-purpose flour
3/4 cup white sugar
1/2 cup brown sugar
2 ounces chopped walnuts, toasted
2 ounces sunflower seeds
1 teaspoon baking soda
1 teaspoon ground cinnamon

STEP 1: Preheat the oven to 350°F.

STEP 2: Mix in a large bowl butter, milk, vanilla, and egg until smooth.

STEP 3: Add the oats, raisins, flour, white sugar, brown sugar, walnuts, sunflower seeds, baking soda, and cinnamon into the creamed butter mixture and beat until it comes together as a dough.

STEP 4: Line a cookie sheet with parchment or waxed paper. Using a scooper or spoon, scoop balls of dough onto the tray.

For full-size cookies, place 2 inches apart, for mini cookies place 1 inch apart. Slightly flatten the dough.

STEP 5: Bake full-size cookies for 22 minutes. Bake minis for 15 to 17 minutes.

This recipe can be multiplied. Cool and store in an airtight container for up to a week or freeze up to a month.

VARIATION:
- Make these an island treasure: add 1 cup chocolate chips, 1/2 cup chopped almonds, and 1/2 cup unsweetened coconut.

Per serving: Calories 260, Calories from Fat 80, Total Fat 9g (14% DV), Saturated Fat 3.5g (18% DV), Trans Fat 0g, Cholesterol 20mg (7% DV), Sodium 75mg (3% DV), Carbohydrates 40g (13% DV), Dietary Fiber 3g (12% DV), Sugars 14g, **Added Sugars:** 9g, Protein 5g, Vitamin A 4%, Vitamin C 2%, Calcium 4%, Iron 8%.

PEACH OR STONE FRUIT CRUMBLE WITH OATMEAL TOPPING

= Makes: 1 crumble   = Active time: 20 minutes

= Serves: 6 to 8   = Total time: 1 hour

Ingredients

4 to 6 cups peaches, sliced (or other stone fruit)

For the Filling:

1 tablespoon brown sugar
1 tablespoon cornstarch
1/4 teaspoon mace or allspice

For the Oatmeal Crumb Topping:

1 cup rolled oats
1/4 cup unbleached all-purpose flour
1/4 cup minced almonds
1 1/2 tablespoons brown sugar
2 1/2 tablespoons butter, softened

STEP 1: Preheat the oven to 325°F.

STEP 2: Mix the peaches in a bowl with the filling ingredients.

STEP 3: Mix the oatmeal crumb topping

in a separate bowl.

STEP 4: Pour the filling into a 6-by-9-inch baking dish and sprinkle with the oatmeal crumb topping. Bake at 325°F for 45 minutes or until the peaches are tender and the crumble is brown. Cool for 20 minutes before serving.

Per serving: Calories 180, Calories from Fat 60, Total Fat 7g (11% DV), Saturated Fat 3.5g (18% DV), Trans Fat 0g, Cholesterol 15mg (5% DV), Sodium 0mg (0% DV), Carbohydrates 26g (9% DV), Dietary Fiber 3g (12% DV), Sugars 11g, **Added Sugars:** 7g, Protein 4g, Vitamin A 8%, Vitamin C 8%, Calcium 2%, Iron 6%.

CARROT CAKE

= Makes:
  1 loaf, 11 slices

= Total time:
  1 hour 10 minutes
  for a cake, 50
  minutes for muffins

= Serving size:
  One 4-ounce slice

= Active time:
  20 minutes

Carrot cake has so much to offer: the mild

sweetness of carrots, the spiciness of cinnamon, the earthiness of nuts, the concentrated flavor of dried fruit. There's really no need to slather it with sugary cream cheese frosting. For a new spin on dessert, try serving this cut in small squares with a platter of sliced fresh fruit, toasted nuts, and a mild cheese.

Ingredients

1 1/2 cups unbleached all-purpose flour
1 cup whole-wheat flour
2 teaspoons baking powder
1 tablespoon ground cinnamon
1 cup grated carrots (approximately 1 large carrot)
1 cup grated red sweet apple (approximately 1 large apple)
1/4 cup honey
1/4 cup white sugar
1/2 cup neutral-flavored oil: rice bran, safflower, coconut, or canola
3 eggs, beaten slightly
1 teaspoon vanilla extract
1/2 cup buttermilk or plain yogurt
1/2 cup chopped nuts
1/2 cup chopped dried fruit (apples, raisins, apricots, or peaches)

STEP 1: Preheat the oven to 325°F.

518

STEP 2: Grease a 9-by-9-inch cake pan.

STEP 3: Whisk both flours, baking powder, and cinnamon together in a large bowl.

STEP 4: Stir remaining ingredients together in another large bowl.

STEP 5: Fold the wet mixture into the dry mixture. Mix, then pour into the cake pan.

STEP 4: Bake for 50 minutes, or until a tester inserted into the middle of the cake comes out clean. Let cool completely and serve.

Keeps, wrapped, in the refrigerator for up to one week, or frozen for up to three months.

VARIATIONS:
- Use a muffin pan instead of a cake pan, filling cups two-thirds full, and baking for 30 minutes.

GOES WELL WITH:
- Sliced fruit and toasted nuts
- Mild cheeses

Per serving: Calories 300, Calories

from Fat 120, Total Fat 14g (22% DV), Saturated Fat 1.5g (8% DV), Trans Fat 0g, Cholesterol 50mg (17% DV), Sodium 260mg (11% DV), Carbohydrates 41g (14% DV), Dietary Fiber 3g (12% DV), Sugars 18g, **Added Sugars:** 12g, Protein 6g, Vitamin A 35%, Vitamin C 4%, Calcium 6%, Iron 10%.

DI NOCI ITALIAN COOKIES

= Makes: 25 cookies = Active time: 15 minutes

= Serving size: 1-ounce cookie = Total time: 30 minutes

These flourless cookies are easy to make and have a satisfying crunch. They have just a touch of sugar and a wonderful hint of fresh lemon. Kids love them.

Ingredients
2 large eggs
Juice from 1 lemon
1/4 cup of sugar
3 1/2 cups chopped walnuts
Zest grated from 1 lemon
1 teaspoon ground cinnamon

STEP 1: Preheat the oven to 350°F.

STEP 2: Line two rimmed cookie sheets with parchment paper.

STEP 3: Lightly beat the eggs, lemon juice, and sugar together in a large bowl. Add the grated lemon zest, cinnamon, and walnuts. Stir until just blended.

STEP 4: Use a 1-ounce cookie scooper or a tablespoon to scoop out 25 round balls of dough. The dough will not be smooth, but don't worry. It holds together when baked. Place the balls at least 1 inch apart on the prepared baking sheets.

STEP 5: Bake in the upper and lower thirds of the preheated oven for 15 minutes, switching and rotating baking sheets halfway through baking. Cool completely before serving.

This recipe can be multiplied. In an airtight container, these keep for two weeks.

VARIATIONS:
- Use a different kind of nut: almonds or pecans would work well.

GOES WELL WITH:
- Milk
- Sliced apples

Per serving: Calories 100, Calories from Fat 80, Total Fat 9g (14% DV), Saturated Fat 1g (5% DV), Trans Fat 0g, Cholesterol 10mg (3% DV), Sodium 5mg (0% DV), Carbohydrates 4g (1% DV), Dietary Fiber < 1g (4% DV), Sugars 2g, **Added Sugars:** 2g, Protein 3g, Vitamin A 0%, Vitamin C 0%, Calcium 2%, Iron 2%.

CHOCOLATE GANACHE
WITHOUT THE CAKE

= Makes: 1 1/2 cups = Active time: 2 minutes

= Serving size: 1 tablespoon = Total time: 15 minutes

Ganache, a sublime mixture of chocolate and cream, is said to have originated in Switzerland. Thick and rich, ganache usually frosts dense European-style cakes that are full of sugar. You can get the same chocolate fix without the cake. Just dip fresh fruit, nuts, or even mild cheese into the frosting. Make sure to use a good chocolate.

Ingredients

1 cup chocolate chips, dark or semisweet according to taste

2 tablespoons honey

1/2 cup heavy whipping cream

STEP 1: Add all the ingredients to a medium saucepan over low heat.

STEP 2: Stir with a wooden spoon until the chips melt and the cream and honey have blended with the chocolate. Do not boil, or the ganache will curdle.

VARIATIONS:

- Use this sauce to make chocolate-dipped strawberries. Wash berries and dry thoroughly with a paper towel. Dip ends of berries into chocolate and place on waxed paper or in paper baking cups. Chill for 20 minutes if not serving immediately.
- If you're making a special dessert, add the cake back in! Make two chocolate cake layers, placing raspberries between the layers and frosting the top and sides with the ganache.

GOES WELL WITH:

- Fresh fruit of all kinds
- Raspberries
- Cheese such as Monterey Jack

Per serving: Calories 60, Calories from Fat 35, Total Fat 4g (6% DV), Saturated Fat 2.5g (12% DV), Trans Fat 0g, Cholesterol 5mg (2% DV), Sodium 0mg (0% DV), Carbohydrates 6g (2% DV), Dietary Fiber 0g (0% DV), Sugars 5g, **Added Sugars:** 5g, Protein 0g, Vitamin A 2%, Vitamin C 0%, Calcium 0%, Iron 2%.

ZUCCHINI BREAD

= Makes: 1 loaf, 8 slices	= Active time: 20 minutes
= Serving size: 1 slice	= Total time: 1 hour 10 minutes

Traditionally, zucchini bread calls for a heavy sugar batter. This version, served at Cindy's restaurant, cuts the sugar by half. Her customers love it.

Ingredients

2 large eggs, slightly beaten

2/3 cup neutral-flavored oil: rice bran, safflower, coconut, or canola oil

1/2 cup sugar

1 tablespoon vanilla extract

1 1/2 cups unbleached all-purpose flour

1 teaspoon baking soda

1/2 teaspoon baking powder

1 tablespoon ground cinnamon

2 cups grated zucchini (from approximately 2 small zucchini)

2/3 cup chopped walnuts

2/3 cup raisins

STEP 1: Preheat the oven to 350°F.

STEP 2: Grease a 9-by-9-inch brownie pan or a 9-inch round cake pan and set aside.

STEP 3: Beat the eggs, oil, sugar, and vanilla together in a large bowl.

STEP 4: Whisk the flour, baking soda, baking powder, and cinnamon together in a small bowl and add to the wet mixture, beating well.

STEP 5: Stir in the zucchini, walnuts, and raisins until just combined.

STEP 6: Pour the batter into prepared pan and bake in the center rack of the oven for

50 minutes, or until a tester inserted into the center comes out clean.

Cool completely and serve.

VARIATION:
- Fill muffin cups two-thirds full with batter and bake for 30 minutes.

GOES WELL WITH:
- A pat of butter
- Yogurt
- Sliced fruit

Per serving: Calories 420, Calories from Fat 230, Total Fat 26g (40% DV), Saturated Fat 2.5g (12% DV), Trans Fat 0g, Cholesterol 45mg (15% DV), Sodium 180mg (8% DV), Carbohydrates 43g (14% DV), Dietary Fiber 3g (12% DV), Sugars 21g, **Added Sugars:** 12g, Protein 6g, Vitamin A 2%, Vitamin C 10%, Calcium 4%, Iron 6%.

APPENDIX:
SPECIAL-OCCASION MENUS

Appetizer Buffet

Keep appetizers simple and light. For most parties, two to three appetizers is plenty.

Kale Chips (p. 181)

Roasted Chickpeas (p. 178)

Edamame Spread (p. 183), served with with cucumber slices, jicama sticks, Triskets, or other whole-grain crackers

Marinated Olives (p. 176)

Cubed cheeses with grapes

Grilled fruit (See Fruit Salad Twelve Ways, p. 217) such as stone fruits (peaches, apricots, plums) and figs

Oven-Grilled Vegetables (See Oven-Grilled Vegetables Four Ways, p. 452) on toothpicks

Spinach and Ricotta Filling (p. 163) stuffed into small mushrooms or peppers and baked

Simple Turkey Meatballs (p. 432) served

with toothpicks and Marinara Sauce
(p. 149) or Barbecue Sauce (p. 152)
for dipping
Homemade "Sausage" (p. 231) served
with toothpicks and roasted peppers
(See Oven-Grilled Vegetables Four
Ways, p. 452)

For a nonalcoholic alternative: Serve
sparkling water or pitchers of water with
lemon, lime, or oranges slices, with
cucumber and parsley, or with fresh
mint leaves.

Sunday Summer Brunch for Twelve

Vegetable and egg scramble with zucchini, chard, fresh tomatoes, and garlic
Roasted sweet and russet potatoes with
fresh rosemary and olive oil
Homemade "Sausage" (p. 231)
Baby spinach with shaved fennel and
grilled figs (See Fruit Salad Twelve
Ways, p. 217) and Balsamic Vinaigrette
(p. 143)
Greek yogurt with Homemade Granola
(p. 205)
Summer fruit platter with melons, stone
fruit, and berries, about 4 pounds total

Chocolate Ganache Without the Cake
(p. 522)

Birthday Dinner Party Buffet — Adult

Tossed salad greens with Homemade
   Whole-Grain Croutons (p. 321) and
   shaved Parmesan cheese
Marinated Olives (p. 176)
Caprese-Style Polenta and Steak (p. 409)
Roasted Chicken: Whole or Pieces
   (p. 425) with Roma Tomato Basil Salsa
   (p. 172)
Braised Greens (p. 460)
"Almost Risotto" Brown Rice Pilaf
   (p. 368) with Basil Pesto (p. 185)
Fresh fruit platter
Di Noci Italian Cookies (p. 520)

Birthday Lunch Party — Kids #1
(Kids Love to Cook and Dip)

Ranch Dressing (p. 141) with carrot and
   cucumber sticks
Multi-Grain Flatbread Pizza (p. 387)

TOPPINGS:
Marinara Sauce (p. 149) with olives,
   spinach, and mozzarella cheese
Barbecue Sauce (p. 152), diced pine-

apple tidbits, Homemade "Sausage" (p. 231), and mozzarella
Marinara Sauce (p. 149) with mozzarella cheese and fresh basil

Sliced fresh apples with lemon juice and nut butters for dipping
Chocolate Ganache Without the Cake (p. 522) with sliced bananas, pineapples, and whole strawberries

Or you can have a pizza bar and lay out the different toppings. Divide the kids into groups of 3 and have them make their own pizza

Birthday Lunch Party — Kids #2 (Oven BBQ and Fries)

Ranch Dressing (p. 141) with jicama, carrot, and celery sticks
Chicken legs (See Roasted Chicken: Whole or Pieces, p. 425) with Barbecue Rub (p. 171)
Sweet potato wedges, tossed in olive oil and herbs, salt and pepper, and roasted (See Oven-Grilled Vegetables Four Ways, p. 452)
Frozen strawberries and peaches

Dinner Party for Eight — Casual #1

Large tossed green salad with chopped jicama, tomato, carrots, and radishes with two dressings: Italian Vinaigrette Dressing (p. 139) and Blue Cheese Dressing (p. 137) or Ranch Dressing (p. 141)

Roasted chicken pieces (See Roasted Chicken: Whole or Pieces, p. 425) heavily rubbed with Italian seasoning

Spanish Brown Rice (p. 373)

Roasted bell peppers, onions, and mushrooms (See Oven-Grilled Vegetables Four Ways, p. 452)

Seasonal fresh fruit platter with dried fruit and nuts

Cindy's Super Awesome Chocolate Chip Cookies (p. 503)

Dinner Party for Eight — Casual #2

Tossed green salad with avocado, shaved fennel, and blood oranges, with Italian Vinagrette Dressing (p. 139)

Salmon Milanese (p. 437)

Creamy Polenta with Fresh Corn (p. 366)

Braised Greens (p. 460)

New York Cheesecake (p. 501) topped with greek yogurt and a large bowl of

Berry Compote (p. 225)
Sliced melon

Dinner Party for Eight — Casual #3

Tossed field greens with roasted onions
(See Oven-Grilled Vegetables Four
Ways, p. 452), cherry tomatoes, and
Balsamic Vinaigrette (p. 143)
Stuffed Bell Peppers (p. 471)
Cracked Wheat Salad (p. 319)
Large fresh fruit platter with grilled
peaches and figs (See Fruit Salad
Twelve Ways, p. 217), sliced melons,
fresh berries, and almonds
Carrot Cake (p. 517)

Dinner Party for Eight — Fancy

Clear broth (See Stock — A Tutorial,
p. 160) with Ricotta Gnocchi (p. 383)
and a dollop of Basil Pesto (p. 185)
Baby romaine with shaved fennel, shaved
Parmesan cheese, and Balsamic Vinaigrette (p. 143)
Creamy Polenta with Fresh Corn
(p. 366)
Pan-seared chicken breast or salmon
topped with Roma Tomato Basil Salsa
(p. 172)

Braised Greens (p. 460)

Four-Berry Pie with Oatmeal Crumb Topping (p. 511) topped with crème fraîche

Tailgate Lunch #1 — BBQ

Tri-tip or flat steak marinated with Basil Pesto (p. 185)

Grilled turkey burgers or grilled chicken breast

Vegetable cubes on skewers

"Almost Risotto" Brown Rice Pilaf (p. 368) made with barley and Basil Pesto (p. 185)

Romaine lettuce, Homemade Whole-Grain Croutons (p. 321), grated Parmesan cheese, and Caesar Dressing (p. 145)

Chopped fresh fruit salad (See Fruit Salad Twelve Ways, p. 217)

Island treasure cookies (See Variation, Oatmeal Cookies, p. 515)

Tailgate Lunch #2

Roasted Vegetables (See Oven-Grilled Vegetables Four Ways, p. 452) and grilled chicken platter

Grilled steak, sliced

Cracked Wheat Salad (p. 319)

Fresh fruit salad (See Fruit Salad Twelve
Ways, p. 217)
Cubed cheeses, Marinated Olives
(p. 176), and toasted nut platter

Picnic at a Music Festival

Grilled eggplant, layered with mozzarella
cheese and Roma Tomato Basil Salsa
(p. 172)
Grilled chicken, sliced
Romaine leaves or butter lettuce for
wraps
Wedges of cheddar and Brie
Sliced carrots, cucumbers, jicama, and
cherry tomatoes
Edamame Spread (p. 183)
Sliced apples with lemon juice
Grapes
Toasted nuts
Marinated Olives (p. 176)
Zucchini Bread (p. 524)

Passover or Easter

Roasted Chicken Soup with Vegetables
(p. 274)
Simple tossed field greens with Pickled
Beets (p. 458), cherry tomatoes, and
Italian Vinaigrette Dressing (p. 139)

Seared and Roasted Leg of Lamb
(p. 407) roasted with carrots, turnips,
sweet potato, red potato, and onions
Grilled asparagus
Apple Pie (p. 508)
Sliced fresh fruit

Summer Dinner Al Fresco

Savory Watermelon and Feta Salad
(p. 312)
Quinoa Turkey Casserole (p. 427)
Mixed field greens with Italian Vinai-
grette Dressing (p. 139) or Ranch
Dressing (p. 141)
Sliced tomatoes, red onions, mozzarella
cheese, and fresh basil Whole-Wheat
Sponge Bread (p. 188)
Oatmeal Cookies (p. 513)
Fresh fruit platter (See Fruit Salad
Twelve Ways, p. 217)

INDEX

Note: Page numbers in *italics* refer to instances in which the item serves as an ingredient in another recipe.

ABOUT THE AUTHORS

Robert H. Lustig, MD, MSL, has spent the past twenty years treating childhood obesity and studying the effects of sugar on the central nervous system and on metabolism. He is the director of the UCSF Weight Assessment for Teen and Child Health Program, a member of the Obesity Task Force of the Endocrine Society, a member of the board of directors of the Bay Area American Heart Association, and the president of the nonprofit Institute for Responsible Nutrition. He is also the author of *Fat Chance: Beating the Odds Against Sugar, Processed Food, Obesity, and Disease* and *Sugar Has 56 Names: A Shopper's Guide.*

Cindy Gershen is an instructor at Mt. Diablo High School in Concord, California; the chef/owner of Sunrise Bistro in Walnut Creek, California; and the founder of Well-

575

ness City Challenge, a community health activist organization.

Heather Millar is a San Francisco–based writer who has covered health, science, and lifestyles for many national magazines. She has written four books for young adults.